MINI
PLEIN
AIR
PAINTING

Quarto.com
WalterFoster.com

First Published in 2024 by Walter Foster Publishing, an imprint of The Quarto Group,
100 Cummings Center, Suite 265-D, Beverly, MA 01915, USA.
T (978) 282-9590 F (978) 283-2742

28 27 26 25 24   1 2 3 4 5

ISBN: 978-0-7603-8807-5

Digital edition published in 2024
eISBN: 978-0-7603-8808-2

Library of Congress Cataloging-in-Publication Data

Names: Robinson, Remington, 1986- author.
Title: Mini plein air painting / with Remington Robinson.
Description: Beverly, MA : Walter Foster, 2024..
Identifiers: LCCN 2024010562 (print) | LCCN 2024010563 (ebook) | ISBN 9780760388075
(paperback) | ISBN 9780760388082 (ebook)
Subjects: LCSH: Plein air painting–Technique.
Classification: LCC ND1342 .R56 2024 (print) | LCC ND1342 (ebook) | DDC 758–dc23/
eng/20240316
LC record available at https://lccn.loc.gov/2024010562
LC ebook record available at https://lccn.loc.gov/2024010563

Design and Page Layout: Morgane Leoni
Photography: Remington Robinson

Printed in China

MINI
PLEIN
AIR
PAINTING

with
Remington Robinson

Walter Foster

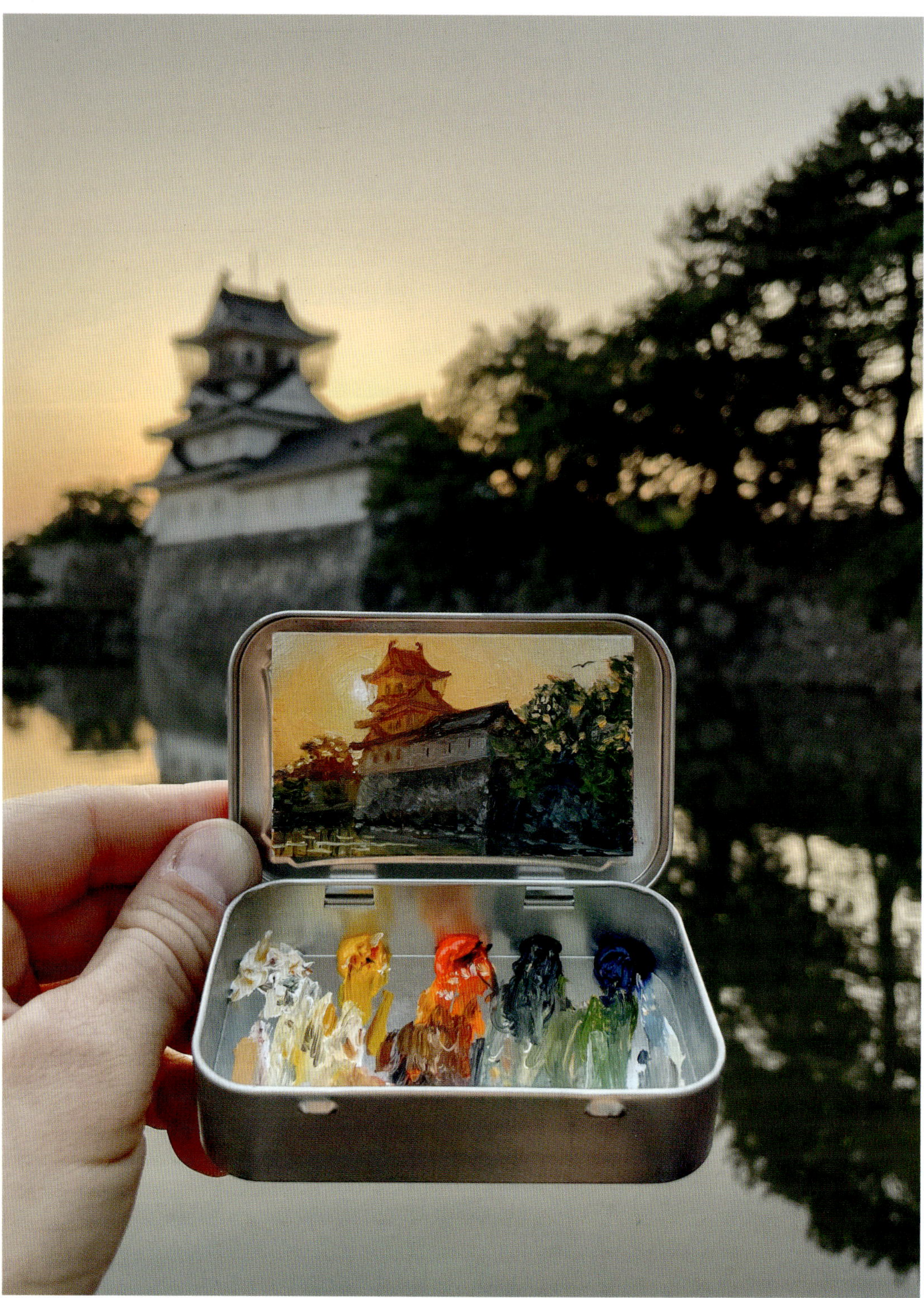

TABLE OF CONTENTS

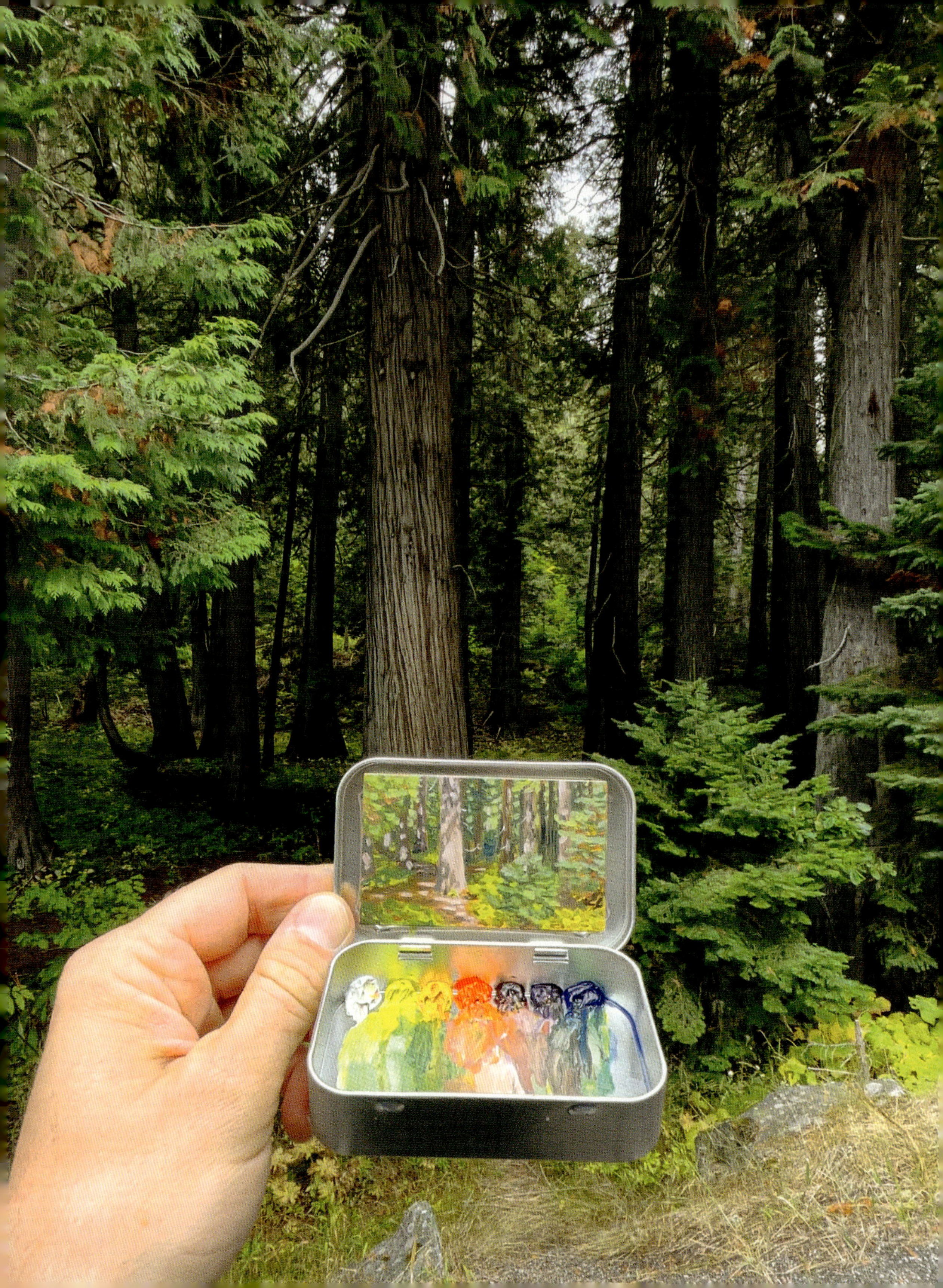

INTRODUCTION

I want to start off by saying thank you for taking the time to open this book. It is intended to be something to casually peruse in your leisure time, or it can be a companion for you wherever you go out and paint. Hopefully, there will be something in here for you, no matter what your skill level in painting is. If you don't paint, that's okay too—it's also fun eye candy.

The style and format of painting that I will demonstrate throughout this book is a type of painting called *en plein air*. That's French for painting out in the open, fresh air, and the English-speaking world has adopted this useful word. *Plein air* painting purists will tell you that it is only done outdoors. I am not a purist and consider all painting from life as *plein air* painting, whether it's outside or inside. I find that there are usually exceptions to most rules, especially in creative endeavors like painting. You might notice some of that attitude throughout this book. After all, this is only painting, and it's nice when it's fun. Mixing it up from time to time helps to keep it from becoming monotonous. There's a saying that I always have to remind myself of: "Perfection is the enemy of progress."

In this book, I'm not going to teach you specifically how to paint a car or a mountain, nor am I even going to teach you how to paint shadows, reflections, or anything else like that. What I will hopefully *encourage* you to do is to think for yourself, and to inspire you to use your consciousness in an attentive and flexible way to paint things that exist out there in the world. Enthusiasm is a key element to this, because if you find a subject beautiful or interesting in some way, you will be more inclined to want to spend time painting it.

The style that I'm showing you in this book is probably the easiest, most inexpensive way to get into *plein air* painting (or even just painting in general). It's a way to be able to paint anywhere, any time. All of a sudden, it's possible to be painting on your lunch break at work, on a backpacking trip, or while waiting for your meal at a restaurant. Just the packed mint tin, one or two brushes, a tiny container of mineral spirits, and a sheet of paper towel are all you really need—and that all fits in the side pocket of a backpack or purse. I've even gotten away with just sticking it all into one pocket of my pants or jacket. Typically, I like to carry a little more than that, which I will describe in the first chapter.

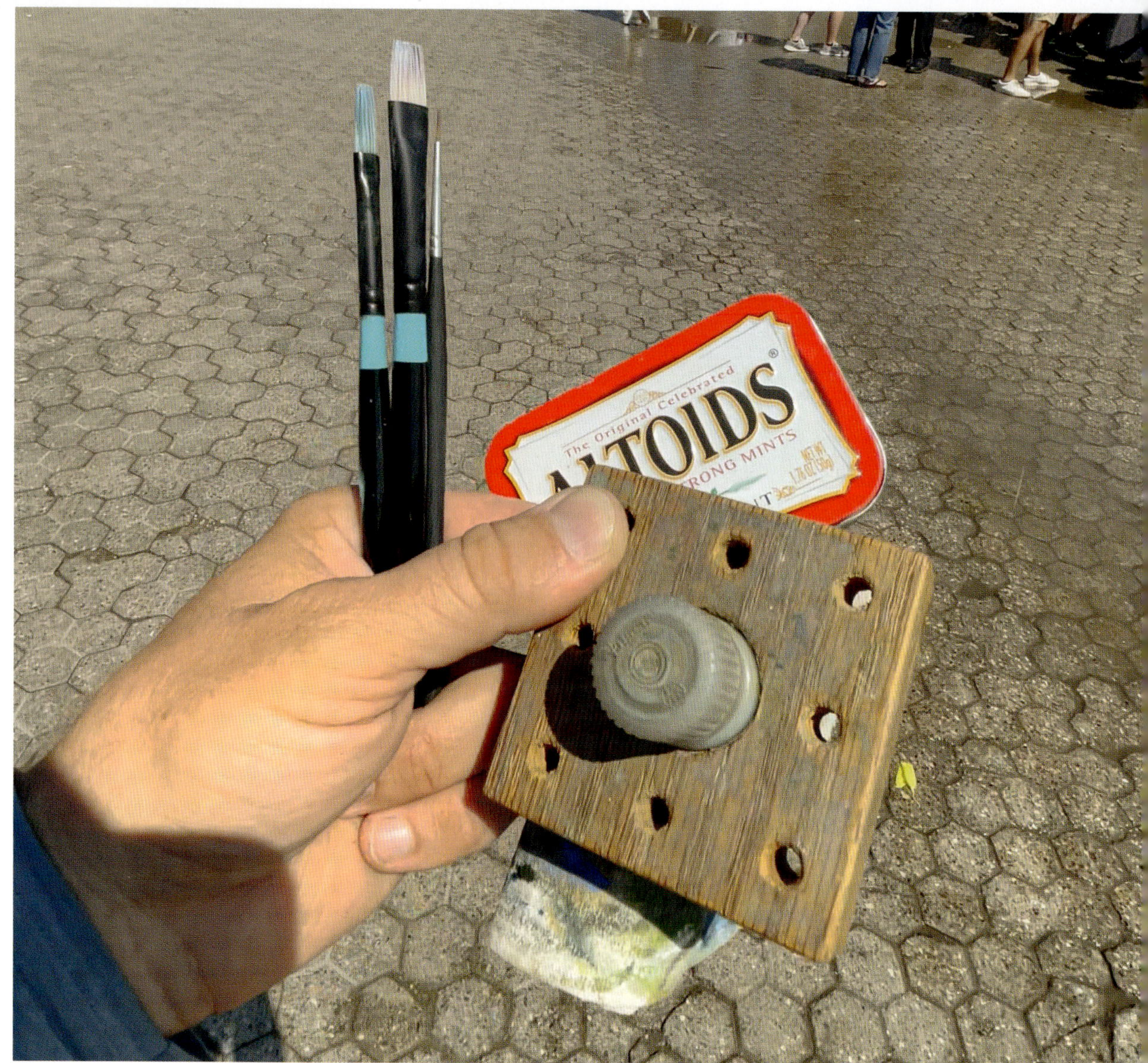

HOW I GOT INTO PAINTING MINI *PLEIN AIR*

When I was younger, I did a lot of paintings in a realistic style that took forever to complete. Sometimes, I didn't even complete them because they took so long. Then I got into *plein air* painting. It made me want to paint all the time, but the result didn't ever feel as satisfying as with my refined studio paintings. When I discovered mini *plein air* painting, I realized it was the perfect combination of speed, accurate colors from life, and a satisfying, nicely rendered final painting. It's basically a way to paint a highly rendered section of a studio painting from life.

WHY I PAINT MINIATURE

Mini *plein air* painting in mint tins has so
many benefits.

Small size

- Less expensive entry point
- Ultra portability
- More risk-taking, because mistakes
  matter less
- Paintings can be finished quickly
- Clear finish line
- Easy storage of many paintings
- Easy to paint frequently

Frequent painting

- Rapid improvement of color mixing
- Keeps things interesting and
  exciting overall
- Rapid growth in work portfolio

MY PHILOSOPHY ON PAINTING FROM LIFE

Painting from life is an activity of the consciousness in which it is possible to directly connect with the reality of nature—the reality we all experience and deal with. Your eyes are showing your consciousness something that physically exists in three-dimensional reality (and may even be changing over time), and your consciousness translates that observation of reality into a two-dimensional image with paint. This process requires concentration and can be considered an active form of meditation. However, unlike many types of mediation, there is a physical byproduct of the process that can be observed afterward. My perspective is that through painting from life, it is possible to get closer both to nature and to reality, as a form of meditation.

A fundamental part of meditation, as I understand meditation in reference to focusing on a specific object, is this: It is of utmost importance to remain as neutral as possible when viewing the object, so as not to form any kind of bias or value judgment of it, in order to gain the purest possible impression. This principle of neutral viewing in focused concentration is beneficial to carry over into drawing and painting accurately from life, because the goal is to record the object as it exists in reality, not what we believe it should look like.

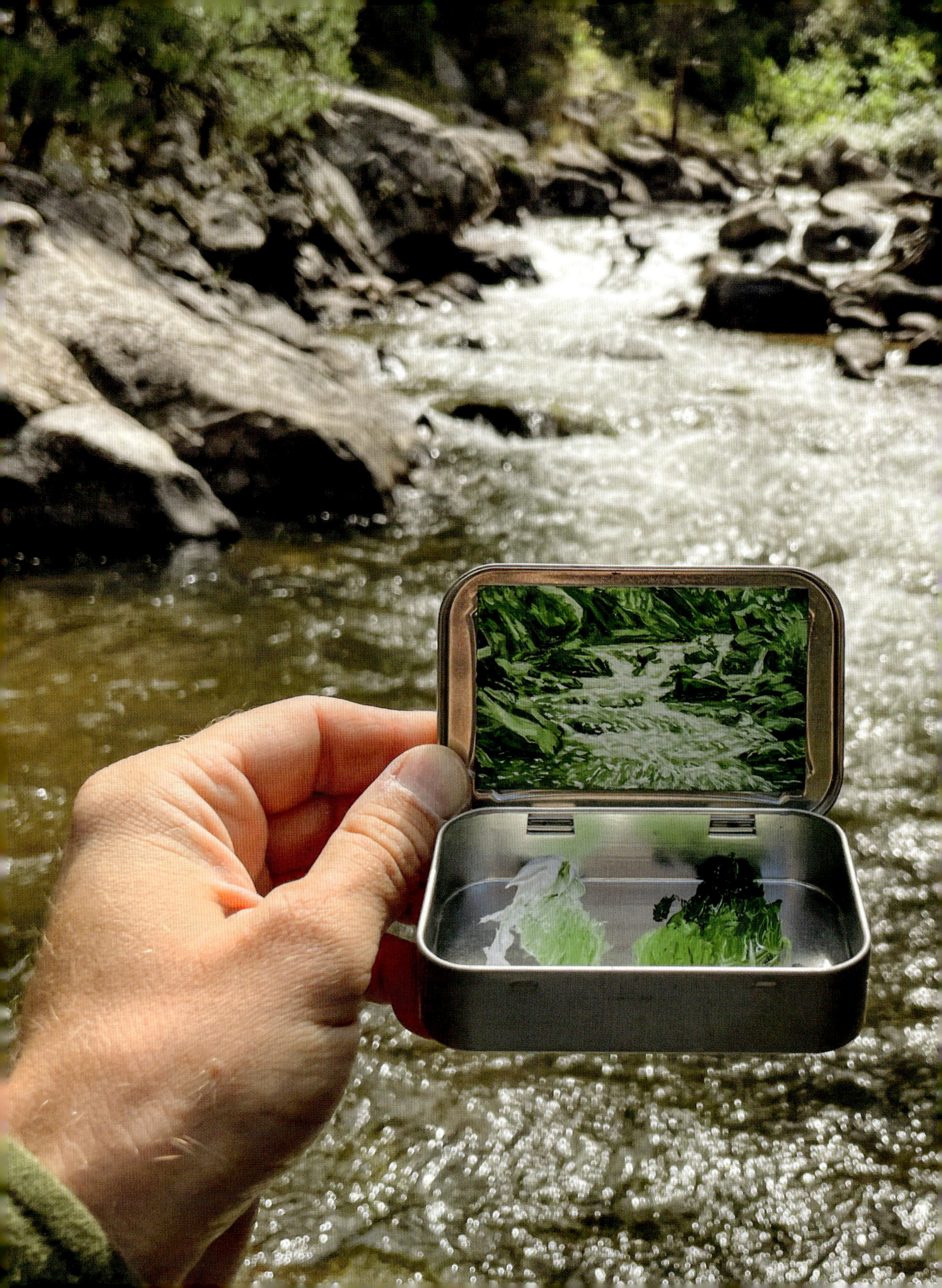

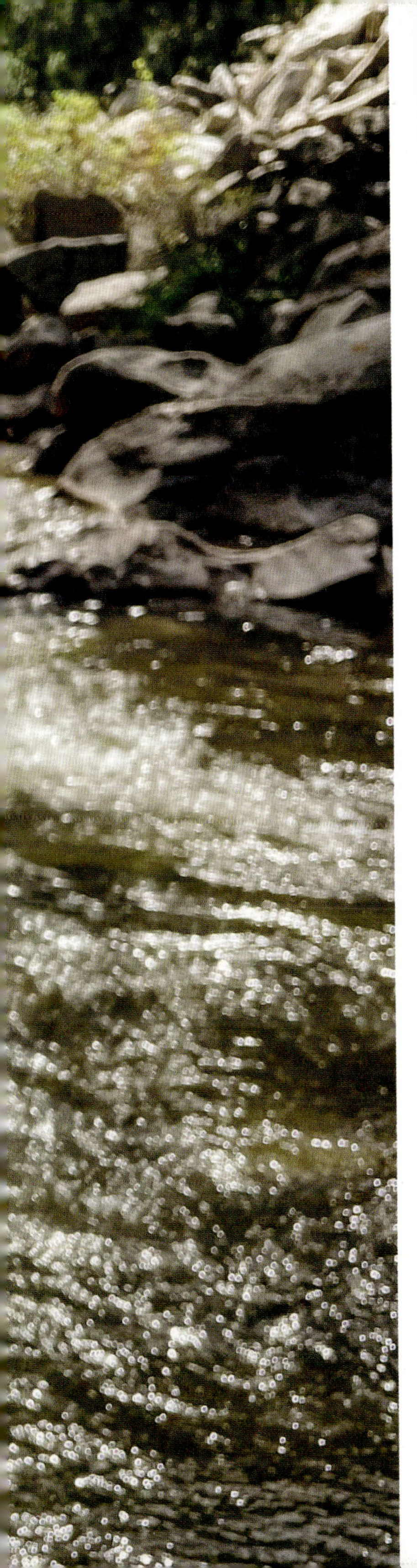

GETTING STARTED

SETTING UP YOUR TIN

Setting up a mint tin to paint in is fairly simple and straightforward, with only a few things needed to convert the actual tin itself into a mini painting station that can be transported practically anywhere. Aside from the actual tin itself, a few other key items are directly required for painting, such as brushes, and several other items that, although not absolutely required to make the painting, certainly do make the experience more comfortable and enjoyable.

NECESSARY MATERIALS

- **Mint tins**. There are many types of tins, but I almost always use mint tins, such as Altoids, because they are abundant and easy to find where I live. The most important quality of the tin is that the lid must have a hinge that lets it open and close. There are also cigar boxes that can be modified to paint in, which are not quite as small, but still cheap and fun. I have several cigar boxes that I have modified for painting.
- **Substrate panel and primer**. This is the surface you paint on. The plywood panels I use are ¼-inch (6 mm) thick underlayment panels from the

hardware store, which are closer to ³⁄₁₆-inch (5-mm). I cut the panels to 1⅞ × 3⅛ inch (5 × 8 cm), which is the same aspect ratio as 3 × 5 inches (8 × 13 cm). I simply cut a bunch of boards with my miter saw at the same time. Then, on each one, I sand all the edges and surfaces with some fine sandpaper to get a smooth finish before priming with spray primer (it goes on evenly). When the board is installed into the lid of the tin, the lid can freely open and close without my art panel hitting any part of the tin.

I have heard of people using aluminum composite sheets, which are more expensive, but will last longer. Masonite and MDF board also work. I do not recommend paper products with oil paints.

- **Substrate attachment**. To attach the substrate to the tin, I use thin, clear, self-adhesive hook-and-loop fasteners, which come in a strip. I cut the strip into small squares. Normal hook-and-loop tape works too, but I don't like how much it moves around. You could also use clear gel mounting tape, but it is hard to remove without damaging the panel.
- **Brushes**. You'll need small brushes with short handles. If there's a long-handled brush you like, you can always cut the handle short. A lot of times I only use two or three brushes in a painting. I like to try out different brushes all the time to see what I like. Some are stiffer and made specifically for oil painting, while others are synthetic nylon. The main

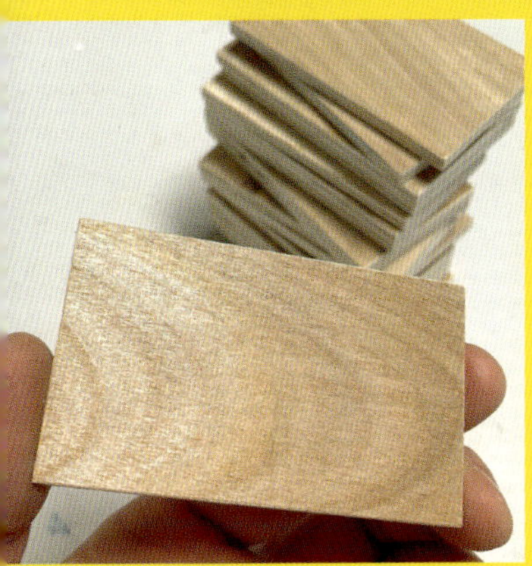
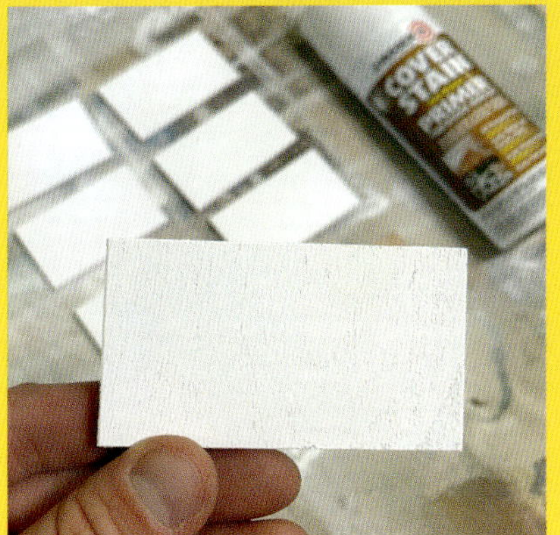
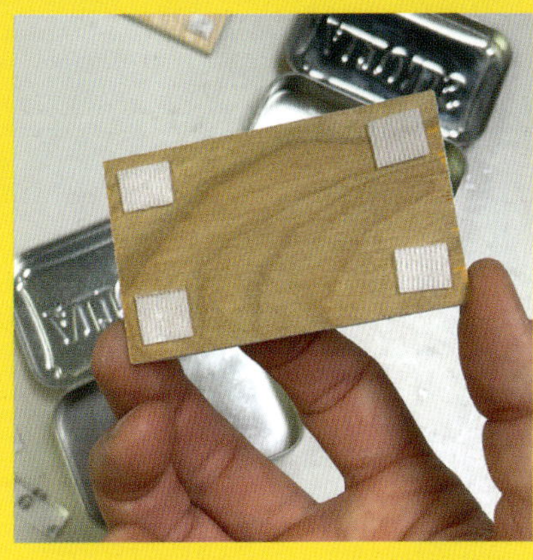
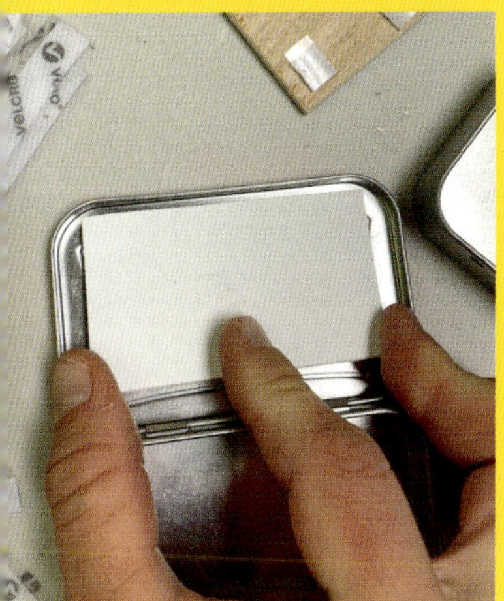
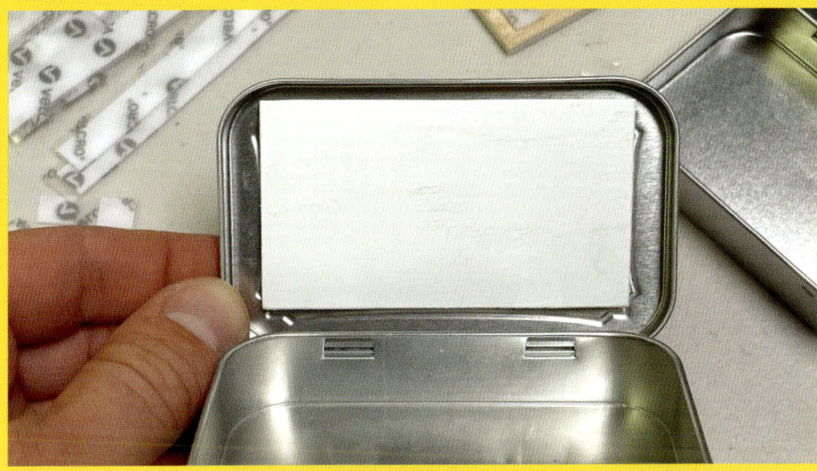
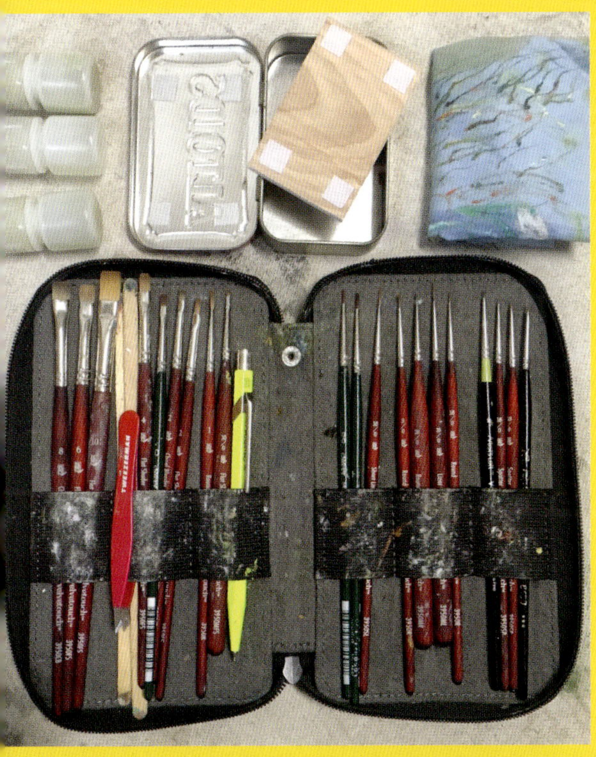
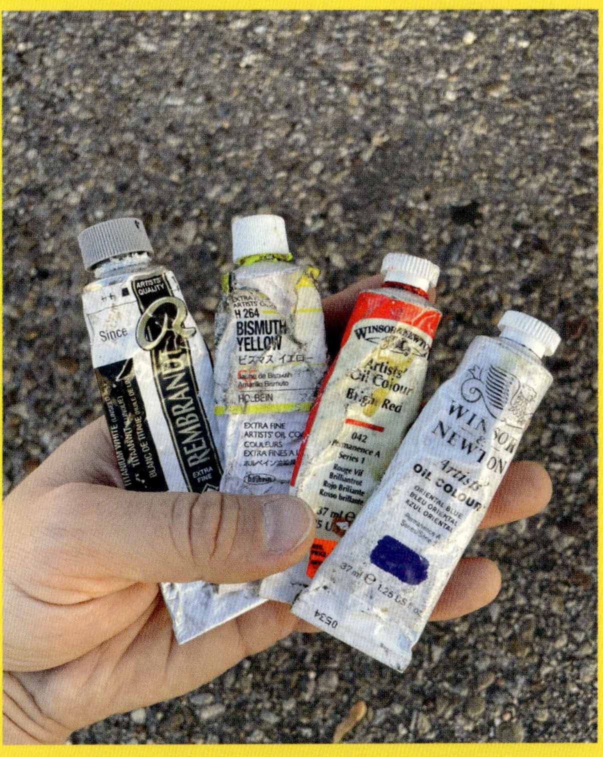

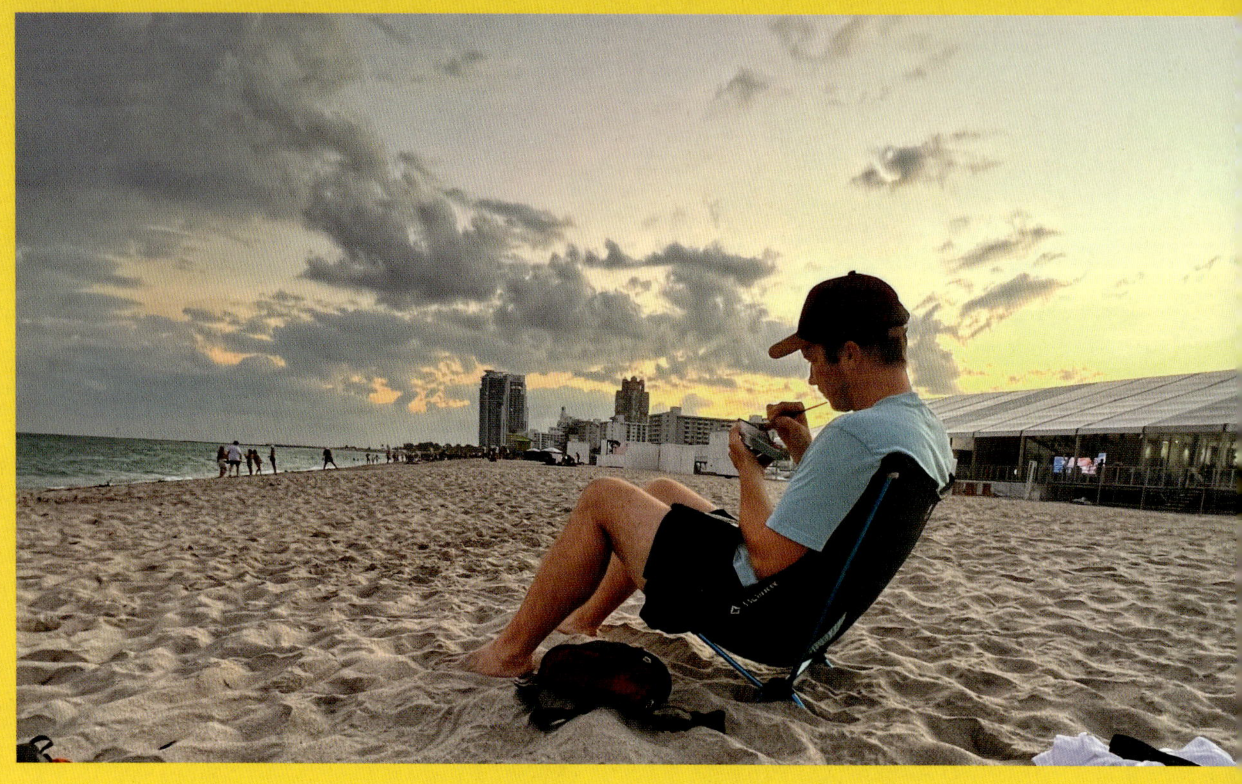

thing that is important with brushes, especially when painting miniatures, is that a round brush has a good tip and a flat brush has a good edge. I like to keep the brush tubes on the brushes while they are in my brush case to protect their tips and keep them good for as long as possible.

• **Paint**. If you're just starting out, a good color selection to begin with is Titanium White, Cadmium Lemon, Alizarin Crimson, Burnt Sienna, And French Ultramarine. Discover what colors you want to paint with by looking through some of the examples in the project section of the book.

I prefer oil paint for small detail painting because of the long drying time. With fast-drying paints at this scale, small mixtures of color dry out quickly, which means having to mix the same colors over and over, which can be frustrating. For oils, I use any and all brands, but my favorite is probably the Winton line of oils by Winsor & Newton, which is their cheap student-grade oil paint. I like it because it comes out of the tube and adheres right to the metal of the tin. Some brands spew out a bunch of extra linseed oil first, so the paint doesn't stick to the tin, but rather slides all around.

If your tin will be bumping around a bit before you paint (like in the project where I painted on a ski slope, see page 89), get some alkyd oils. They stay in one place on the tin instead of slowly moving around as traditional oil paints would.

If using acrylic paint, I recommend slow-drying acrylic, such as Golden Artist Colors' OPEN Acrylics.

- **Odorless mineral spirits and a container.** You'll need some to clean the oil paint off your brushes. (If using acrylic paints, don't use mineral spirits—just use water.) You'll also need a small container to hold the cleaner. I like Nalgene's ½- and ¼-ounce jars for this purpose. You only need one, but it's good to have at least one backup jar in case one tips over and spills while you're painting.
- **A sheet of paper towel.** Really, any paper towel, napkin, or cloth will do. You want to wipe as much of the paint off your brush as you can onto the paper towel before cleaning your brush in the mineral spirits. (This prevents the mineral spirits from getting too mucky, which will eventually affect your color purity.) After you clean your brush, you will need to use the paper towel again to dry your brush.

NICE, BUT NOT NECESSARY

- **Fanny pack.** A small pouch that attaches around the waist is ideal to keep all of your materials together in one place.
- **Pencil case.** This additional storage item keeps your brushes nice. Painting at this scale means you don't want stray bristles.
- **Mineral spirits container base.** It is easy to tip over your mineral spirits container. I cut a small block of wood and drilled a hole into it, which the jar fits into. I also drilled some smaller holes into it in case I ever want to put my brushes there.
- **Portable camping chair.** You'll need a nice camping chair—I use the Helinox Chair Zero because it is comfy, small, and lightweight (under 1 pound [½ kg]). Alternatively, I sometimes use a small tripod chair.

ADDITIONAL ITEMS

- **Reading glasses.** If you can't see small things, grab a cheap pair of reading glasses. I have some even though I don't need them for reading.
- **Headlamp.** Headlamps are great for painting in low light.
- **Gloves.** If you do a lot of painting when it's cold out, you'll want a pair, because the metal tin sucks all the heat away from your hands!
- **Sun protection.** A broad-brimmed hat may look goofy, but it provides very good sun protection, along with a sun shirt. Sun protection is key when painting outside on a sunny day, and I prefer to cover up rather than to wear a ton of sunscreen.

TECHNIQUES

In this section, I will show you some fundamental techniques of painting. As you learn to paint and keep painting, you will find that there are thousands of tips and techniques. Some of them work better in different situations than others. Being a versatile painter means trying different techniques based on different circumstances, and the best technique for you doesn't always mean it's the one that produces the best result—it might simply be the one that feels the most fun.

Painting on a small scale, like I am doing in this book, offers the opportunity to easily start over, and the lower level of commitment of time and materials means that the consequences of mistakes are easier to deal with. (Though a good tip to remember is that mistakes are the best tool for learning.)

UNDERSTANDING COLOR

When I first began painting in high school, the process unlocked a new way of seeing and grasping color. The relationship that colors have with each other became apparent through the simple knowledge of the color wheel and the direct experience of mixing colors of paint together. My entire way of seeing the world changed, because suddenly I was trying to imagine how I would mix paint colors for anything and everything I was looking at, wherever I was.

I was always taught to never (or very rarely) use colors straight out of the tube. But why? Because color exists in nature in an almost infinite variety, and tubes of paint do not. As a painter, you do not need to own every possible color of paint that exists—you just need to know how to mix your own colors. This is where the color wheel comes in.

The Color Wheel

A basic color wheel shows the three primary colors (red, yellow, blue) and the three secondary colors (orange, green, purple). Any color that exists in the real world is a mixture of certain hues of those colors, with the addition of white and/or black. This mixture usually includes at least some amount of an opposite color to either darken it or to simply tone down its intensity. For example, a green leaf may have some amount of red in its color mixture.

Any time I am mixing colors, I am thinking about the relationship different colors have with each other. What's special

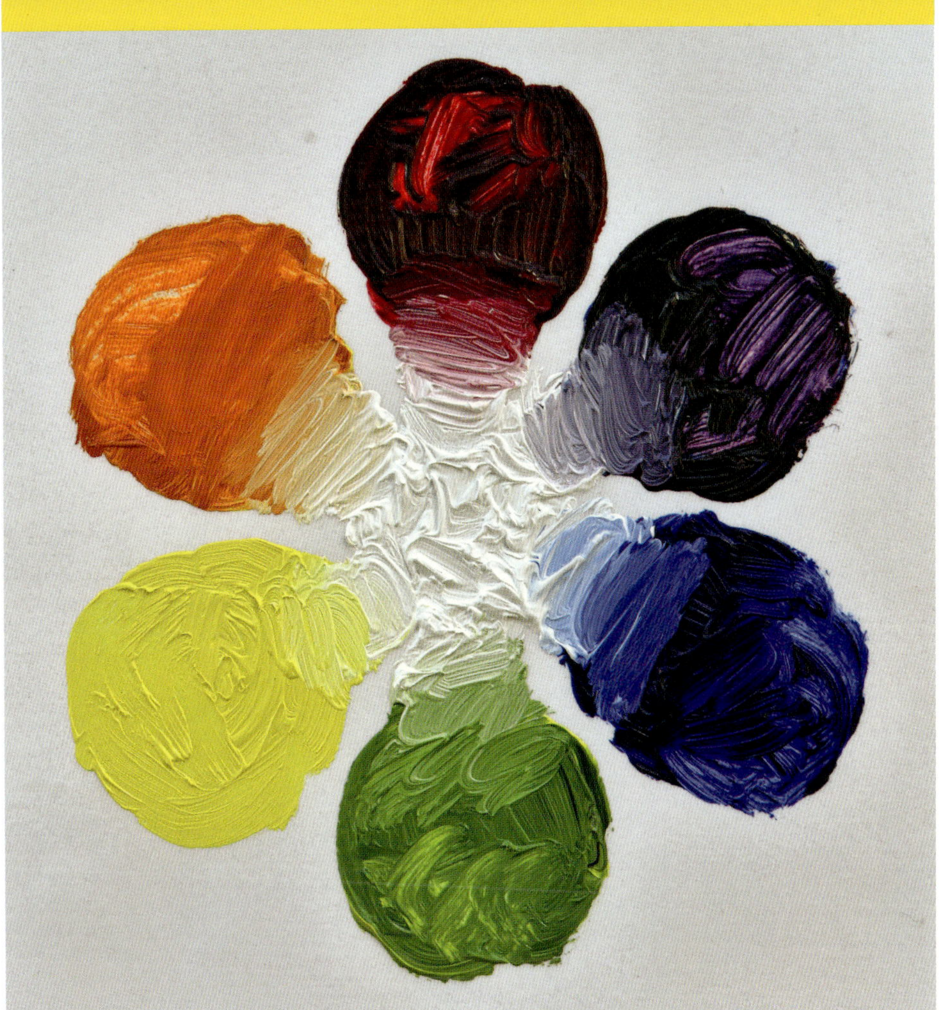

about the color wheel is not the fact that it is a wheel of organized colors, but that this wheel shows you those color relationships—what each color's opposite is, as well as adjacent colors that harmonize with one another. It's pretty straightforward and simple, and it is the basis for all color relationships.

This simple color wheel is painted with the primary colors Bismuth Yellow, Alizarin Crimson, and Oriental Blue. The secondary colors green, orange, and purple are mixed with the primary colors. Titanium White is in the middle to show what each one looks like mixed with white, and each color pool has a scraped-away area showing the white mixing surface underneath.

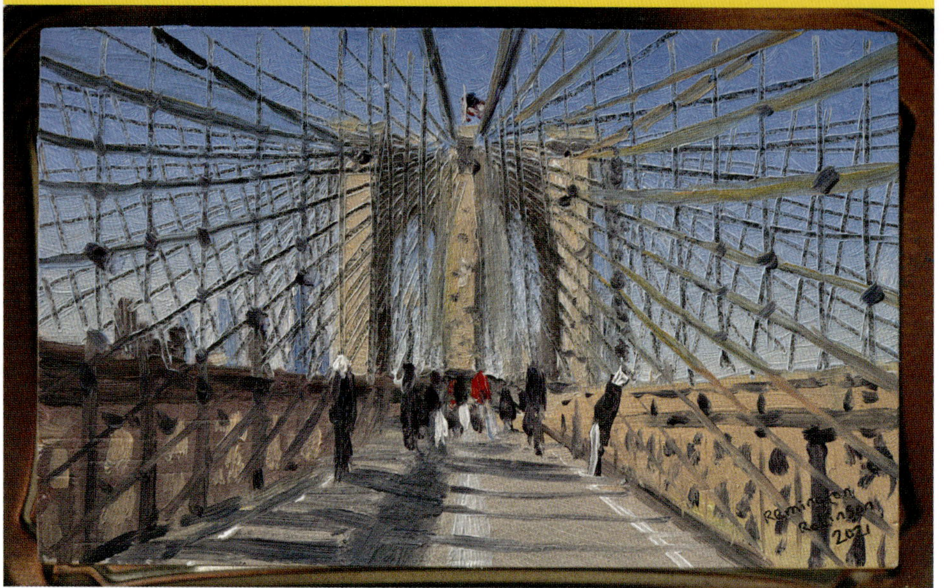

BRUSH TECHNIQUES

There are probably hundreds of brush techniques for painting. Here are a few fundamental techniques I use frequently when doing my miniatures in oil paint.

The most important information to know about painting with brushes is this: Make sure you always know what pigment is on your brush at all times, and *where* it is in and on the bristles! *This matters* with all painting, but *especially* detail painting!

Lifting Pigment

The first technique is lifting pigment up into the bristles by pushing the brush. A technique best suited for brushes with stiff bristles, this is how I quickly establish light areas in my underpainting technique. It is also useful for eliminating a painted area before the paint dries, especially when working in oil. The brush should be clean, and can be dry, but damp is even better because it will wick the moisture of the color up into the bristles more easily. A

sopping-wet brush is not good because that means the brush is occupied with liquid and there is little or no room within the bristles to pick up paint.

Painting Thin Lines

Laying the brush at a low angle, or nearly flat, is useful for gently painting a color over top of another layer of color. This is especially useful for small details painted over other paint that is still wet. Soft bristle brushes lay paint more gently over other paint.

Holding the brush at a steep angle makes the bristles plow down into the color underneath. The stiffer the bristles are, the more it plows through the paint underneath.

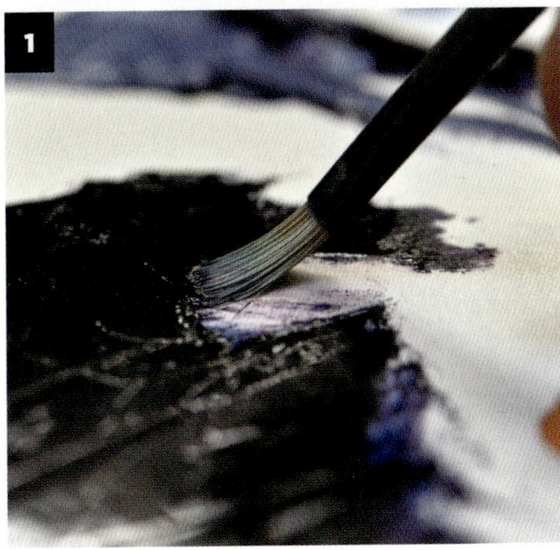

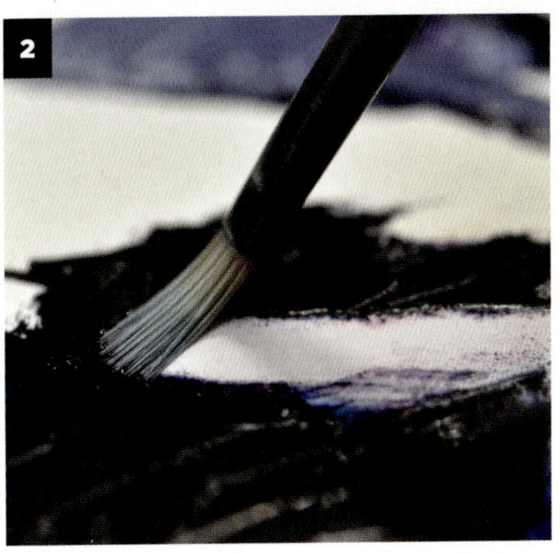

1. Place the brush down with the bristles pointing toward where you want to go.

2. Push the brush bristles-first to lift away the paint.

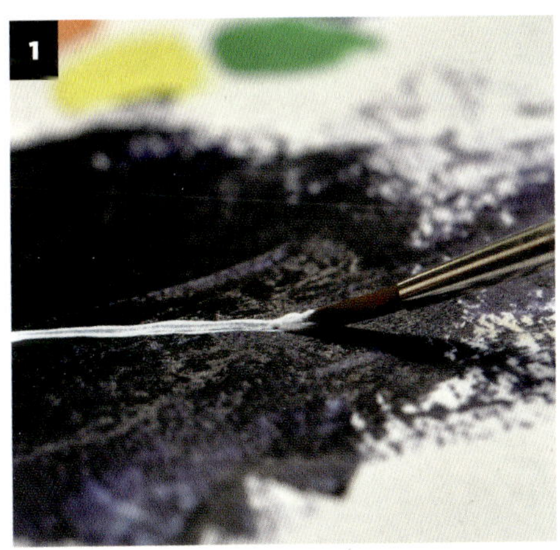

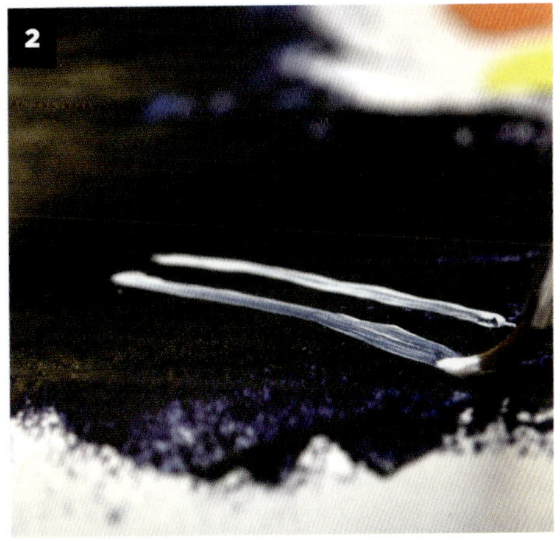

1. Painting with a thin brush at a low angle works well for adding light colors over dark, still-wet paint.

2. Painting with a thin brush at a steep angle forces the paint through the color underneath.

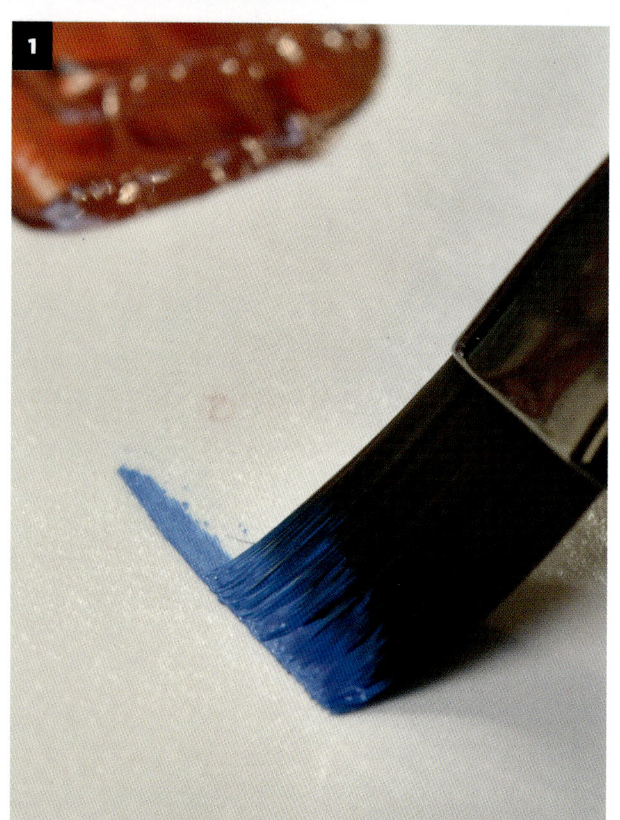 

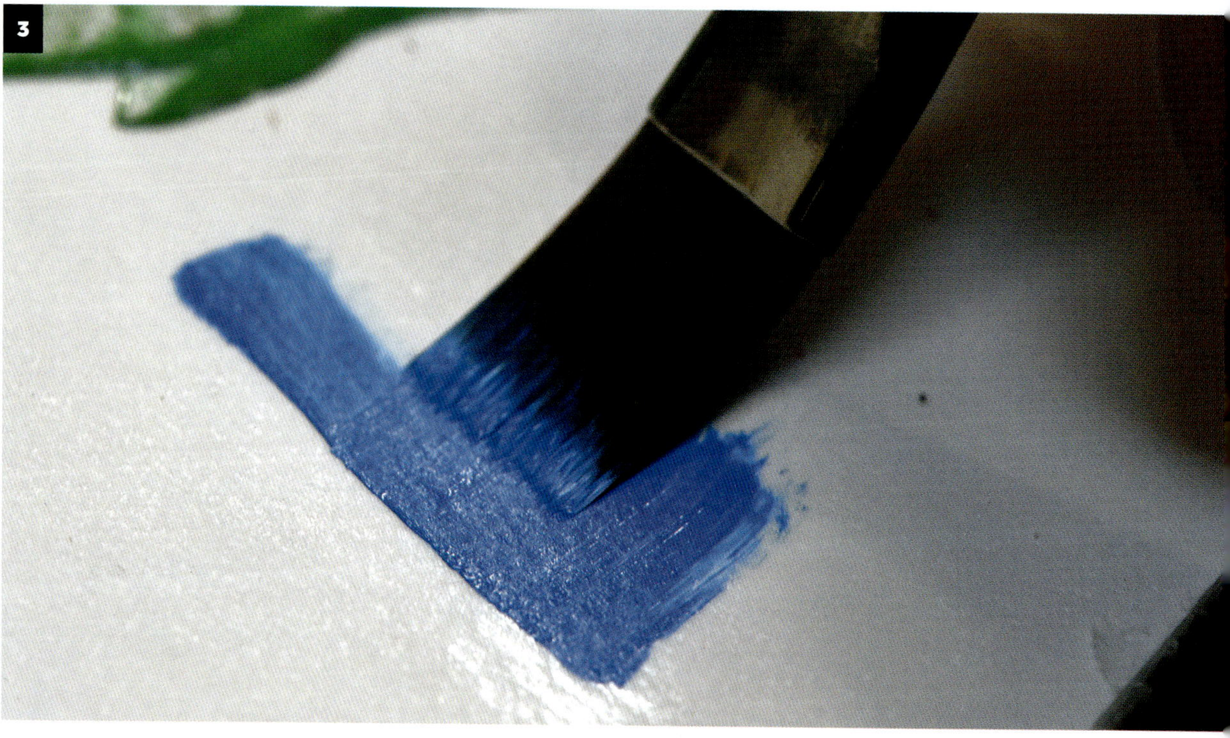

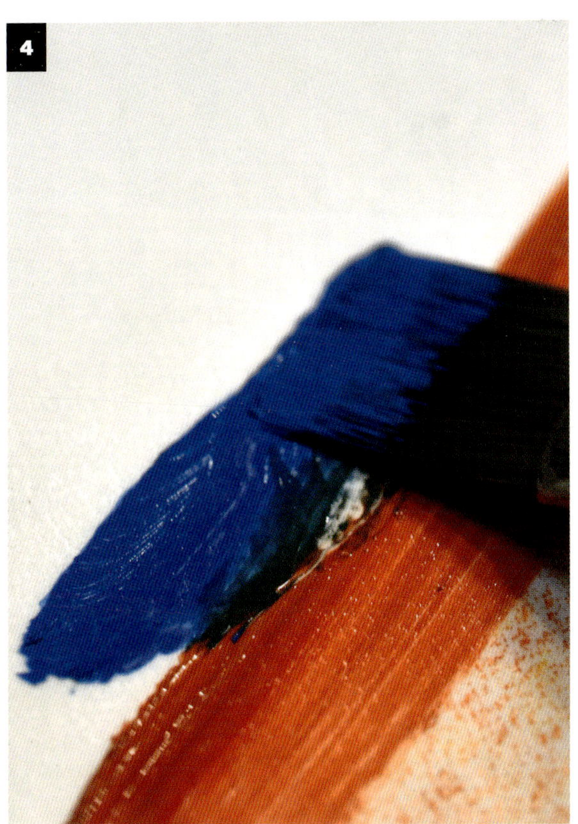

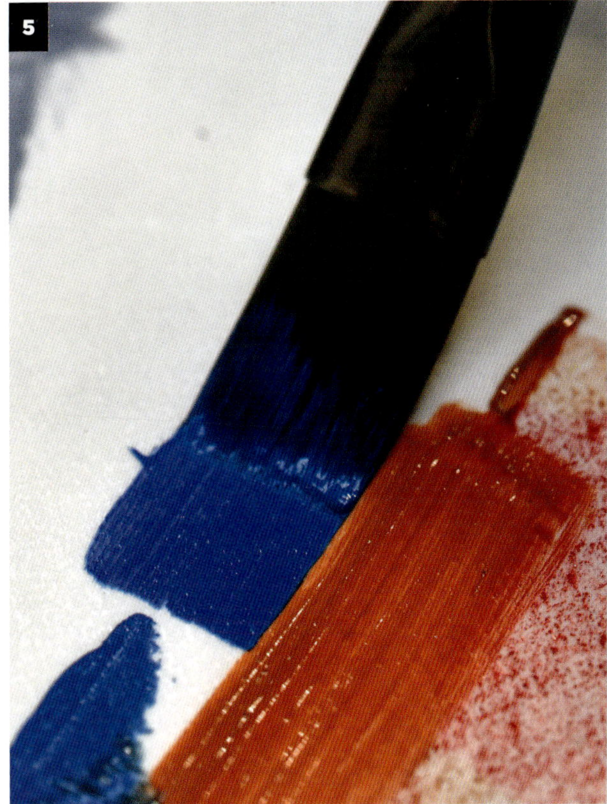

Edge and Fill

Use a flat brush vertically to make a thin line (here, the brush size is ⅜-inch [9.5-mm]), or at an angle to achieve a nice, crisp edge on a color fill. Once that edge is established, a color fill can be applied with several broad strokes pulled away from the clean edge you just made. When painting next to another color, always be mindful of the current color in your brush bristles and where the brush edge is in relation to the other color, to ensure a clean color separation without overlap.

1. Make the first pass with a flat brush to start a crisp edge.

2. Build the edge up with another pass.

3. Work from the edge to create a big color fill with the same brush.

4. When painting one color next to another color, *do not* hold the brush this way, unless making a messy edge is what you are going for.

5. Paint one color next to another in a clean way, without overlapping.

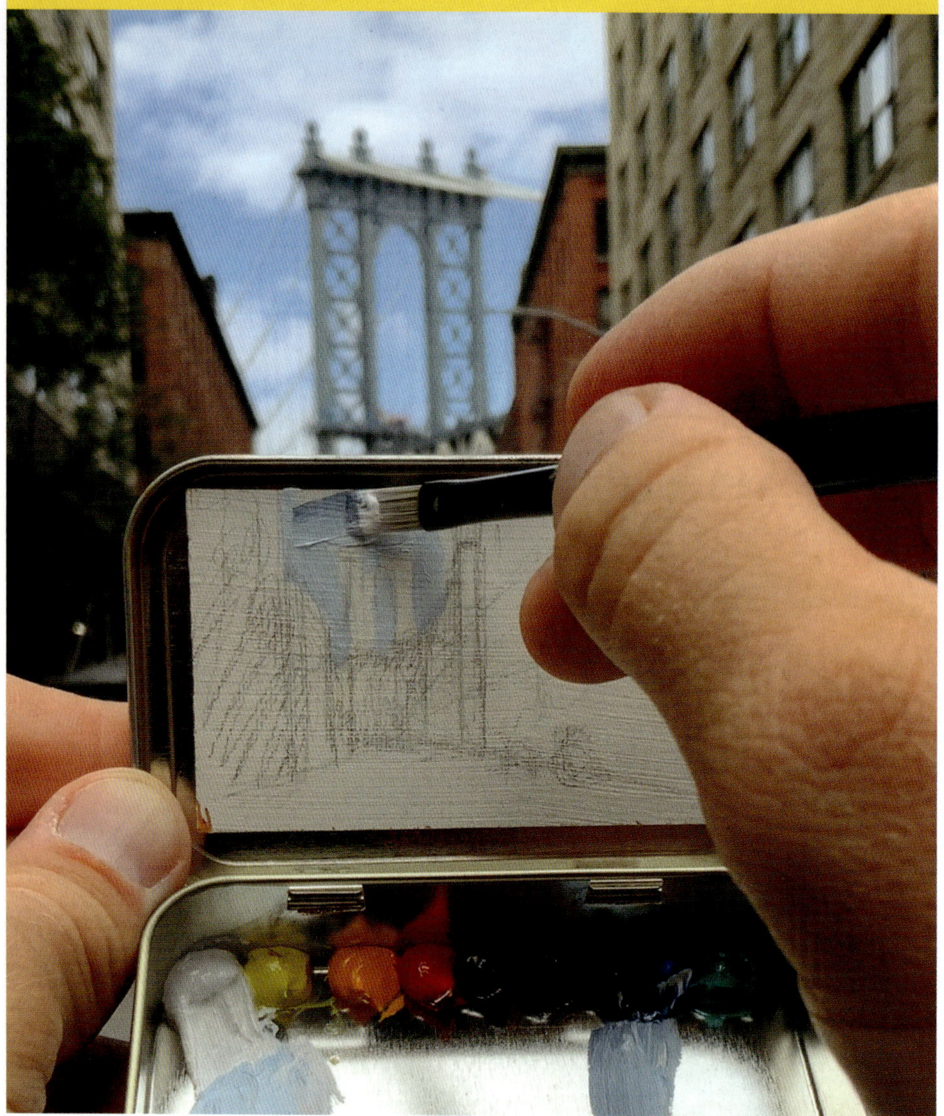

In-Brush Gradient

This is a very useful way to paint a sky on a small scale, or anything else where there is a color transition. It can be done with a large brush or on a smaller scale with a small brush. The most important thing with this technique is to be mindful not to twirl your brush. First, apply a small pool of two colors to the mixing area. It's a good idea to leave space between the colors to give room for them to mix. Several brushstrokes mix the colors together into a nice, even gradient fade within the bristles of the brush. This can then be applied to a painting in countless ways.

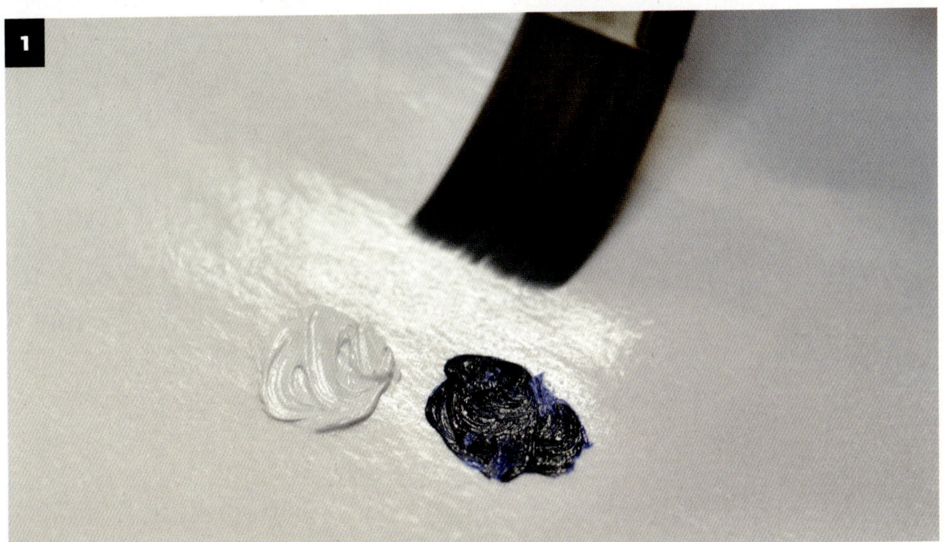

1. Add two small pools of color—in this case, Titanium White and Oriental Blue.

2. Brush across the colors several times to load the brush with the gradient fade.

MY PROCESS

In the over twenty years I have been painting, my process has changed continuously. In the last several years, while painting miniatures, parts of my process have become more and more refined. I currently work according to several basic steps, which isn't necessarily a magic formula or a key to all doors, but it is a great way to construct a painting.

Not all of my paintings follow an absolutely identical process from start to finish. However, if I were to break it down, there are seven basic steps I almost always rely on in some way, and a lot of artists follow a similar approach. Sometimes these steps bleed into each other. The first two steps come before anything is applied to the surface at all, and the remaining five steps create the actual painting.

STEP 1: SUBJECT MATTER

The first thing is to come up with an idea of what to paint. What do you feel like painting? It could literally be anything. Set out with a goal, like, "I want to paint a coffee cup," or "Since it's summer, I want to paint a scene at the park," or "Today, I want to paint the mountains." A lot of times, what I choose to paint is influenced by where I am, what season it is, what the weather is like that day, or what colors I feel like painting with. Every once in a while, I just drive, walk, or ride my bike for a little bit until something I see strikes me, because the world is full of beautiful and interesting things to paint.

Here are some good things to think about when picking a subject to paint:

While choosing your subject, it is very important to consider if it's something you can execute in the time you have available. I find that the average day can be broken into 2-hour painting increments, where the angle of the sun is still similar, and the weather hasn't changed that much. Sunrise and sunset are difficult times, because the light changes constantly in a short amount of time.

Recognizable subjects—like specific buildings, cars, and people—are more difficult to execute. If the structure is slightly off (proportions and perspective), it looks wrong. This is why faces are particularly challenging. Everyone has a head with eyes, ears, a nose, and a mouth, but if any of these are even the tiniest bit off, it can look weird. On the other hand, neutral subjects and distant objects are easier to execute. Trees, flowers, and mountains are good

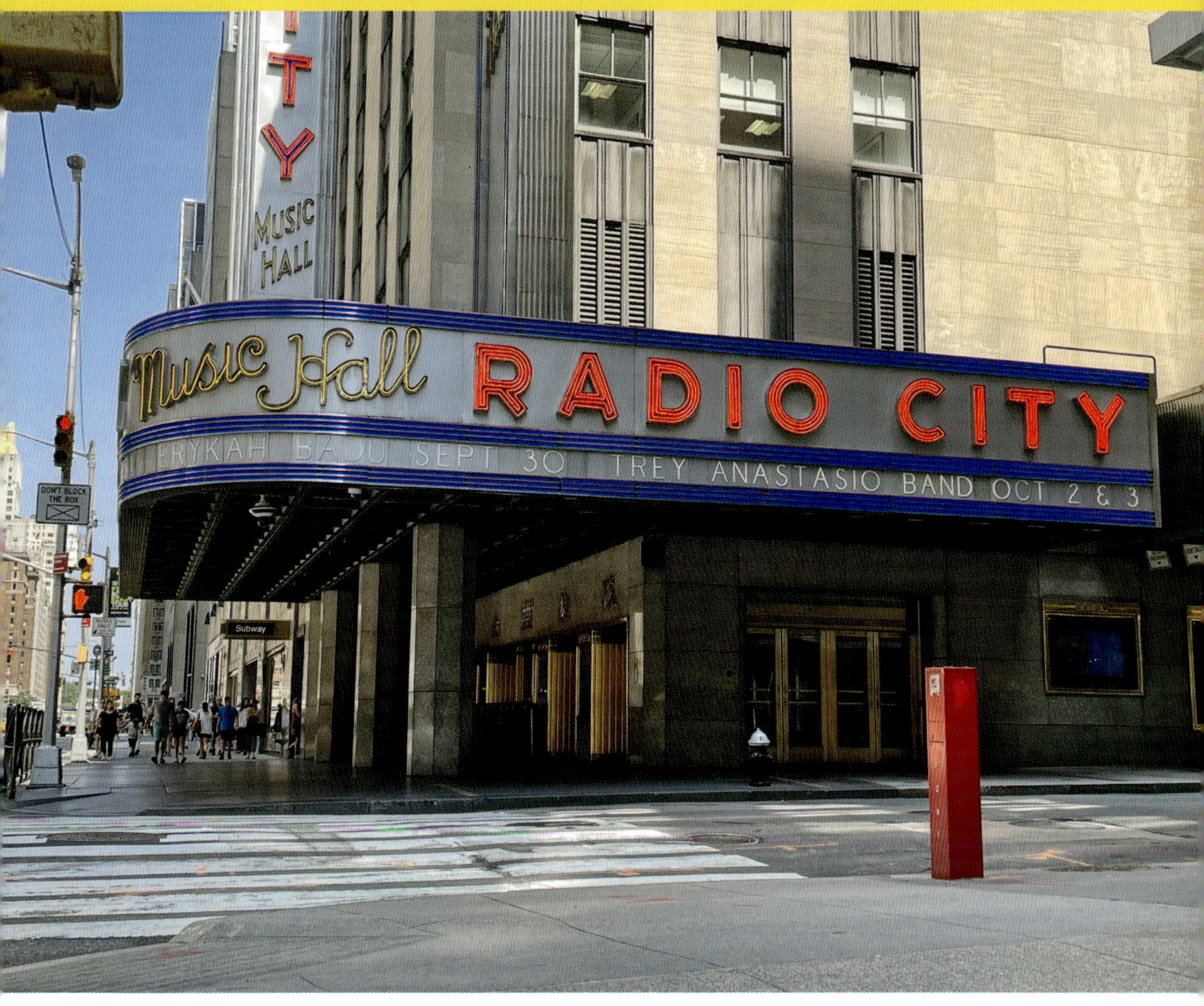

One morning when I was in New York City, I thought to myself, "Today, I want to do a painting of Radio City Music Hall."

examples of things found in nature that are more forgiving.

In terms of painting miniature, a simple, graphic subject tends to work better on a small scale. When people are looking at a painting that is roughly the size of a credit card, it tends to have more visual impact if everything is clearly recognizable without too much clutter. So, one key to success is to keep it relatively simple.

STEP 2: COMPOSITION

Imagine how you want to lay out your painting. How do you want to organize your subject(s) onto your picture plane? There are several composition styles to choose from, and many of them can even be combined. Composition styles can be the impetus to paint something, or a guide to use after finding the subject. You might also have a set of things you want to

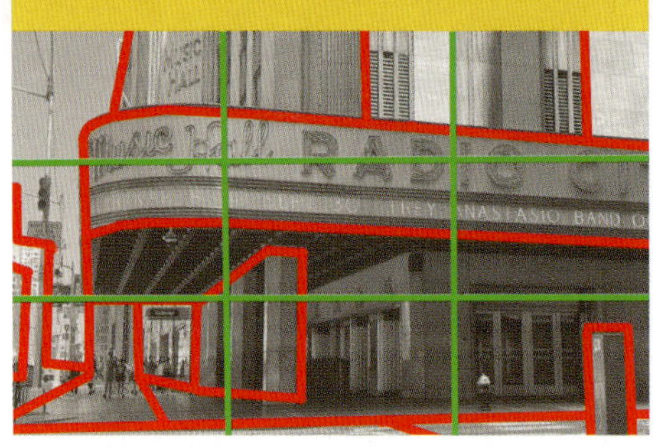

While imagining how this view will turn into a painting, I have a desire for compositional balance while also showcasing my subject. In this case, my main subject is the marquee with the text. While imagining my composition, I want the marquee to land on the top horizontal line of the rule-of-thirds grid, while the corner of the building lands approximately on the left vertical line. The red lines denote one possible approach to color blocking the main forms, which help simplify this otherwise complex scene.

include in your composition. Some people use a viewfinder to help them visualize a composition, and sometimes it's helpful to take a photo to help figure out the composition.

STEP 3: STRUCTURE

Whether it is an amorphous blob and a few lines sketched in pencil, or a bit of negative space carved out of an underpainting, the structure needs to be defined from the basic forms of whatever you are painting. It doesn't need to be perfect—there will always be the possibility for adjustment later.

This step, in which you are finally making some kind of mark on your substrate, can be approached in various ways: one involving a pencil sketch, and another involving an underpainting.

I prefer sketching with a pencil when there is a lot of man-made structure, like with architecture; some other situations also call for a pencil sketch. Generally, I find that it's more fun to do the underpainting technique; instead of making a sketch, I like to make a wash of color first, and then I can add to and subtract from this underpainting. It's also faster because the structure and value stages can be combined. With the underpainting technique, it's easier to adjust on the fly.

Sometimes, defining the structure can even be a combination of both techniques, where I sketch something—either loosely or with precision—then cover the entire surface with a light wash of color before moving on to the other steps. Sometimes, it's the other way around, where I cover the surface with color and sketch on top of that.

STEP 4: VALUES

Indicate values lightly, and keep it simple: just lights and darks. I usually start with dark values, which creates contrast against the white background surface and helps me see my image better.

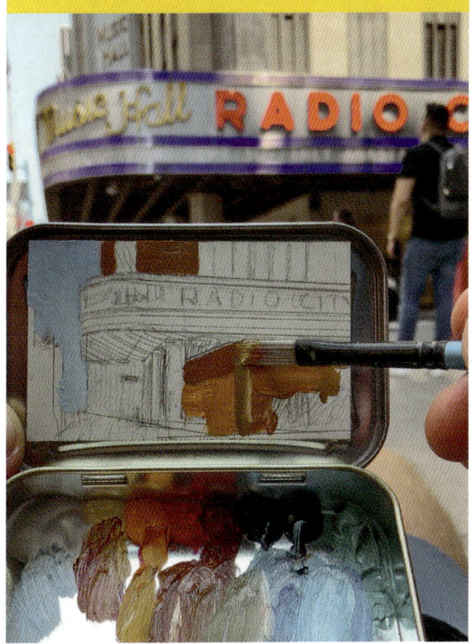

I've started blocking in the colors.

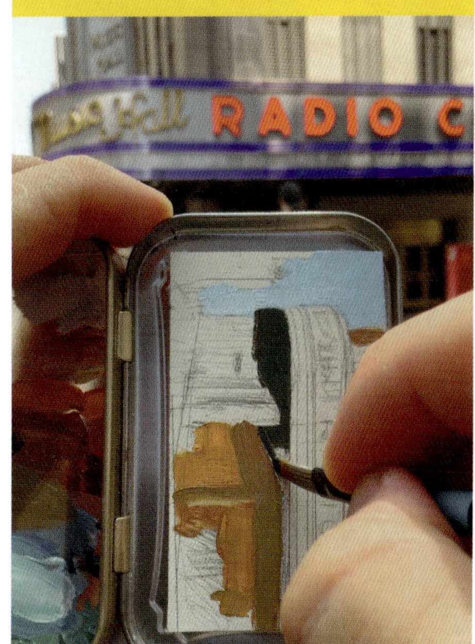

Don't be afraid to rotate the painting vertically if it helps you.

If using a pencil to indicate values, the darks can be defined with a few lightly shaded areas. If you can help it, don't spend forever rendering a perfect drawing. It's all going to be covered up.

As I explained in the last step, the underpainting technique I use involves making the structure of the painting with the values, so that is two steps in one. The dark areas can be indicated with more pigment, and the lighter areas can be created by lifting away pigment with a clean, slightly damp brush.

STEP 5: BASIC COLOR BLOCKING

Starting with the largest brush that makes sense for the size of your painting, fill all major areas on your whole surface with a fairly thin layer of color. With the miniature paintings I do, the largest brush I use is typically ½" (13 mm)–wide flat brush, but ¼" (6.5 mm) works, too.

As the first step of the actual painting process, this part should be an extremely simplified version of the final image. A goal for this part is to take as little time as possible. If you can shoot for blocking in all your base colors in ten to twenty minutes, this will ensure that the colors you're seeing are nailed down before the light changes too much, and the rest of the time is spent tweaking and detailing.

If any structural problems are revealed while creating the basic forms of the painting, it's not difficult to fix them since everything is still looking very basic. The more detail that is added, the more difficult it is to fix major structural issues. The less detail there is, the less emotionally attached you are to what you have created, and making changes is easy.

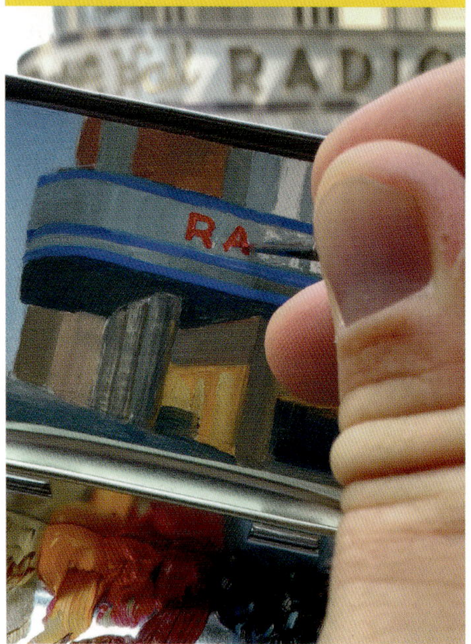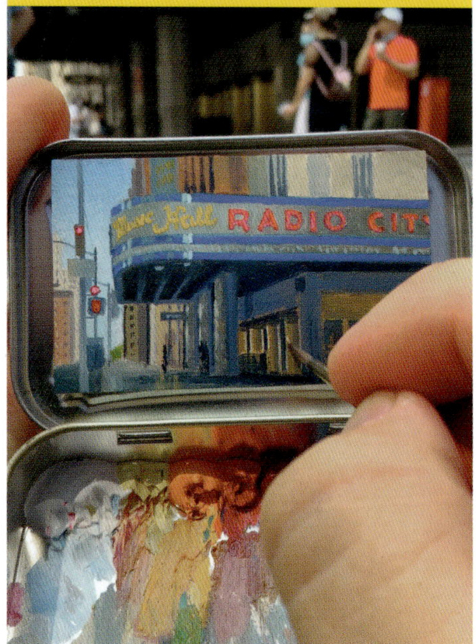

Now is the time to add the smaller areas of color.

Some final highlights wrap up this painting.

STEP 6: SMALLER COLOR BLOCKING AND TINTING

This step involves painting smaller color areas within the larger blocks of color from the previous step, or tweaking the colors that are already there. This can either be done with the smaller edge of the large brush, or with a different, smaller brush. On my miniature paintings, I often use a small #2 or 2/0 round brush for this stage.

The best part about using oil paint is that for this step, you can easily mix the colors you need by slightly altering the large pools of existing colors on your palette, since the paints in your palette are still wet and workable.

STEP 7: DETAIL

With your smallest brush, you can now paint any final touches that you feel will make the painting complete, such as a few stray leaves, some small twigs that may catch your eye, or some small areas of extreme highlights or shadows that were missing.

I don't count documenting a painting as part of its creation, but it is always a good idea to document what you create. If for nothing else, you can use this to see your own progress over time.

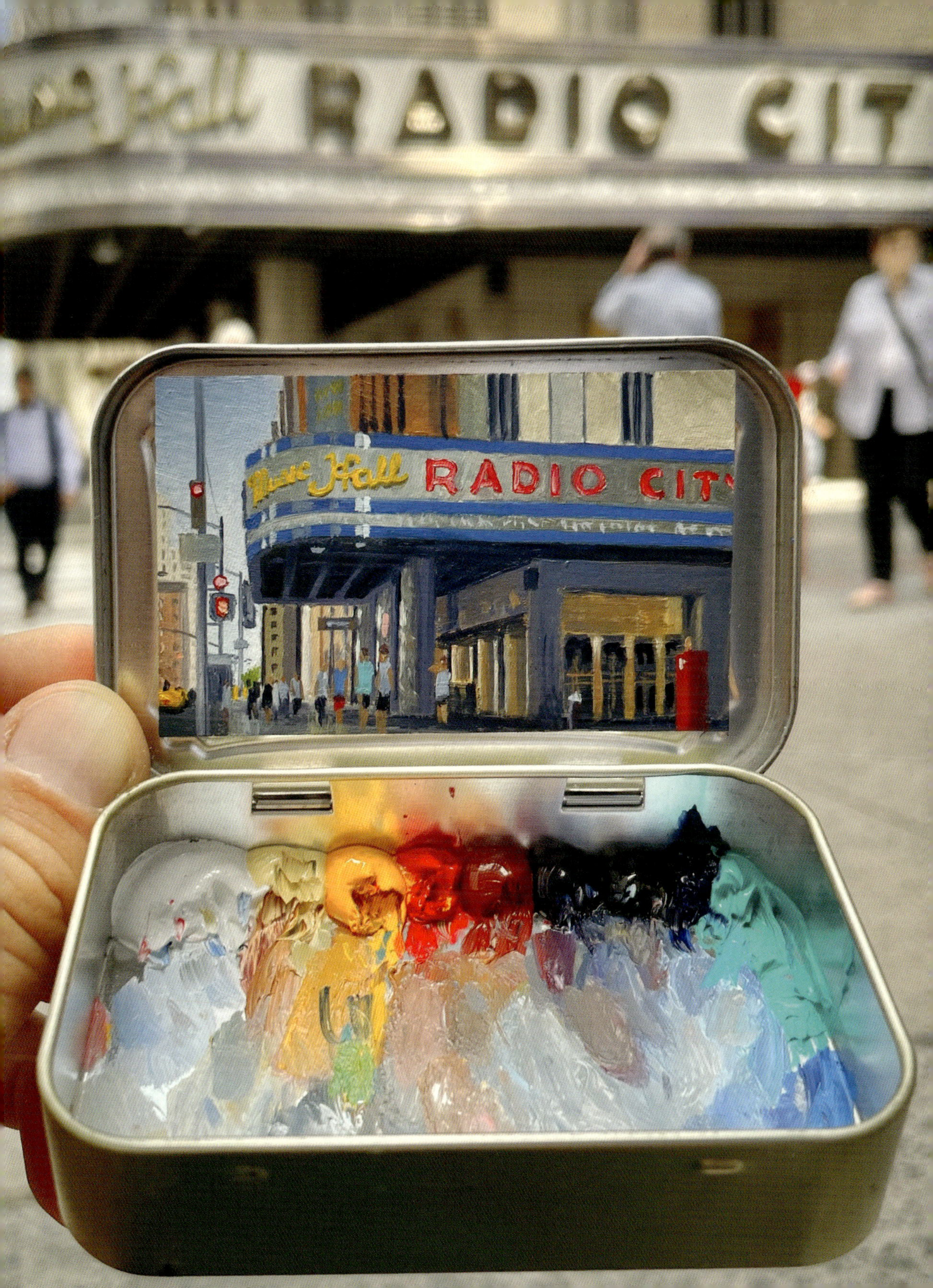
Music Hall RADIO CITY

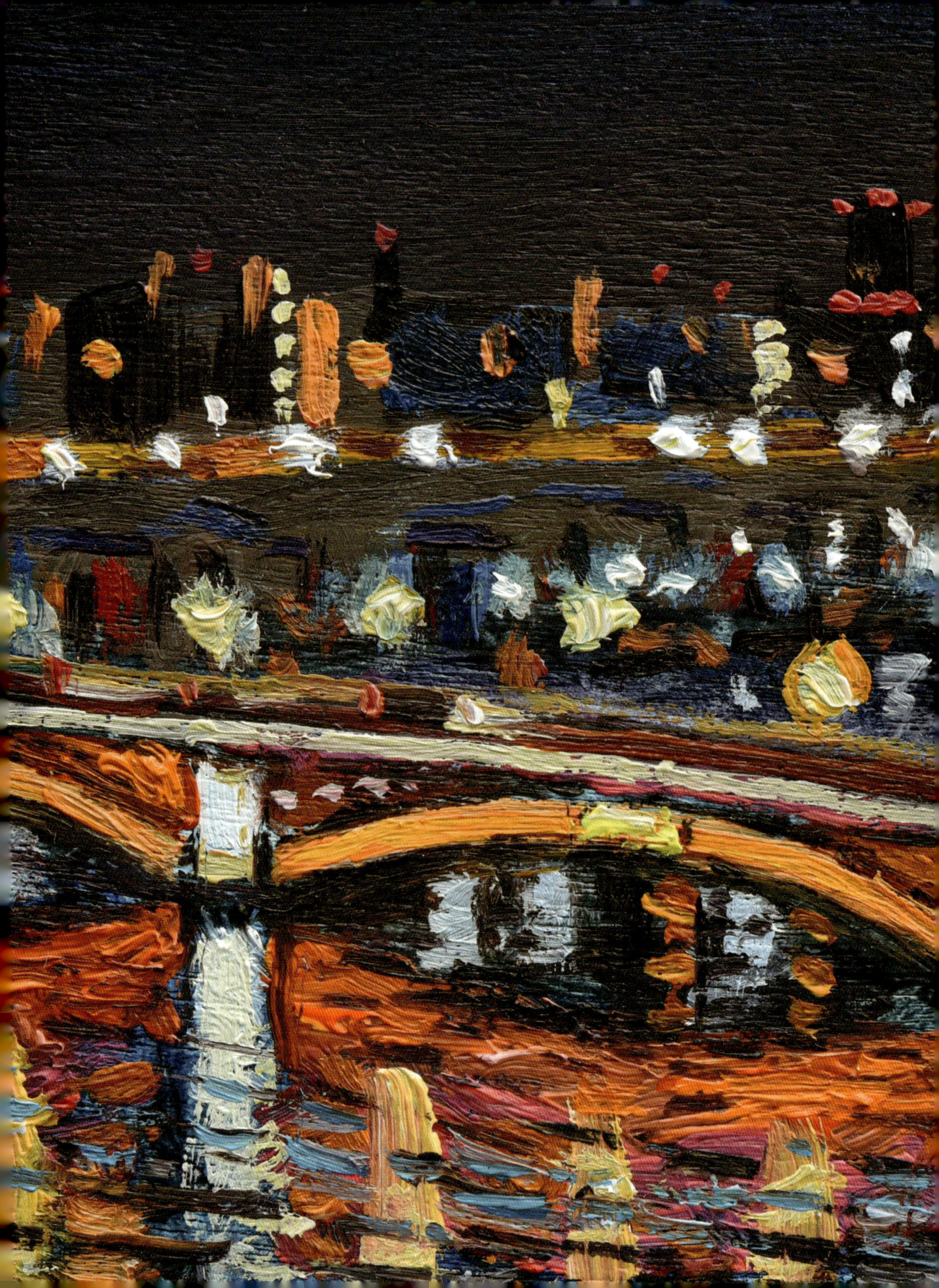

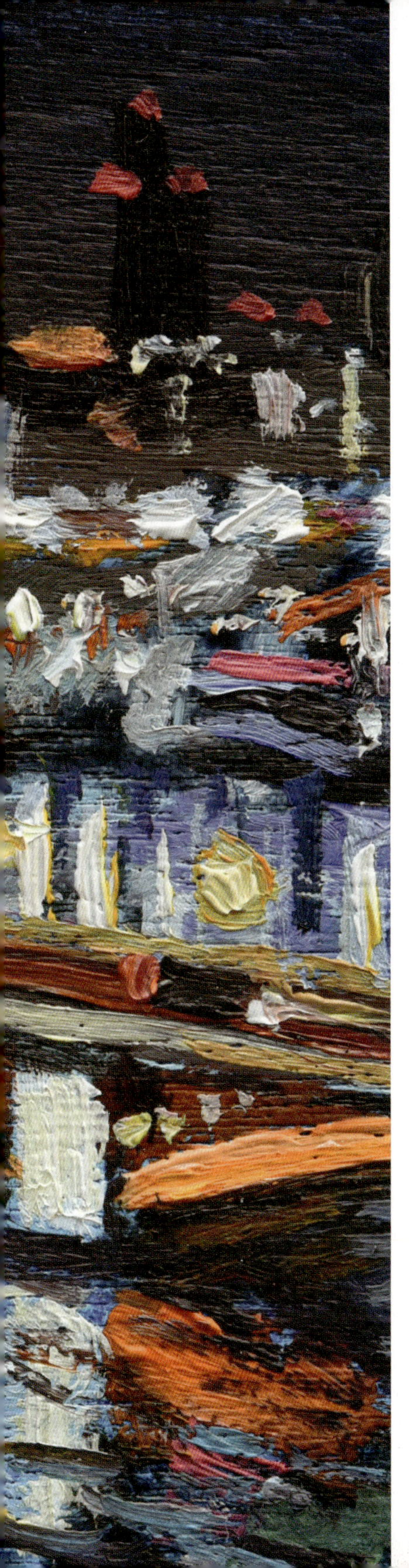

PAINTING TUTORIALS

MONOTONE: STANDING IN A CREEK

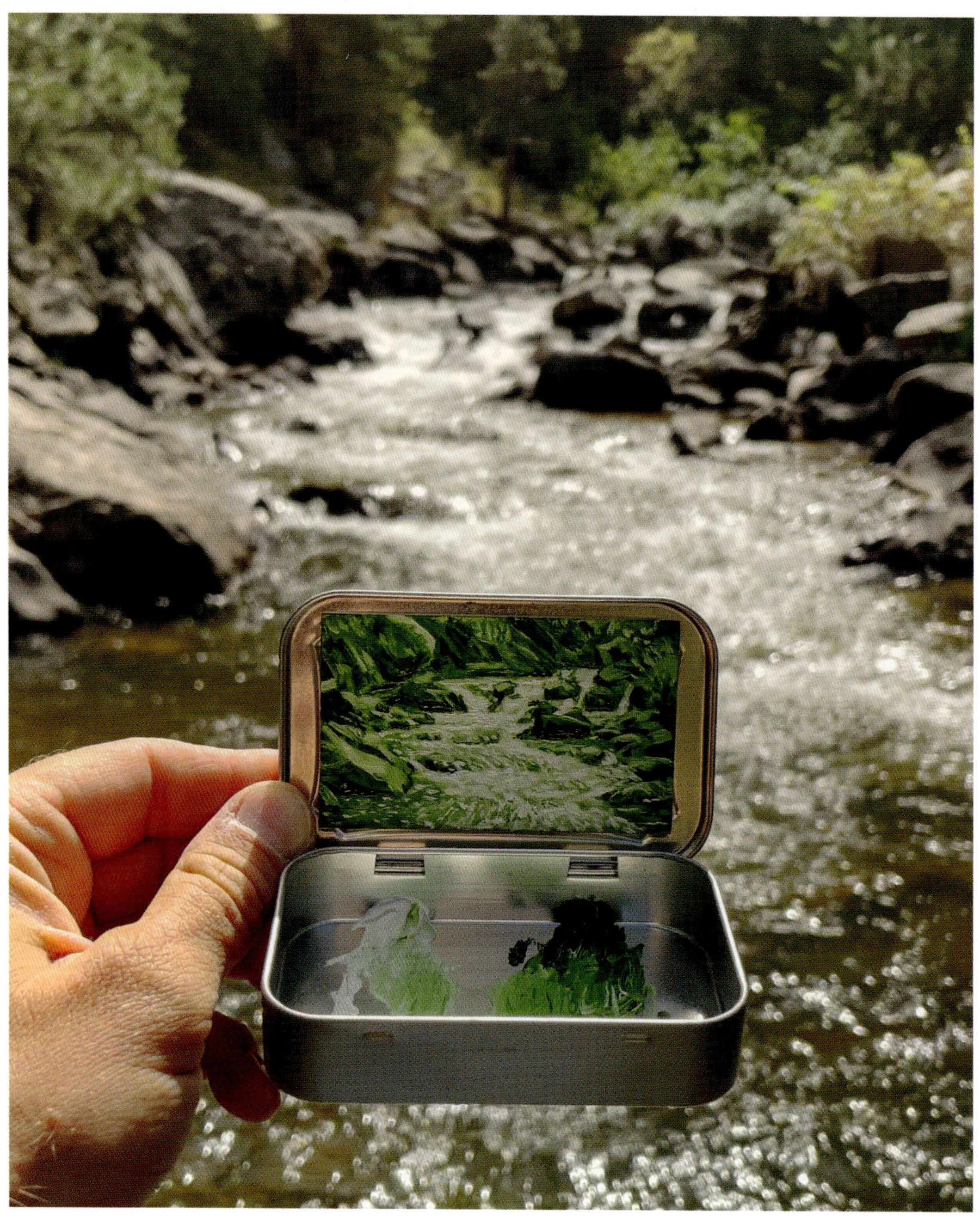

Working with a single color plus white is a great way to get practice at seeing and recognizing values, as well as painting them more effectively.

Monotone paintings have been created for centuries by countless artists, not only as a less expensive way to get into painting, but as a practice in and of itself. It is also used as an underpainting technique before painting in full color. While monotones can be painted with any color, historically they have been painted in brown (also known as a brunaille), gray (grisaille), or green (verdaille). In this exercise, I will be painting a verdaille, or a monotone painted in green. Check out the gallery on page 37 to see some more examples of monotones.

I will be painting from an unconventional vantage point, which also speaks to the portability of this style of painting. I have my fishing waders on, and I am standing in the middle of a creek. I improvised a way to hold my painting supplies while I stand in the water. Attached to the front of my waders is something I found at a thrift store—a silly thing called a "tactical travel tray." It's basically a flat piece of robust fabric that snaps together into a little tray, which I can clip to the front of my body. When I'm done, I simply unsnap the corners and put it into my backpack.

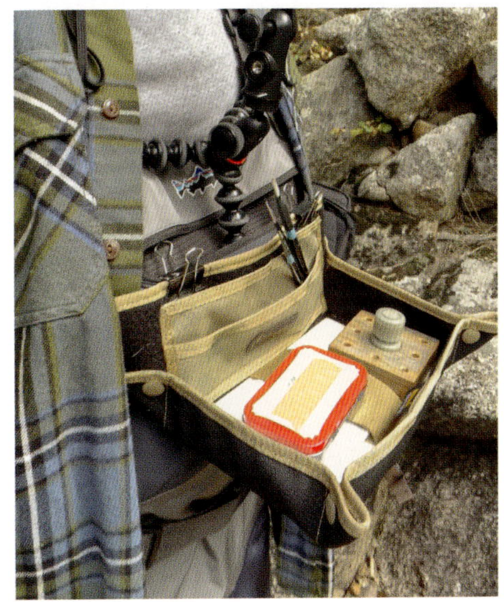

Check out my standing painting rig—the useful "tactical travel tray." You can also see what I use to record all of my videos. It's a phone-holding tripod with bendy legs.

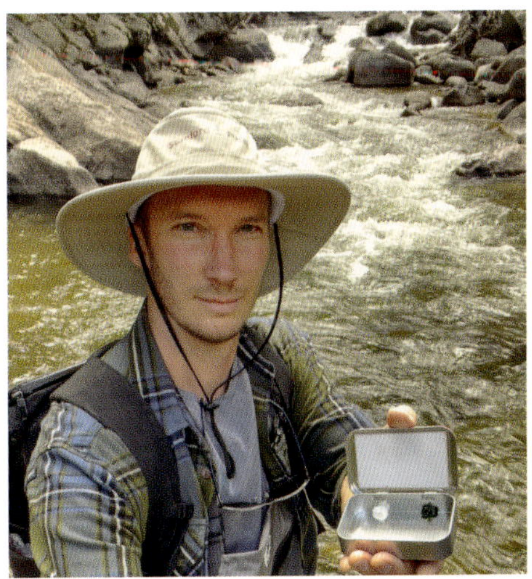

I took a quick selfie with my mint tin before I began painting. This is really an unconventional place to be doing art!

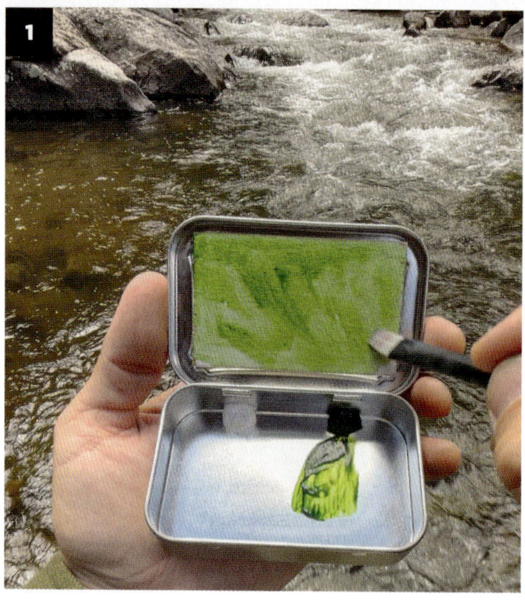

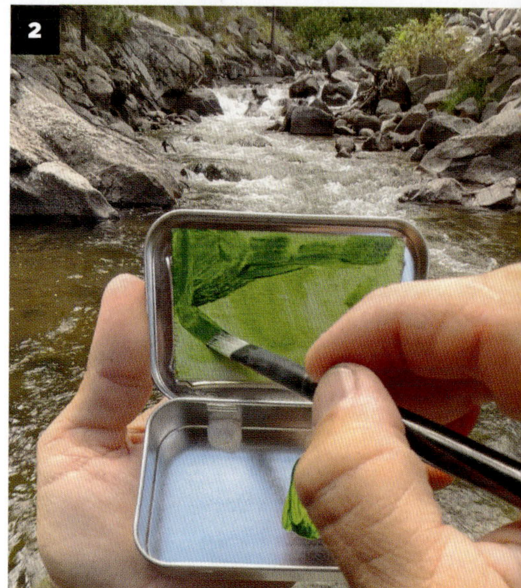

1. My only two paints here are Titanium White and Sap Green. I begin by toning my whole surface with a thin wash of Sap Green using my ½" (13 mm) flat brush.

2. Using the same brush, I begin mapping out my composition by establishing my dark values. Before painting, I decided on a composition that zooms in tightly on this area of rapids in the creek.

3. I'm not using full-strength dark values—just somewhere in between 50 and 75 percent dark.

4. Once I've done a basic blocking-in of the main dark areas without going into too much detail, now I can establish the lighter areas. As with the darks, I am not using a full-strength light value at this stage, but rather a value that is about 10 percent away from pure white. I want to leave room for any lighter highlights in the water.

5. Just a few highlights on the rocks in the background is all that needs to be done there for now, as this painting does not focus on those details.

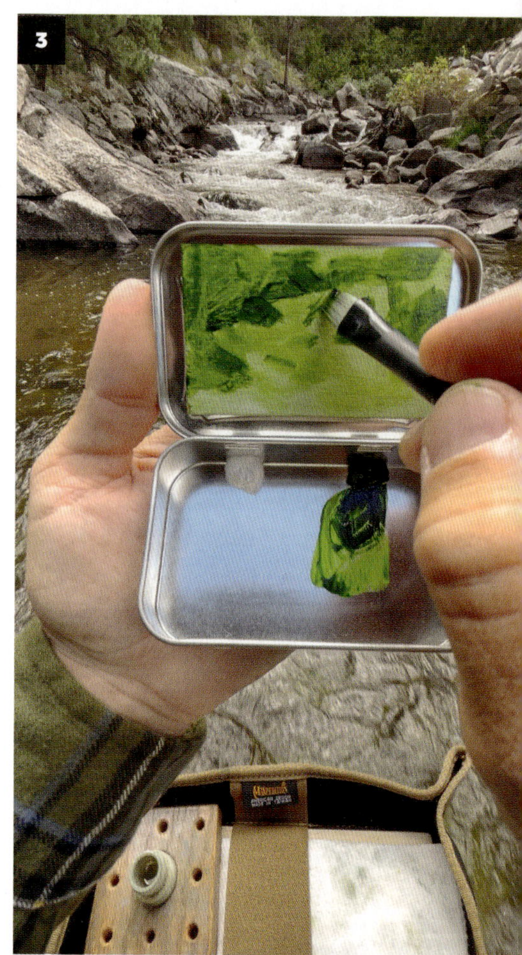

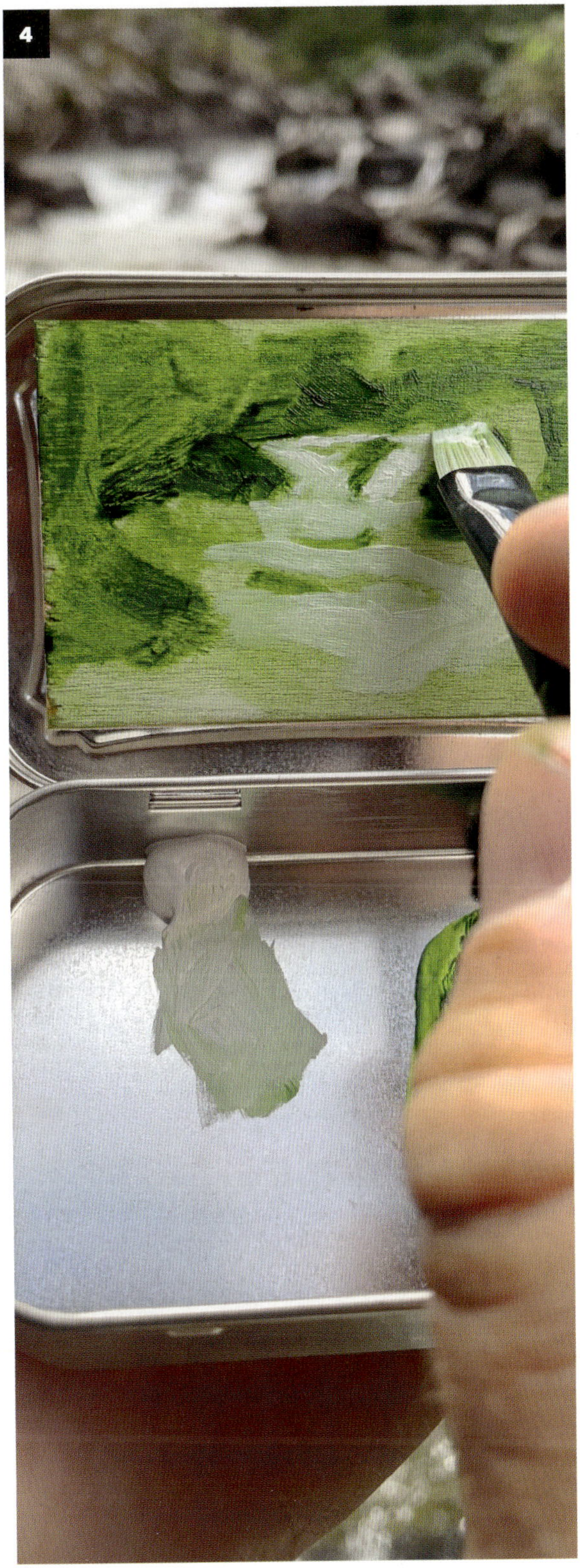

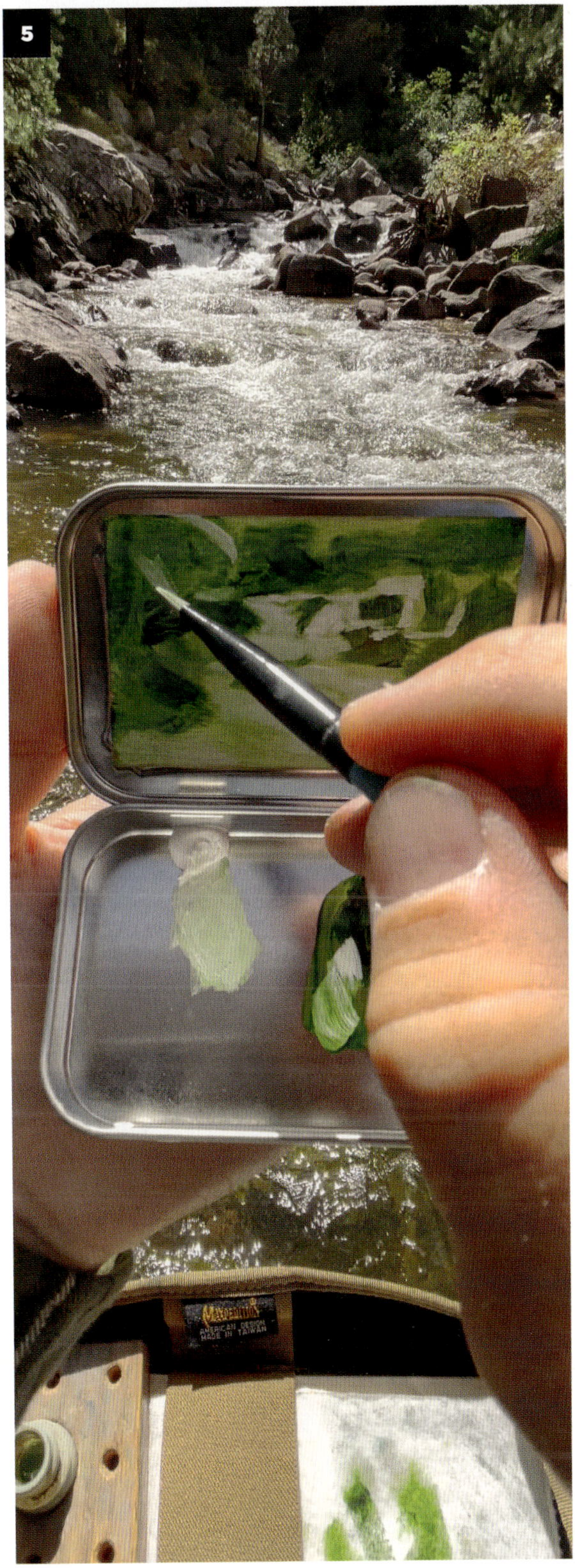

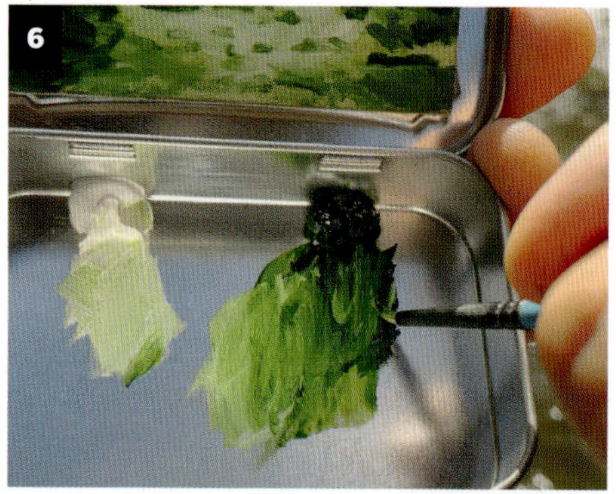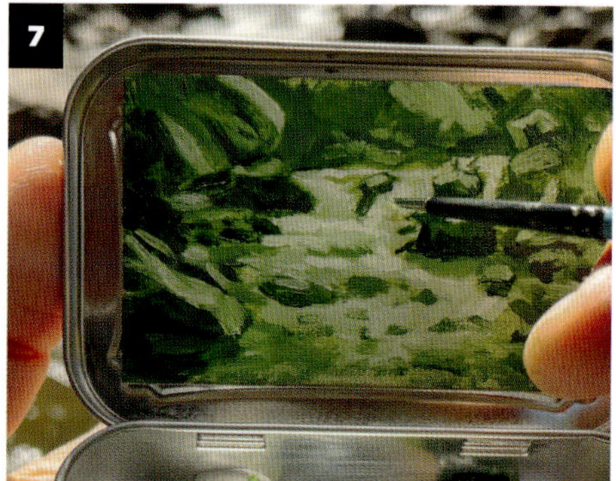

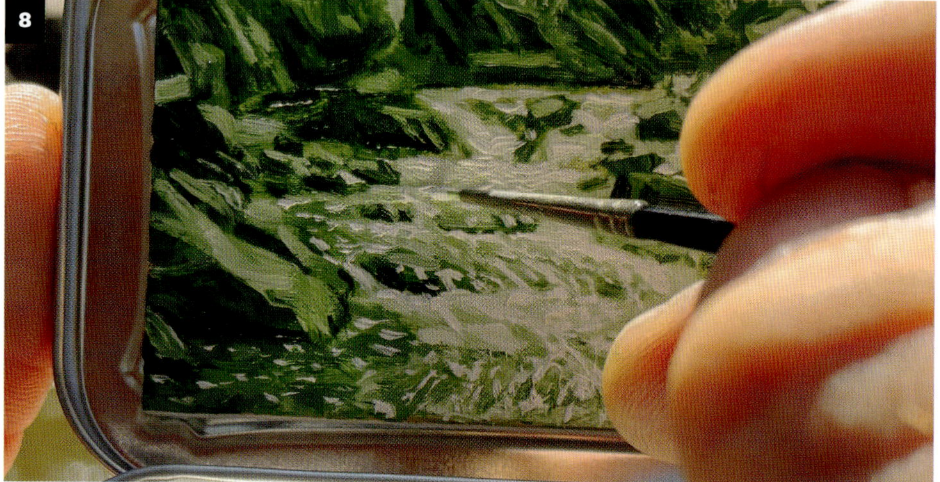

6. If you look at my palette, you can see that I'm mixing my paint as a value scale, light to dark. The more I look back and forth between my painting and the real thing, the more nuance in value I notice.

7. Now I'm really starting to focus on and refine on some of the darkest sections in my composition with full-strength Sap Green, using a smaller round brush.

8. The last thing is moving to my smallest brush, where I paint the brightest highlights in the water and any other small details that are necessary to complete the painting.

GALLERY: MONOTONE PAINTINGS

The following is a small selection of paintings made with a single color plus white.

The final painting from the previous section.

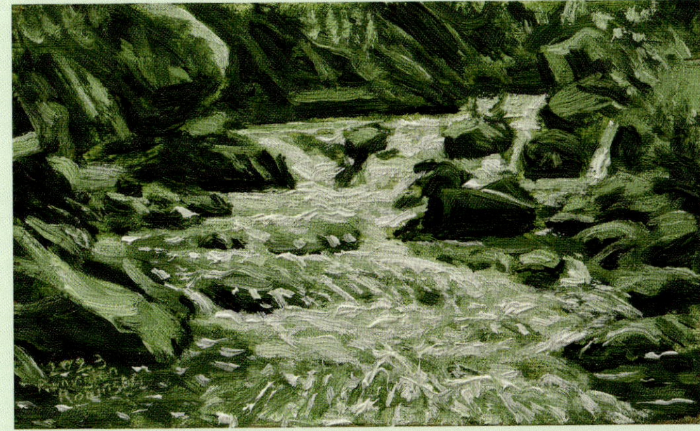

A coffee cup and saucer painted with Mars Black and Titanium White.

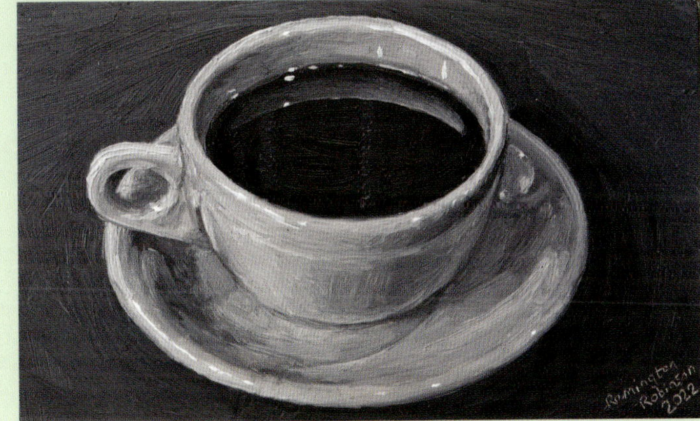

Rain over the Flatirons on Boulder, Colorado, painted with Torrit Grey and Titanium White. This was tricky, involving a lot of subtlety in the color mixing.

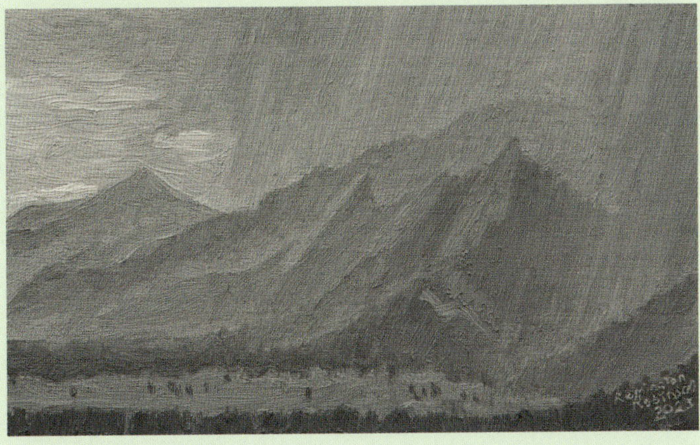

PRIMARY COLORS: POPPIES AT THE FLATIRONS

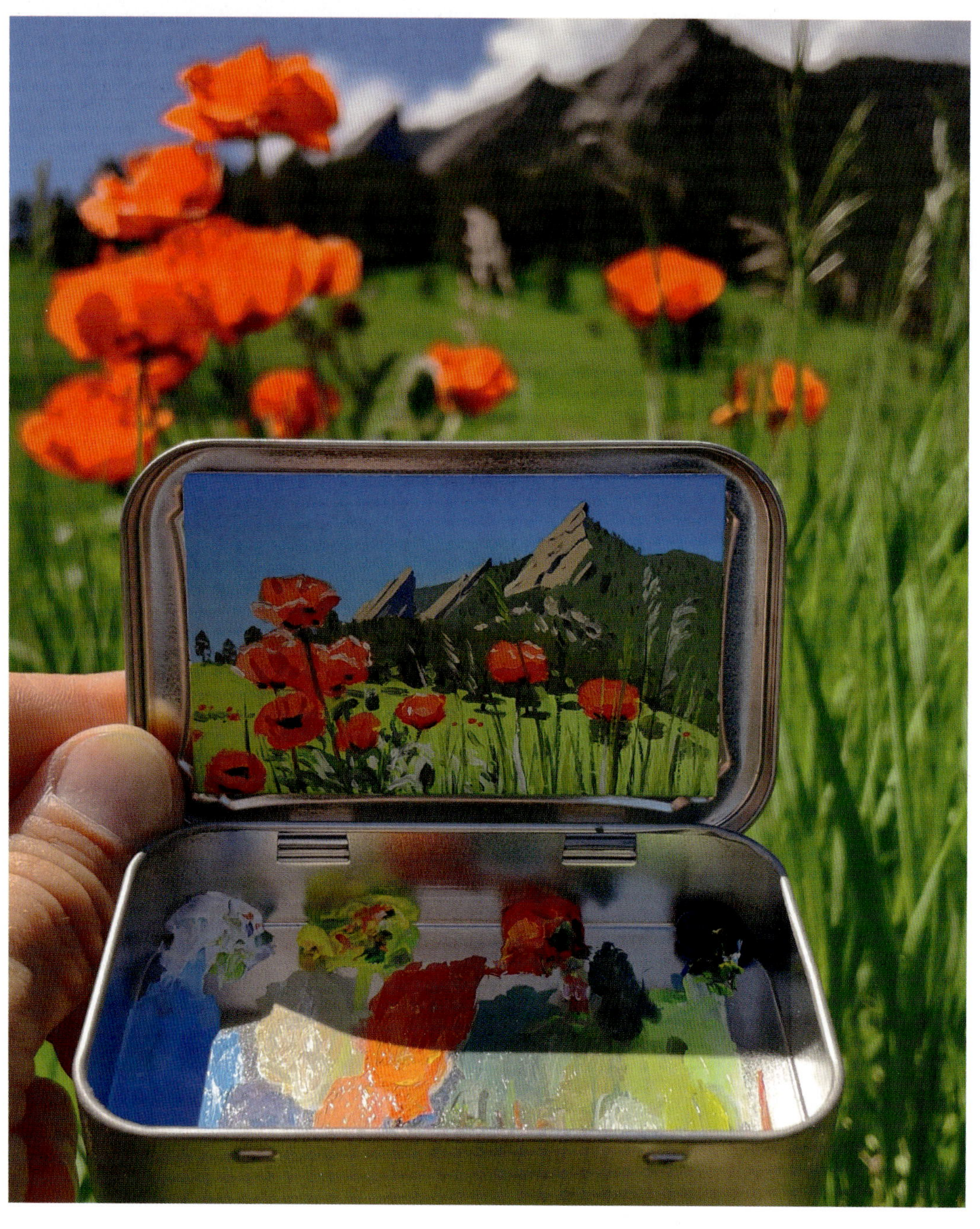

In almost any painting situation, it is possible to make a painting that is fairly true to the colors that exist in real life, using only primary colors. This is an example of painting with primary colors. I think it is a relatively easy landscape to paint because it is made up of only a few very graphic forms, with not too much fine detail. What's nice is that there is an opportunity to paint some fine detail if desired.

There are many versions of a primary color palette. For this exercise, I picked pure, saturated pigments that I thought could produce a fairly realistic representation of the colors that exist in reality: Bismuth Yellow, Bright Red, and Oriental Blue. Check out the gallery on page 46 to see some more examples of paintings made with primary colors.

This painting is a great example of one that I sketched first, before I painted it. As I mentioned when discussing my process (page 25), I usually have a composition in mind first, and sketching is a familiar way to try out what the composition will look like before committing to paint.

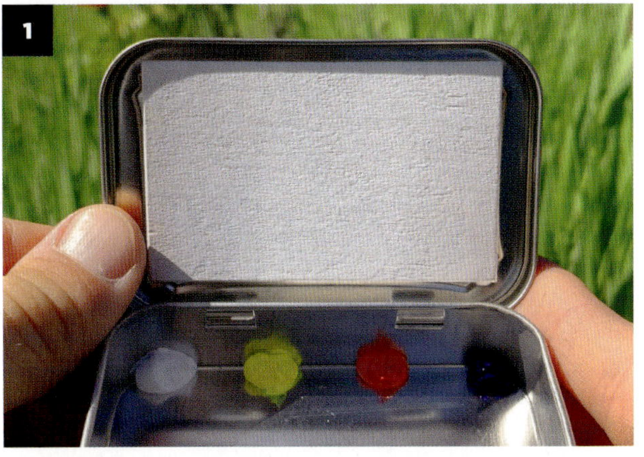

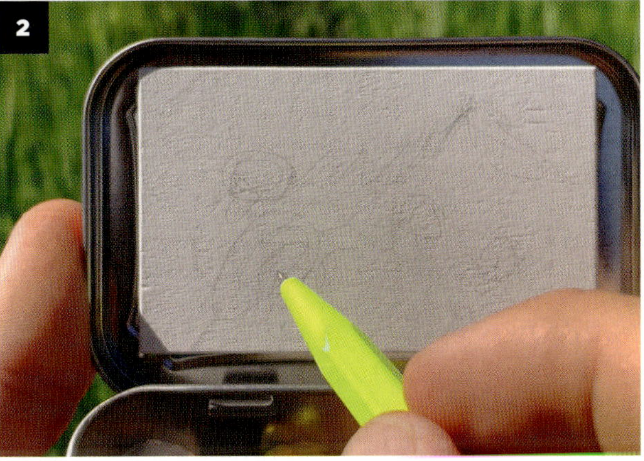

1. Here you can see my tin with the colors for this painting—Bismuth Yellow, Bright Red, and Oriental Blue.

2. The beginning of the sketch is always very light and gestural. I'm just getting a feel for my subject and envisioning how the final painting could look. This stage is fast, and I can always erase it if I don't like it.

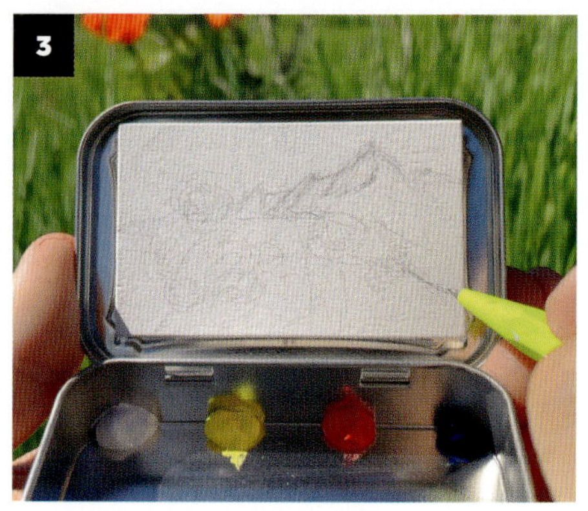

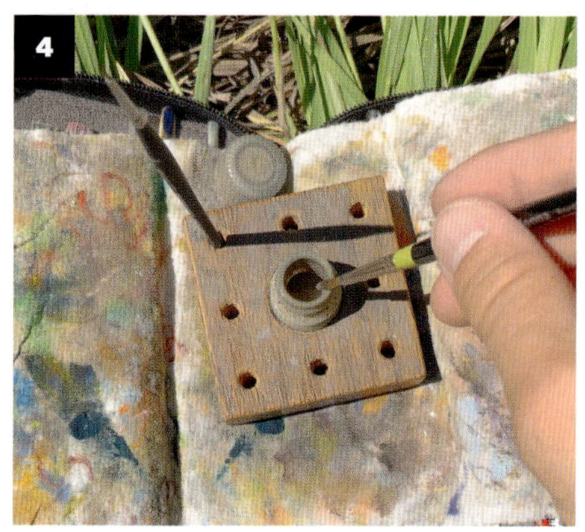

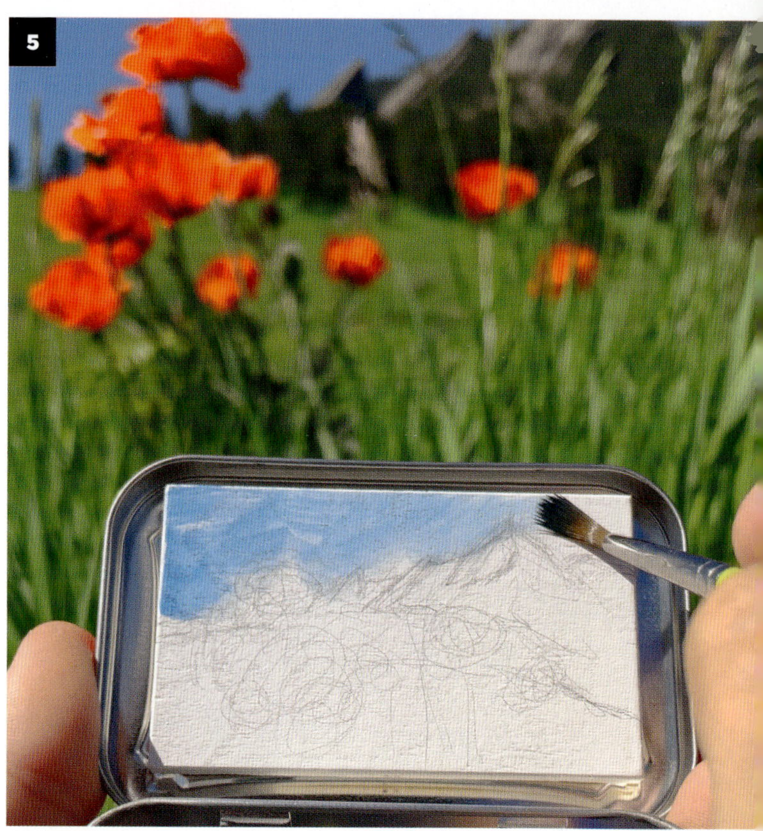

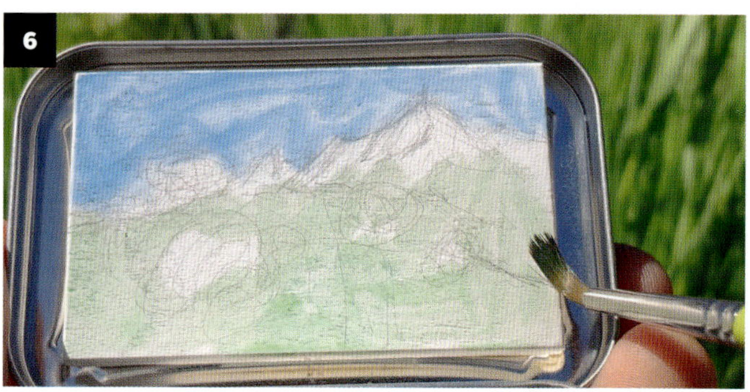

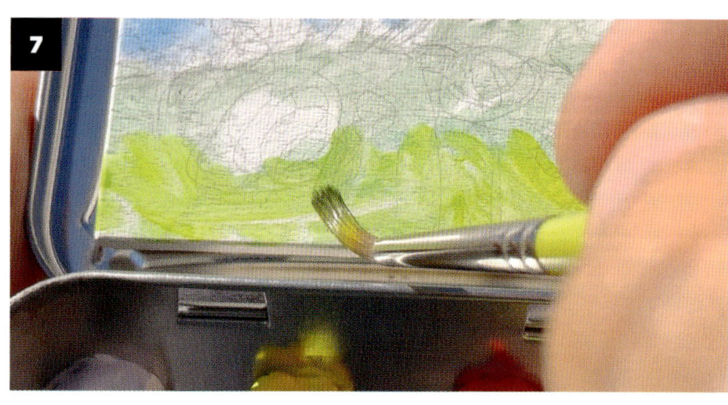

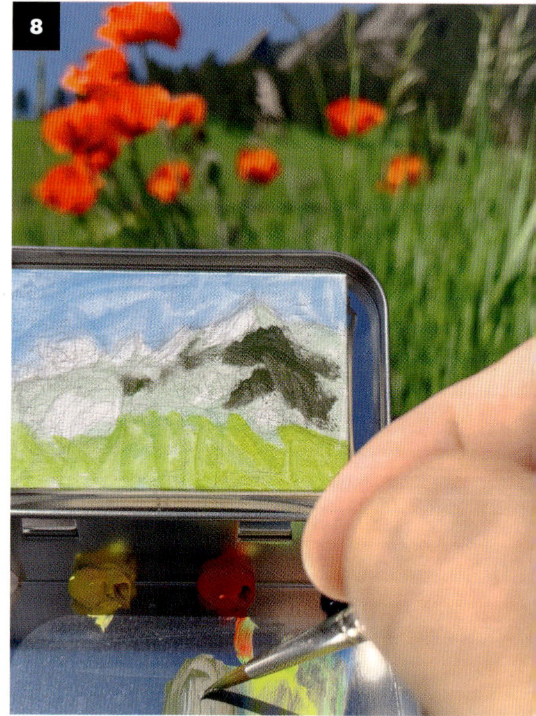

3. The sketch is becoming finalized, as I distinguish the rock formations and the tree line. One thing to keep in mind with using a pencil is that it should be done lightly, because the gray pencil lead can wash into the paint and affect the color of the paint if it is overdone.

4. Now that my sketch is done, I can pick up a paintbrush. This is a medium-sized round brush with soft synthetic fibers. The first thing I do is dip it in odorless mineral spirits to wet the brush. Since I am going to populate the shapes in my composition with some light washes of color, the brush needs to be fairly saturated with liquid.

5. At this stage, it doesn't really matter which order I go about filling in colors. The main goal is to quickly and loosely cover some of the white up in my largest areas of color. Having some color on the surface makes it easier to see how the final painting is going to end up, and the wet surface allows the paint to spread a little easier when filling in those large areas.

6. Notice that I'm not being very meticulous or careful with where I put my pigment, because at this basic color-blocking stage, everything is still approximate. I'm also being fairly liberal with my mineral spirits.

7. I'm going a little heavier on pigment now with the grass color, but it's still a fairly wet mixture. This is basically just yellow with the smallest touch of blue.

8. For the pine trees on the mountain, this is the first time I've employed all the paint on my palette. This particular color is heaviest on the blue and yellow, with a touch of red and a tiny bit of white. The red is crucial here. When mixing green for conifers, depending on the variety, they typically have more orange or red in their color mixture. Deciduous trees usually have less red or orange mixed into their green color mixture.

9. Now that all the largest areas are filled in with a base layer of color, I can start to lock in the final direction of the painting by applying a layer of paint at full opacity. This layer of paint is thick enough that it covers up what's underneath, but is still thin enough to be able to lightly add detail over the top of later.

The sunlit side of the Flatirons is a warm, light yellowish-brown color, which is mostly white and yellow but has a tiny touch of red to shift it towards orange. I muted the color just slightly, to make it a little muddy and brown by adding the tiniest amount of blue, since blue is the opposite of orange in the color wheel.

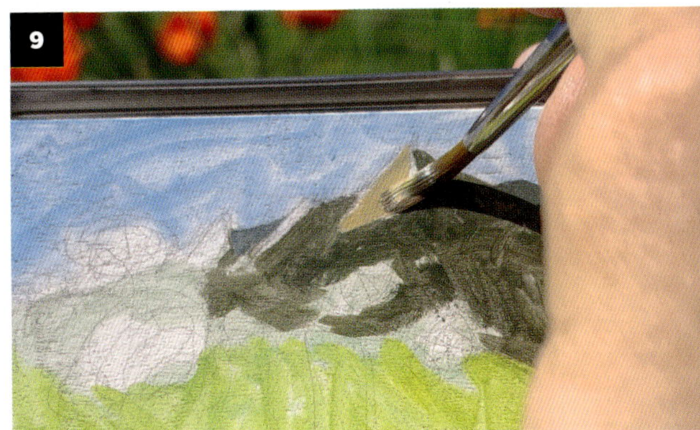

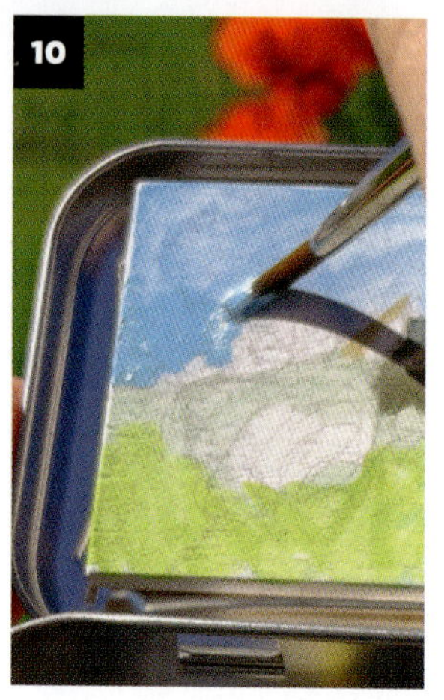

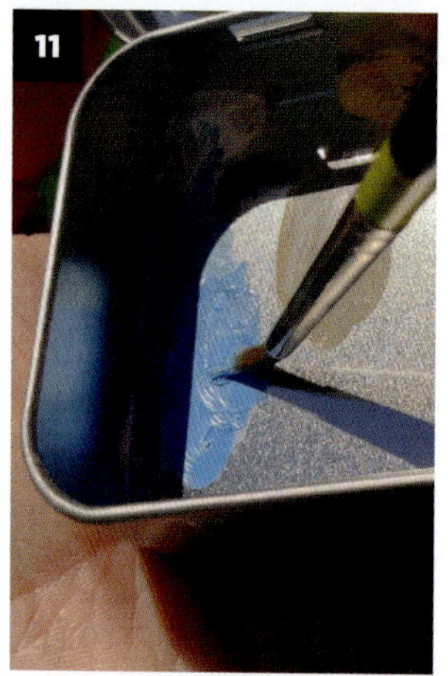

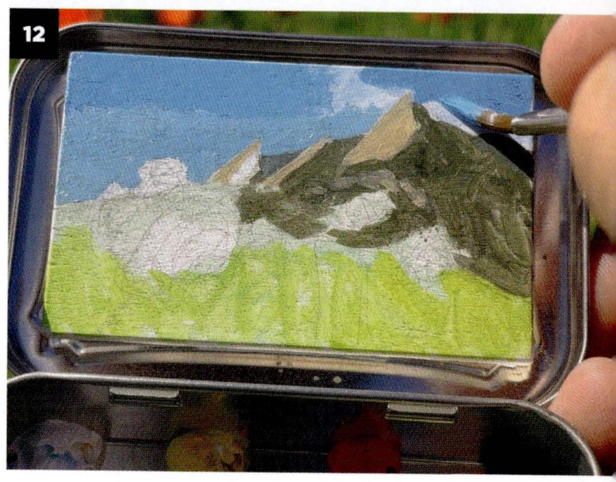

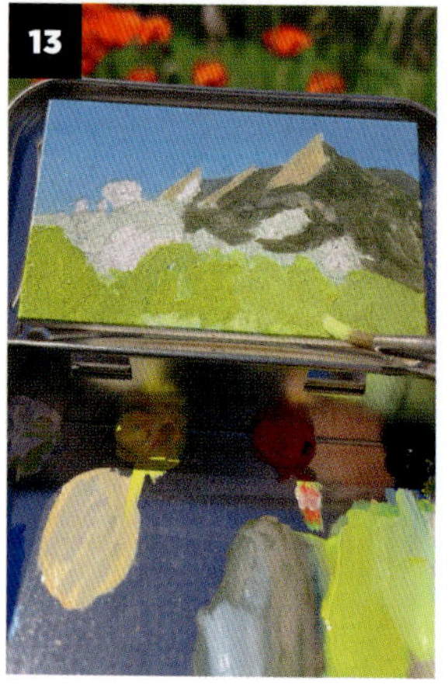

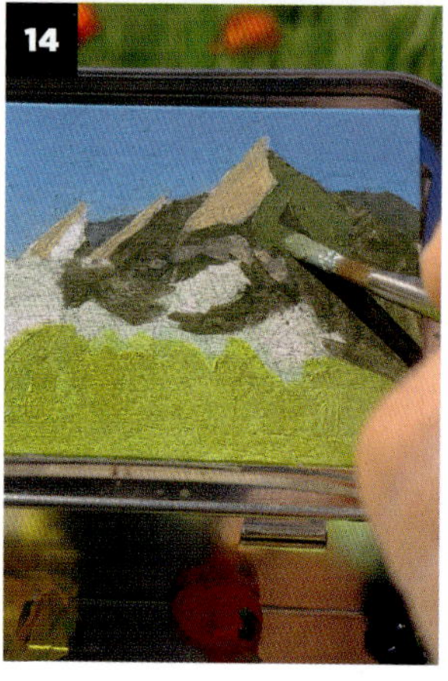

12. I ran out of my mixture and had to mix another batch of blue, which ended up darker than my original mix. That's totally fine since I'm going to blend it all together later anyway. It's actually good though, since the sun is off to the left, and the sky really does gradually get darker the further right I look.

13. The grass is next for the thicker paint. You can see I had to mix a new color a few times, and each time it was slightly different. That's fine since I am going to be adding grass texture to this later.

14. Now I add thicker paint application to the conifer forest on the mountain. There is not very much moisture in the air, but still enough that some atmospheric perspective can be observed. The farther away each part of the mountain is, the more atmosphere is between it and me. The color I apply for the mountain corresponds to that—the parts of the mountain that are farther away will be lighter and slightly more blue.

10. The clear blue sky is almost always lighter the closer you get to the horizon, and shifts in color toward green. I mixed a light blue and touched a little yellow into the mixture to achieve that.

11. Now that the lower part of the sky is painted in, I'm mixing the upper part of the sky with just blue and white, but slightly heavier on the blue in this mixture to make a darker and more saturated blue.

15. Up until now, I've painted in midtones, but that is all about to change with the shadows on the Flatirons. I started out a little darker than I wanted, so now I lighten it up. The color is a slightly muted dark bluish-purple.

16. The time is right to mix that saturated red-orange color for the poppies, and to begin painting them into the scene.

17. As soon as I put some color down, I realized I made an error in my excitement. My brush, with that saturated red-orange color, touched the blue paint of the sky and mixed into it. Because blue and orange are opposites, this muted the color and robbed it of its saturated quality. Instead of continuing on, I'm going to start the flowers over and do them properly. The first step here is to wash and dry my brush.

18. With my dry brush, I carefully lift away the muddy orange color, scraping away the paint into the bristles and washing my brush as I go, until all of that pigment is lifted away.

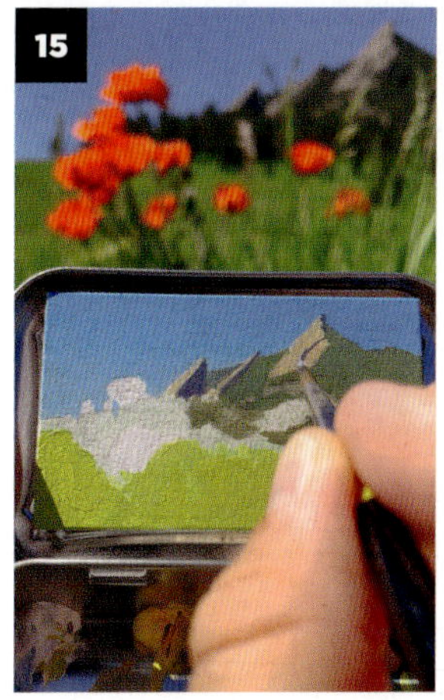

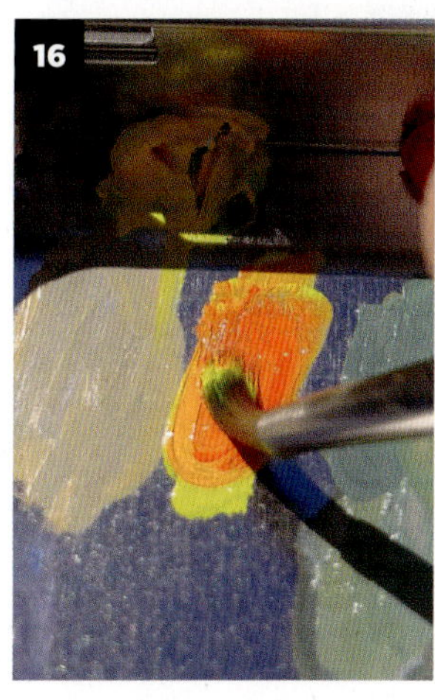

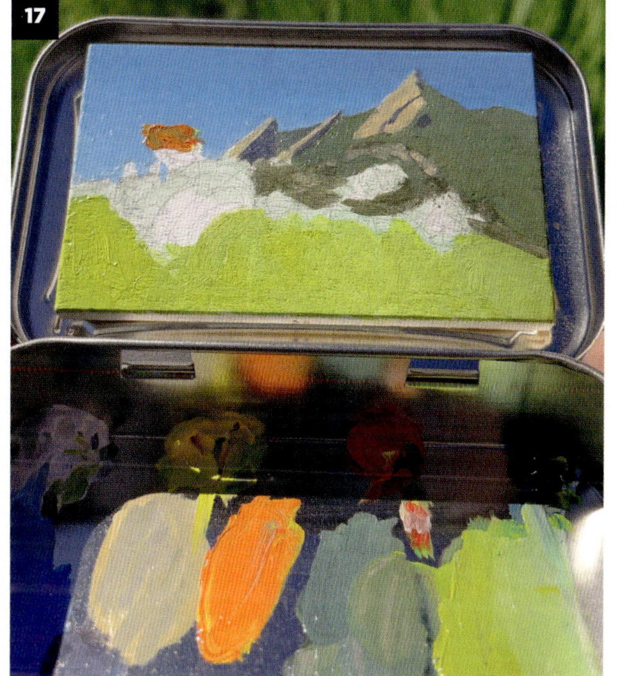

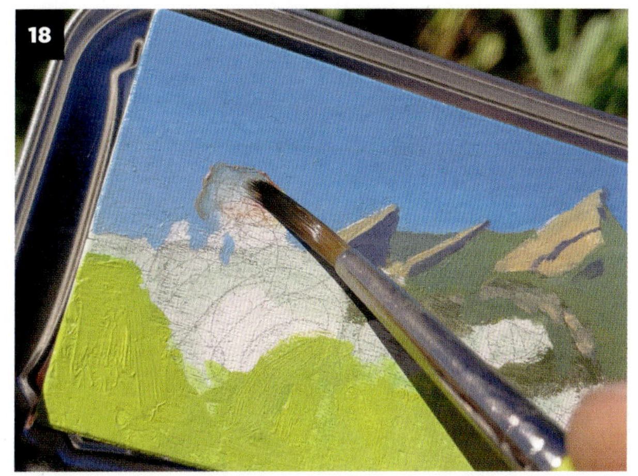

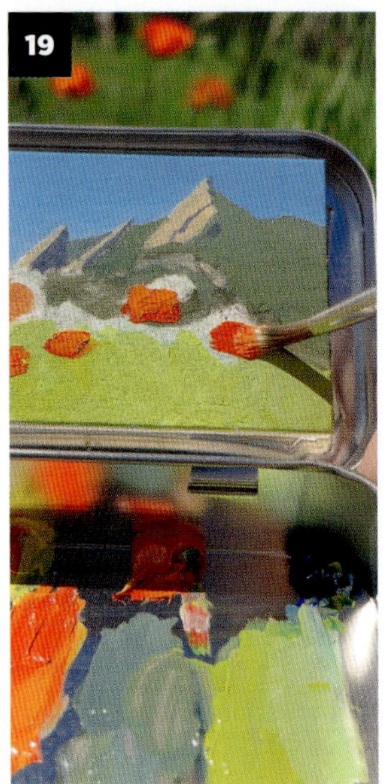

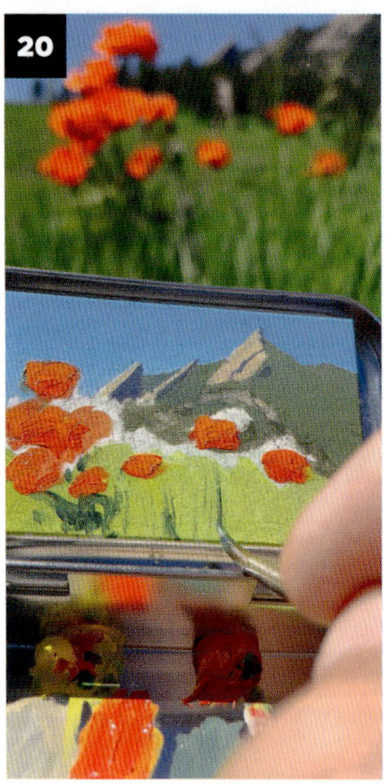

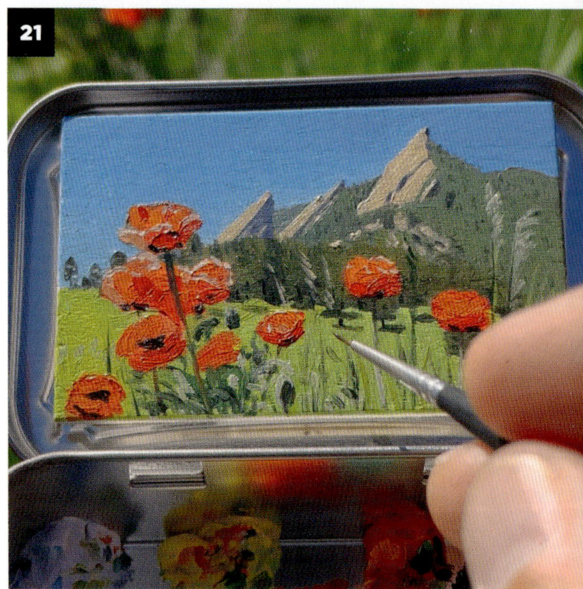

19. Now I can apply that color again more carefully. One thing to add here is that I intentionally left filling in the red poppies for after the sky and the grass. Had I painted the red before the sky, the smallest amount of that very saturated color would have contaminated the sky and compromised my plan to make a nice gradient that is lighter on the bottom. Likewise, had I painted the red before the light green grass color, it is likely that the red would have contaminated that color.

You can see that the powerful red pigment can be painted over the light green with little consequence, as long as the paint is applied with a brush at a low angle. The poppies are not filling up all the space I had allocated for them, and that's okay, as I can close in on them later with the other colors that are still mixed in my palette.

20. Now for the darker green poppy leaves and some grass details, which are in shadow.

21. I've now moved to my smallest round brush to fill in details all around this painting. In the background, you might notice that I put in tree shadows on the mountains, more light and shadow detail on the rocks, some trees on the far left, and brought the sky color into the areas where it was missing. In the foreground, I added the dark spots on the underside of the poppies and some light areas on the red petals, painted in the light bluish-green highlights on the poppy leaves, and added more grass details.

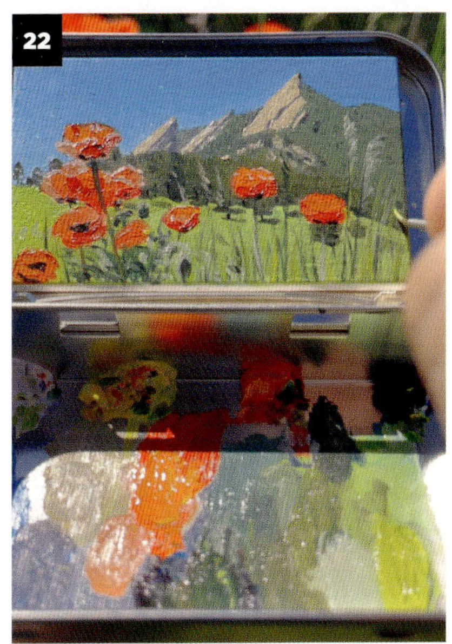

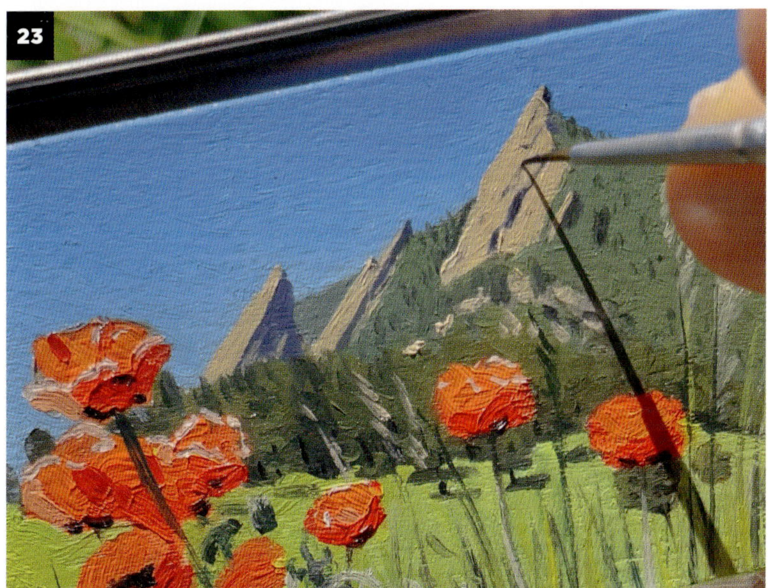

22. To finish up this painting, I'm adding more variation into the grassy foreground.

23. I'm putting some shadow details on the Flatirons, which are the main subject of this painting, with the poppies providing a very nice accent of color.

24. Here is a view of the finished painting.

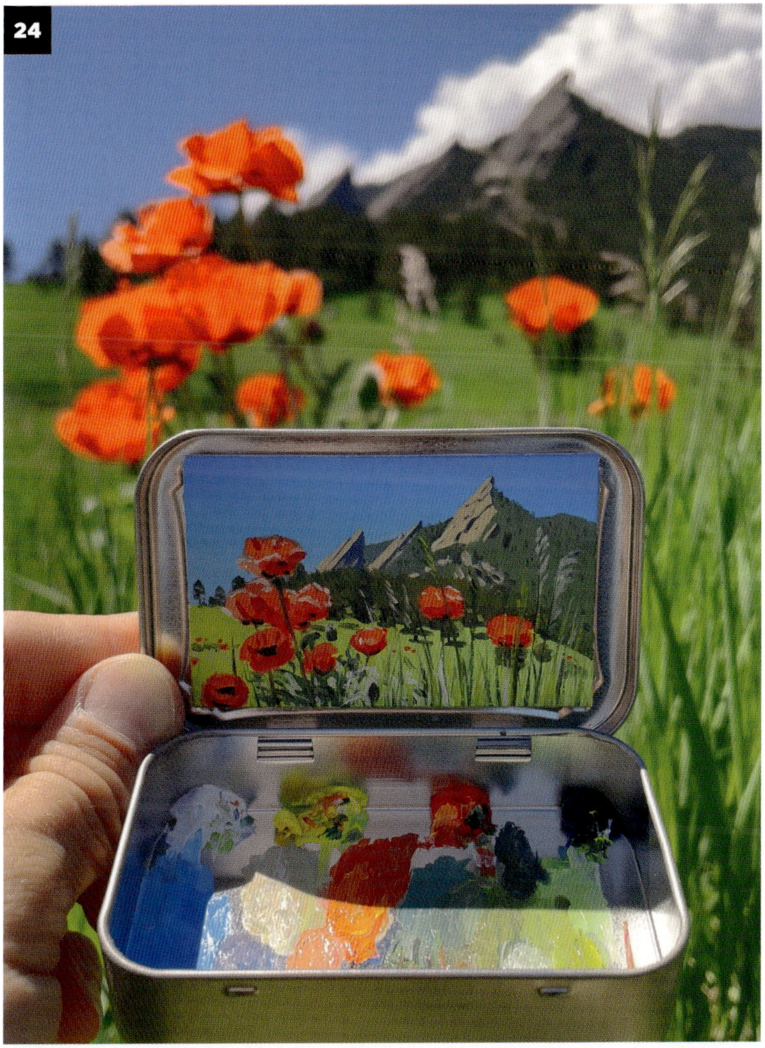

GALLERY: PRIMARY COLOR PALETTE

The following is a small selection of paintings made with a primary color palette.

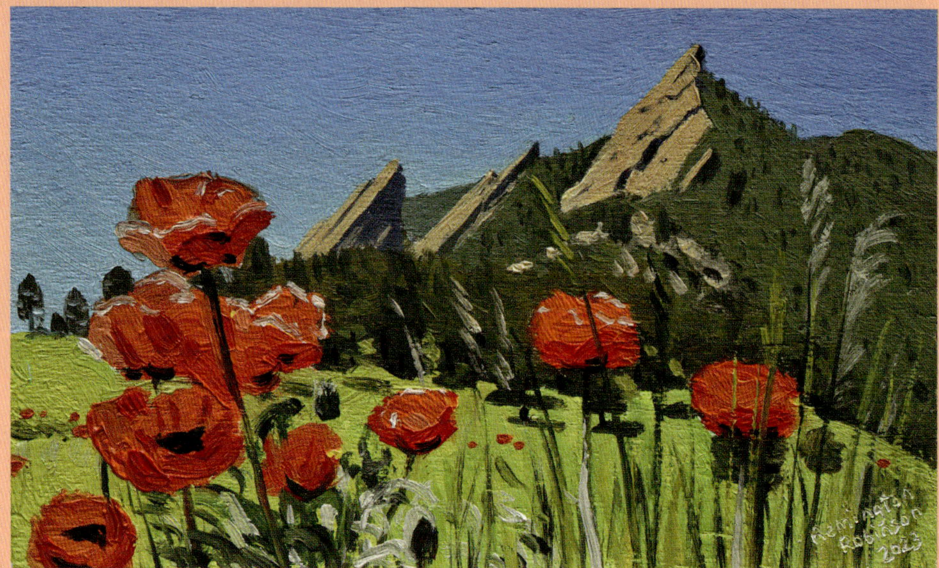

Poppies at the Flatirons in Boulder, Colorado. This was painted with Titanium White, Bismuth Yellow, Bright Red, and Oriental Blue.

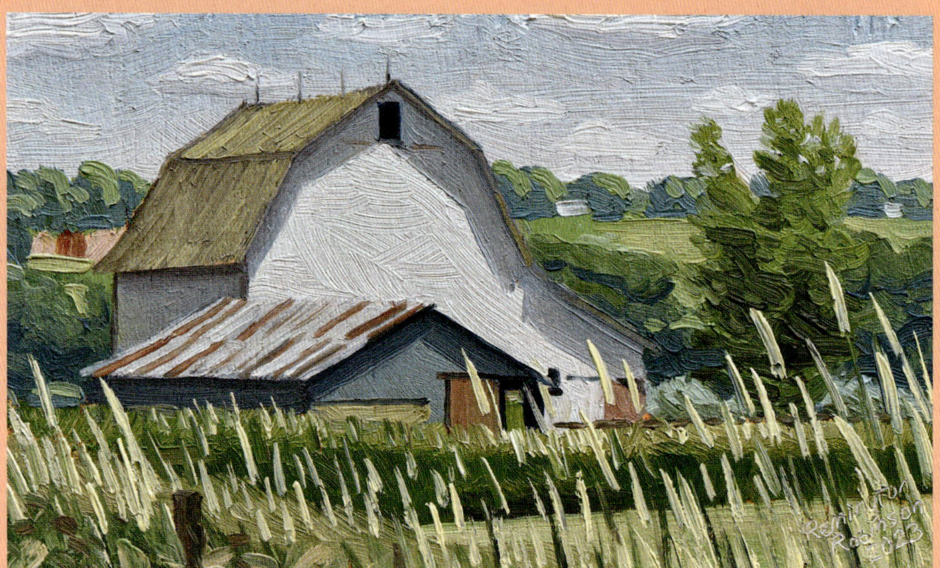

A barn in Boulder, Colorado. This was painted with Titanium White, Chrome Yellow Deep, Mars Red, and Prussian Blue.

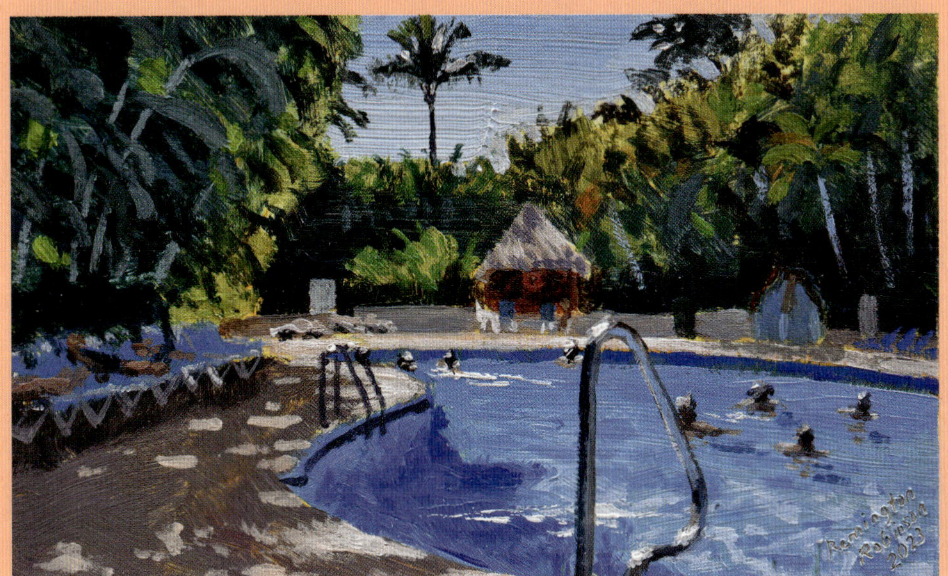

A swimming pool in Puerto Vallarta, Mexico. This was painted with Titanium White, Winsor Lemon, Permanent Geranium Lake, and Phthalo Blue.

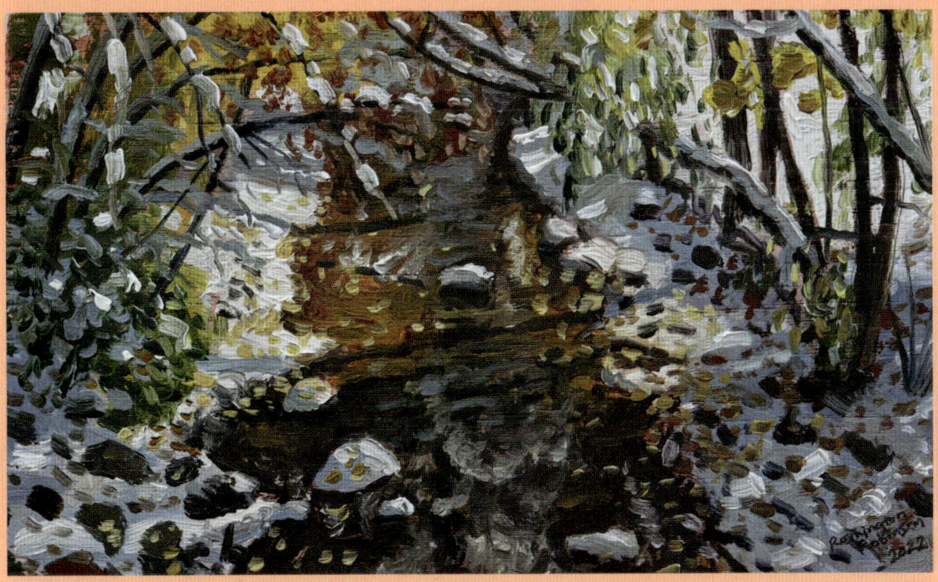

Fall colors and snow on Boulder Creek in Boulder, Colorado. This was painted with Titanium White, Indian Yellow Deep, Venetian Red, and Indanthrene Blue.

FOLIAGE: TREE NEXT TO THE ROAD

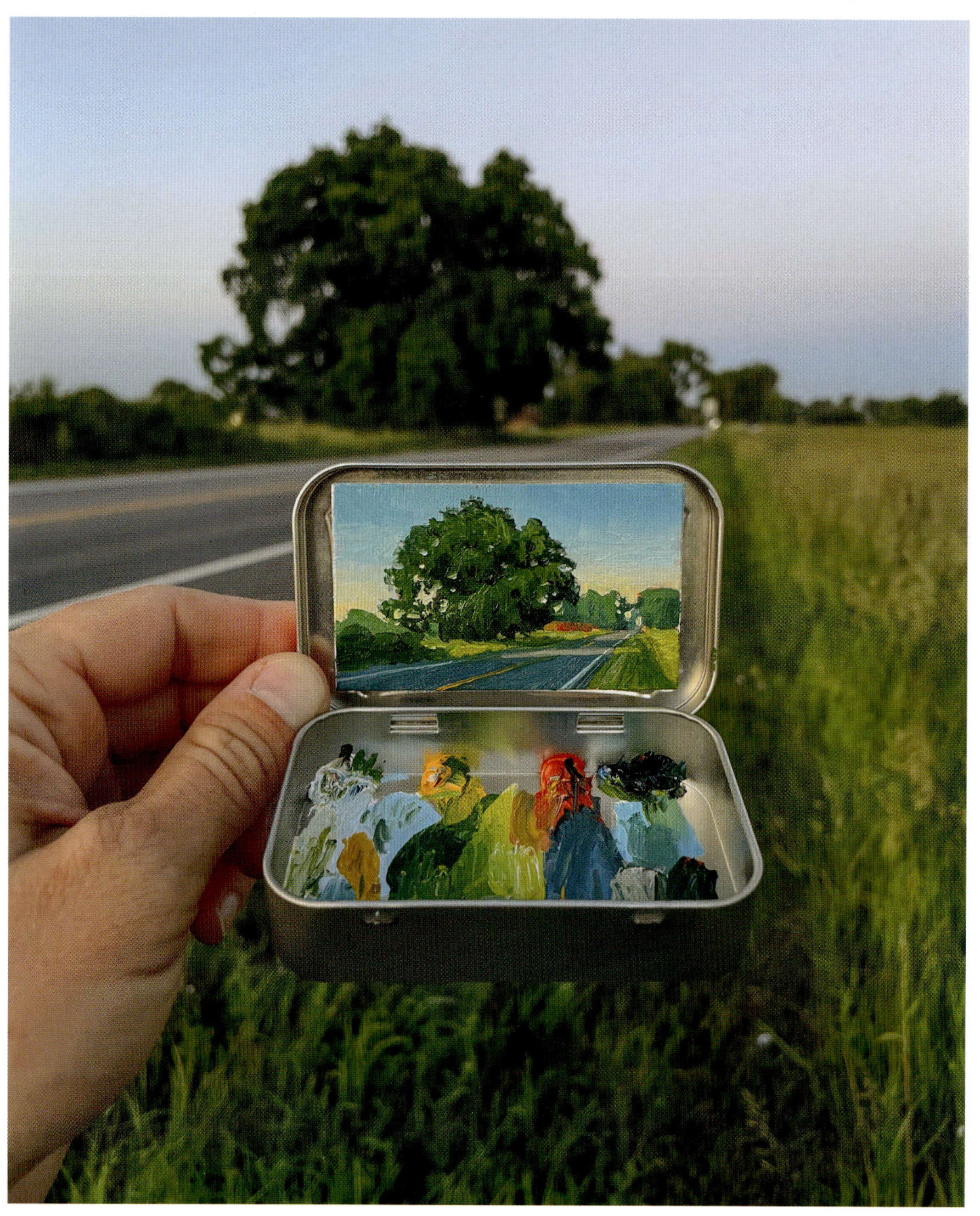

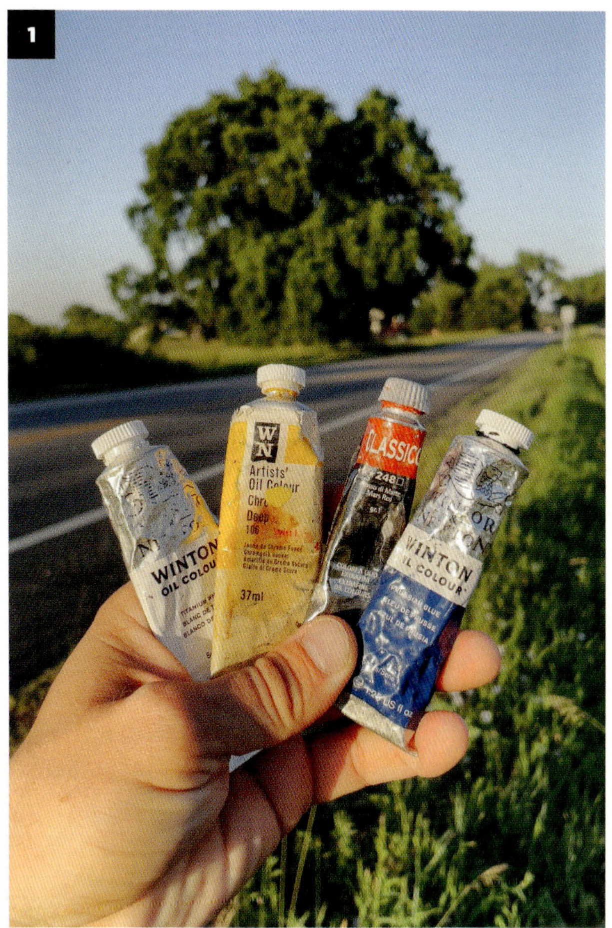

1. For this session, I'm using a color palette of warm and slightly impure versions of the primary colors: Titanium White, Chrome Yellow Deep, Mars Red, and Prussian Blue. Chrome Yellow Deep is a very strong and opaque, slightly orange yellow; Mars Red is an opaque, slightly brownish earth-tone red. Prussian Blue, as a very concentrated pigment with a high tinting strength, is a very saturated blue on the greenish side, similar to Phthalo Blue. It looks a tad bit more rusty than Phthalo Blue though, because it is derived from the oxidation of iron.

2. I'm starting with a very light wash of Mars Red, diluted with odorless mineral spirits, to cover my whole surface.

3. Now I am defining the form of the tree, placing it nearly in the center of my composition. This stage is very loose and playful, and I am finding joy in the controlled chaos while I get a feel for my subject, empathetically connecting with it. This stage corresponds to Step 3 of establishing the structure (page 26).

4. Now addressing values, I have loosely indicated where the darks are in my composition in a very loose and basic way. Likewise, I am now lifting away pigment for my light areas with a clean, semi-dry brush. I am skipping the part where I build out the values within the tree itself, because the light is fading quickly and I want to save time. I will establish the darks at the color-blocking stage.

The simplicity at this stage allows room for easy adjustment. If you compare this to the previous step, I have already adjusted the tree shape by lifting away some pigment from the right side of it. Since there is not very much detail to become too attached to at this stage, I could even wipe away the whole thing and start over without shedding too many tears.

5. Here I am fixing the tree in place by blocking in the basic sky color. The sky is the lightest value in this composition, and light values are easy to contaminate with other paint. (I know what you might be thinking—what about the pigment of the underpainting? It is so thin that the pigment there doesn't make too much difference.) So, instead of trying to paint the tree first and then the sky around it, I am painting the sky first, then will detail the tree edge later.

6. Here I am mixing the first green for the tree. Trees come in endless variation, but generally they are green, right? The quick and easy answer is yes, but green also comes in seemingly endless variations. That doesn't always mean you can mix that shade of green just with yellow and blue paint. Like other painting situations, light influences the green of the leaves. They can be in direct sun, they can be in shade, they can be backlit, or even lit by diffuse light on a cloudy day. Generally, they are lit from above or the side, but sometimes they can even be lit from below—naturally or artificially. (See Tips for Painting Green Foliage on page 54.)

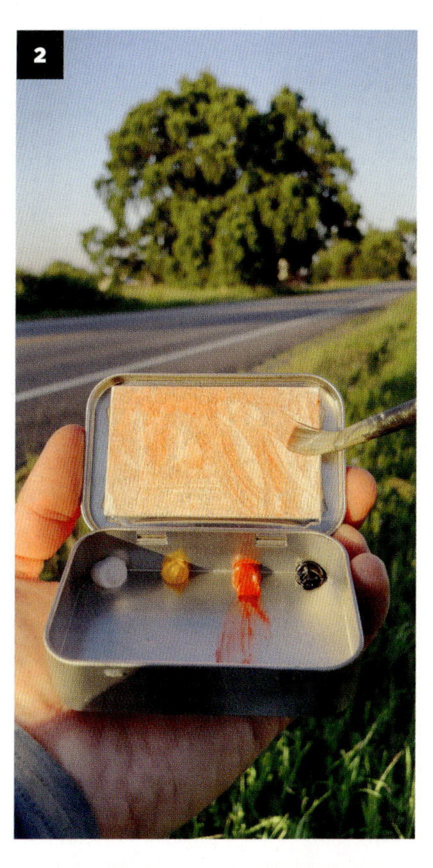

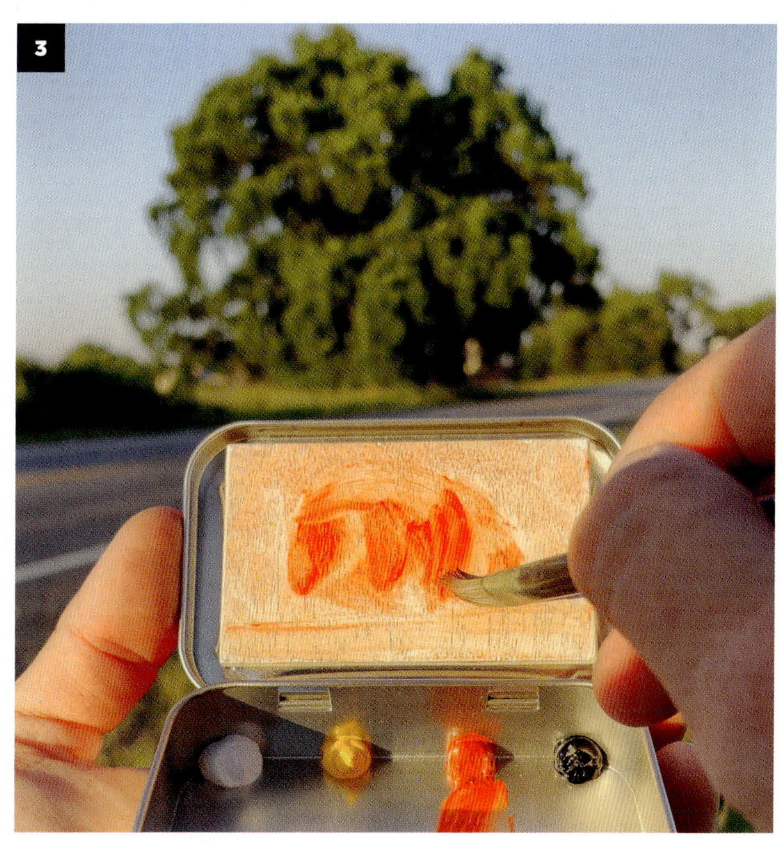

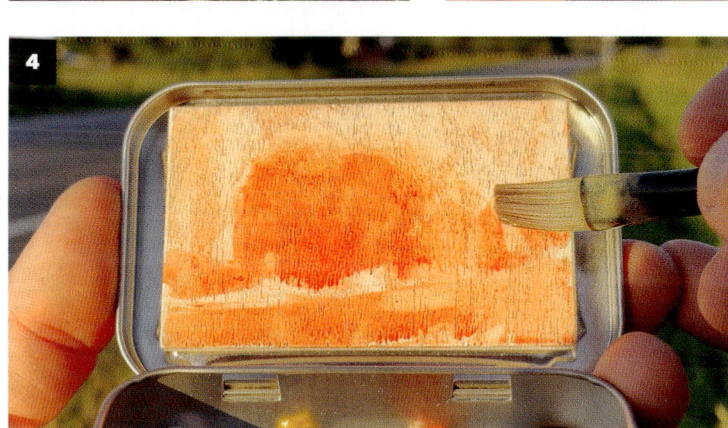

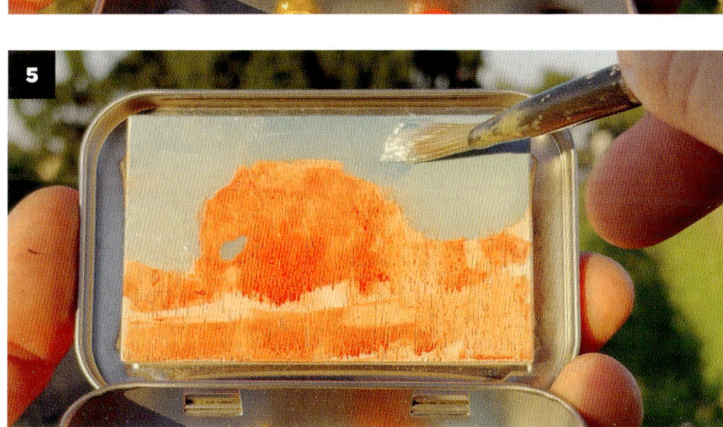

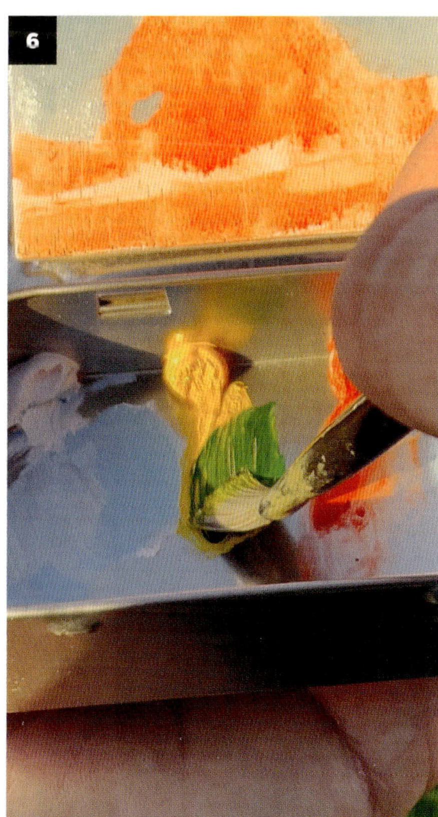

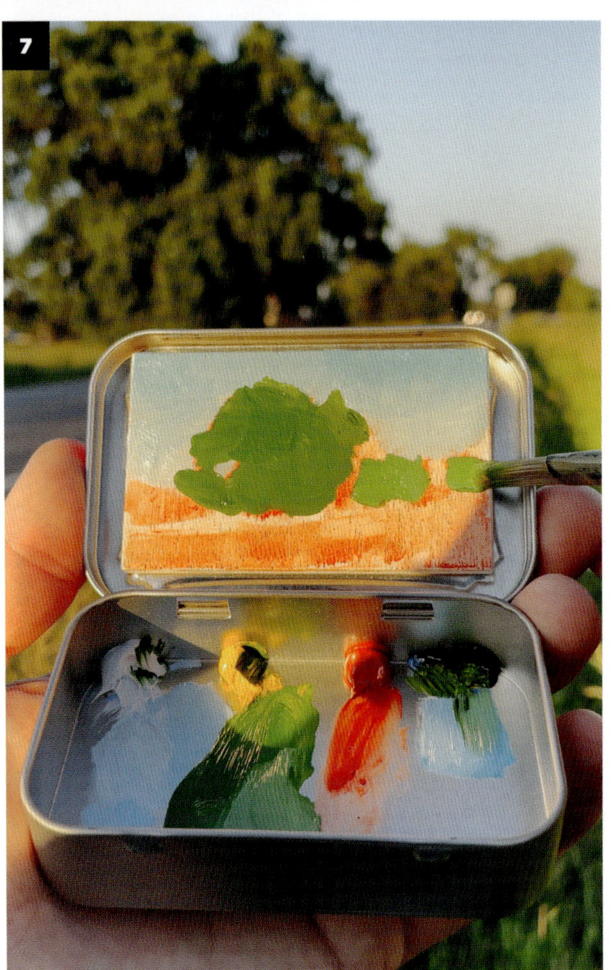 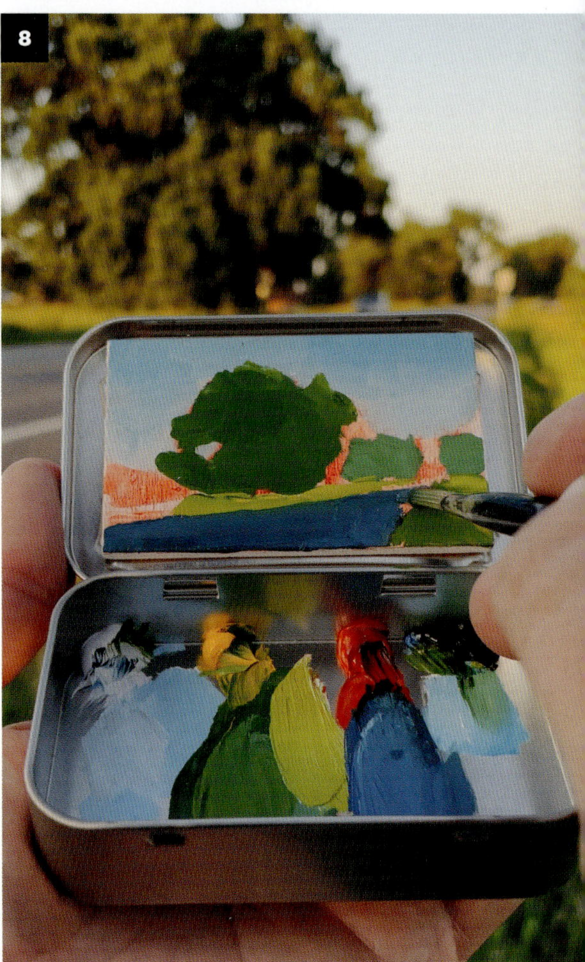

7. The main tree shape is blocked in. If you look at my palette, I tinted a small section of that existing color with white and blue to block in the green tree line in the background. The shaded part of my palette also more clearly shows the real difference between those two colors.

8. I'm continuing the blocking-in process for the rest of the painting. I've built on the green tree color with a generous helping of white and yellow, plus a tiny tint of red, to make the color of that nice golden yellow–green grass lit by the golden-hour sunlight. I also blocked in the green grass on my side of the road, and am currently finishing the initial block-in of the road itself. I am choosing to start with the shadow color—a dark blue muted down with Mars Red—and am planning on putting some streaks of sunlight across it later.

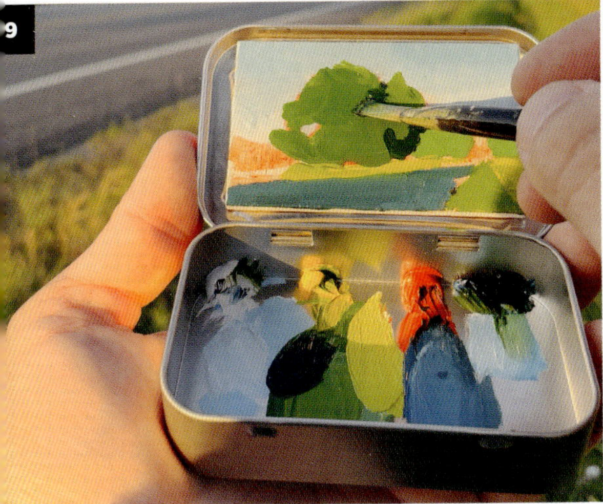

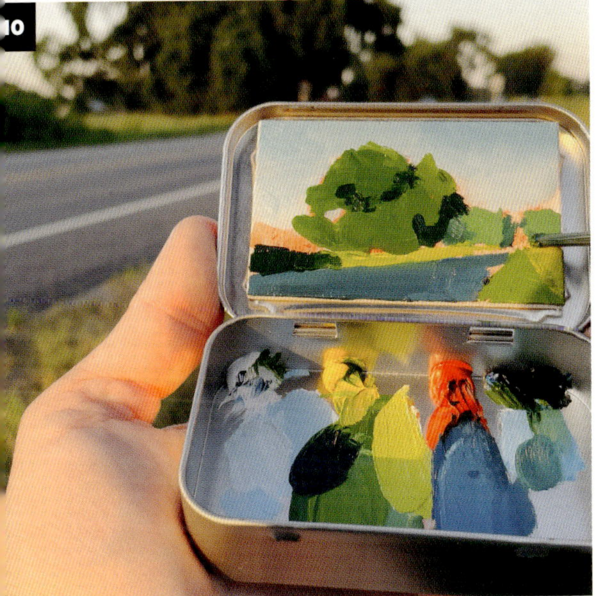

9. Now is the stage where I am establishing the darkest darks in my tree. You can see the spot in my palette where I mixed the color by adding a thick swath of Prussian Blue to the already-existing green tree color. If the trunk were visible on this tree, this is probably the time where I would paint it in.

10. The shadowy part of the trees in the distance is blocked in with a significantly lighter greenish-blue color, which is still darker than the light green of those trees. This value is slightly lighter and bluer in the painting than in real life, as a way to use atmospheric perspective to enhance the distinction between the foreground and the background.

11. I've now mixed a warm, light gray color for the sunlight streaks that are making their way across the road. They just disappeared because the sun went down, so I am doing this part from memory. I studied where they approximately were, as well as how the color would be mixed, so I think it should look all right.

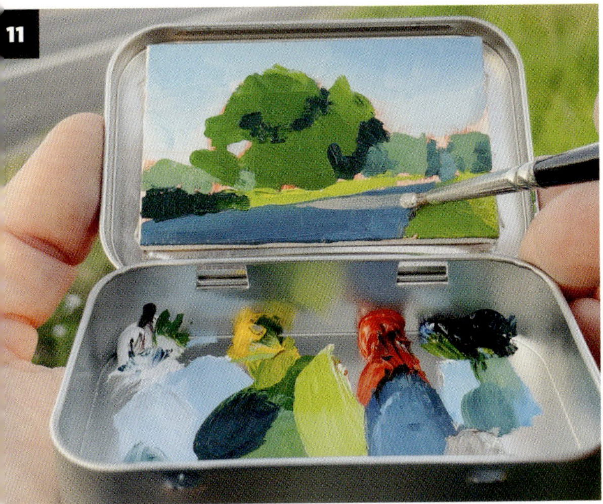

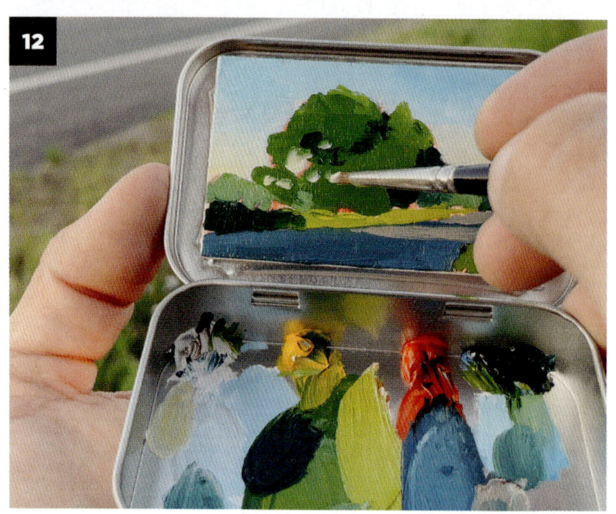

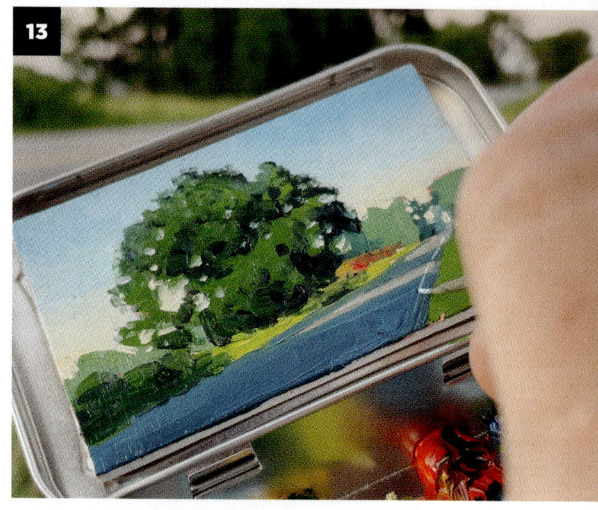

TIPS FOR PAINTING GREEN FOLIAGE

General rules to remember when color blocking: When mixing light green, begin with yellow and add blue in small increments. When mixing dark green, it's ok to start with blue and add a little yellow at a time.

There is often orange in leaves: Deciduous trees typically have less orange, while evergreens have more. In both cases, this means either adding a small amount of orange or an even smaller amount of red.

Full sun: In sunlight, the green contains some white, from sunlight reflected off the surface.

Shade: In shade, the green mixture is heavier on blue.

Backlit: Individual leaves that are directly backlit with sunlight are often a very pure, bright green—almost appearing fluorescent. This effect is more apparent when other parts of a backlit scene are in deep shadow.

Study: Next time you go outside where there are trees, take a moment to imagine how you would mix their colors and paint them. Also, study the way different painters treat trees.

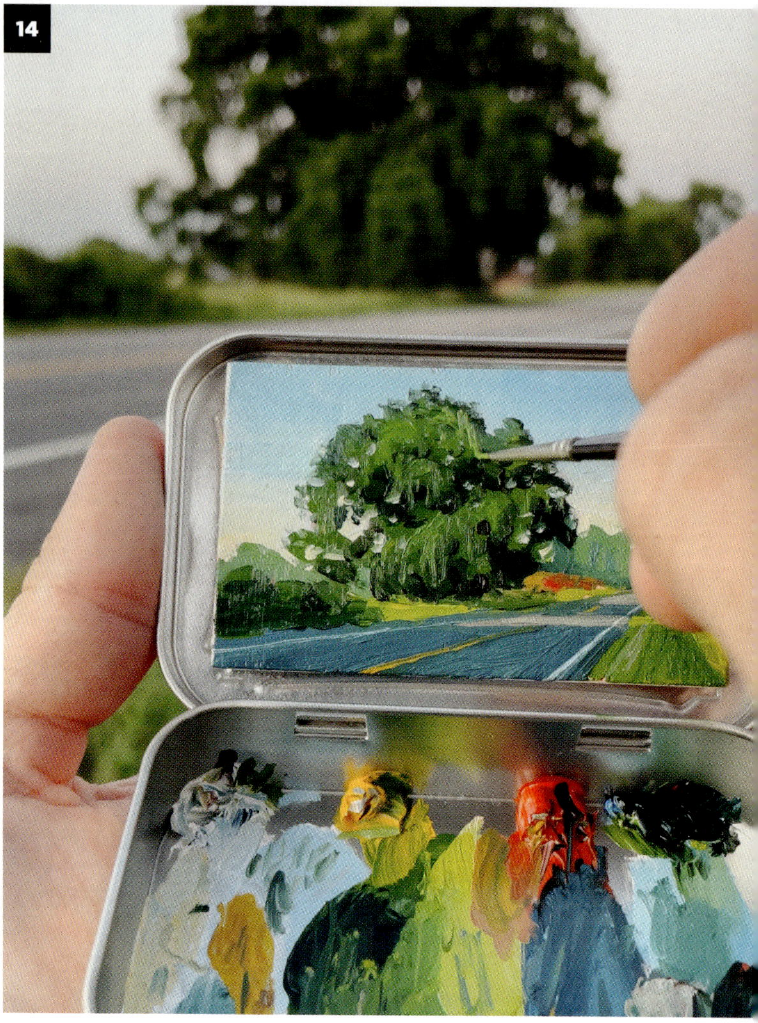

12. I washed my brush and mixed a light brownish-orange, similar to the color I just had for the road, but mainly orange with only a hint of brown. You can see my color mixture on the far left of my palette, below the white. This color is for the sky just above the horizon, which has that warm color from the setting sun, but a bit on the brownish side due to pollution in the atmosphere. I am also using that color for a few gaps in the tree that are located in that same low part of the sky. Any other tree gaps above will be painted with the blue of the sky at the corresponding height.

During the time between the last frame and this frame, I added a bit of color nuance in the green foliage, giving the leaves more dimensionality. In addition to that, I built out some texture on the edge of the tree where it meets the sky.

All those variations of green are pretty straightforward, as various proportions of Chrome Yellow Deep and Prussian Blue mixed together. The dark shadows of the tree contain a touch of Mars Red to make that green even darker. Remember that red is the opposite of green on the color wheel.

13. Now I am using my smallest brush to paint in the smallest details. I used it to break up the top edge of the tree and now I am in the process of painting the lines of the road. The white line in the sunlit part of the road is pure Titanium White tinted with a touch of Chrome Yellow Deep to add warmth, and the white line in the shade is mixed with a touch of that muted blue of the road. I am making sure that the value of the white line in the shade is slightly darker than the warm white of the line in the sunlight.

14. I'm finishing up this painting with some final texture in the tree, painted in a lighter green. I have been noticing this lighter value for a little while, and this is basically the last thing on my mental checklist. This is just a slightly lighter value created by adding just a little more of the yellow-white mixture on my palette.

This was a nice primary color palette to work with for this scene because it produced fairly accurate color matches to reality. Even a secondary color palette of orange, purple, and green would have worked for this, which would have produced an interesting outcome, although I can imagine that the blue would not have been noticeably less vibrant. A close-up of the finished painting is on the following page.

GALLERY: FOLIAGE

The following is a small selection of paintings of foliage used in different ways.

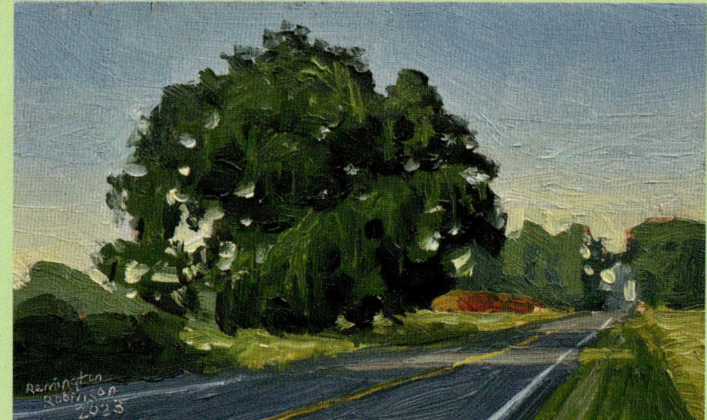

Here is the final painting from the previous project. A large cottonwood tree in Boulder, Colorado.

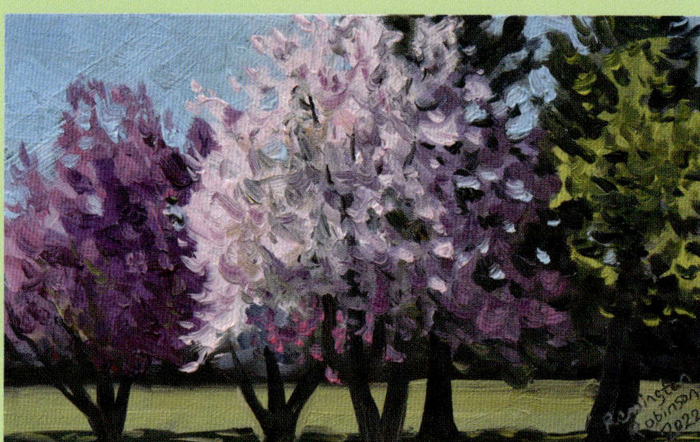

The same technique to make foliage can be used in different seasons, as in the spring when the blossoms are out.

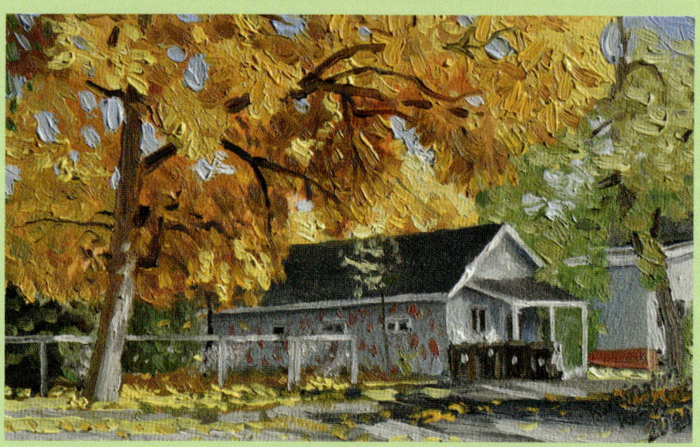

Very often, trees can be found near manmade structures, as with this yellow ash tree looming over a small house in autumn. I find vibrant yellow shadows to be one of the most difficult things to get right.

Some types of foliage require a different approach, as with these palm fronds in Maui, Hawaii. The overall light green and yellow color of the fronds were painted first then cut back with the dark background colors. The highlights were mostly added last.

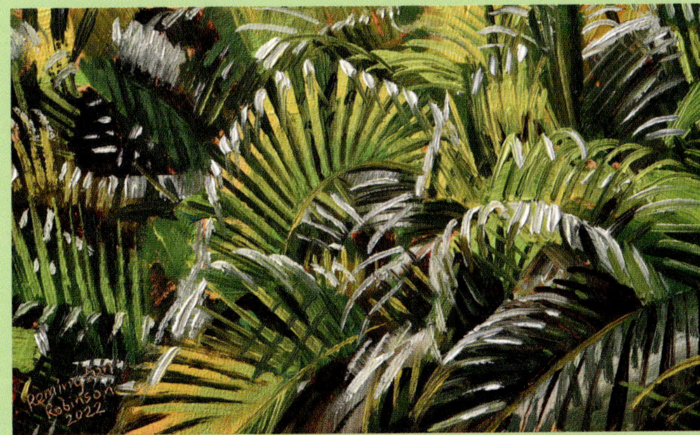

Trees can be used to frame a subject – in this case it is the Flatirons in Boulder, Colorado which are flanked by two red maple trees in the fall.

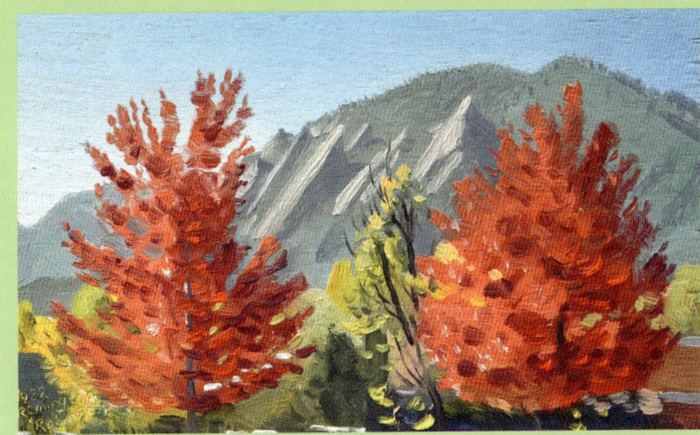

Trees in a park in Denver, where the focus is more on the shadows and dappled light on the ground than the trees themselves. Note the atmospheric perspective used to create depth in the distance (page 78).

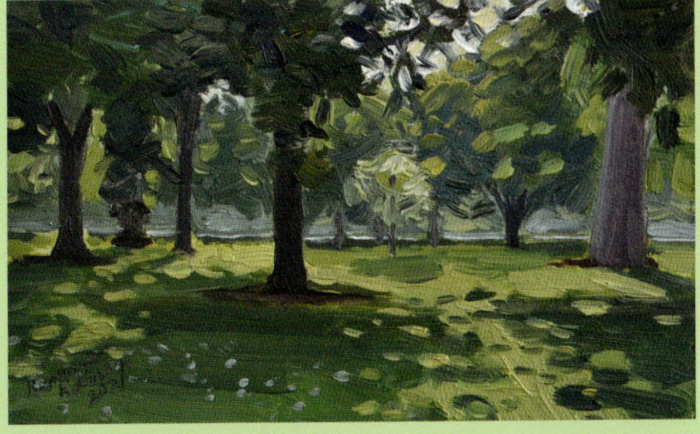

TOURIST DESTINATION: NIAGARA FALLS

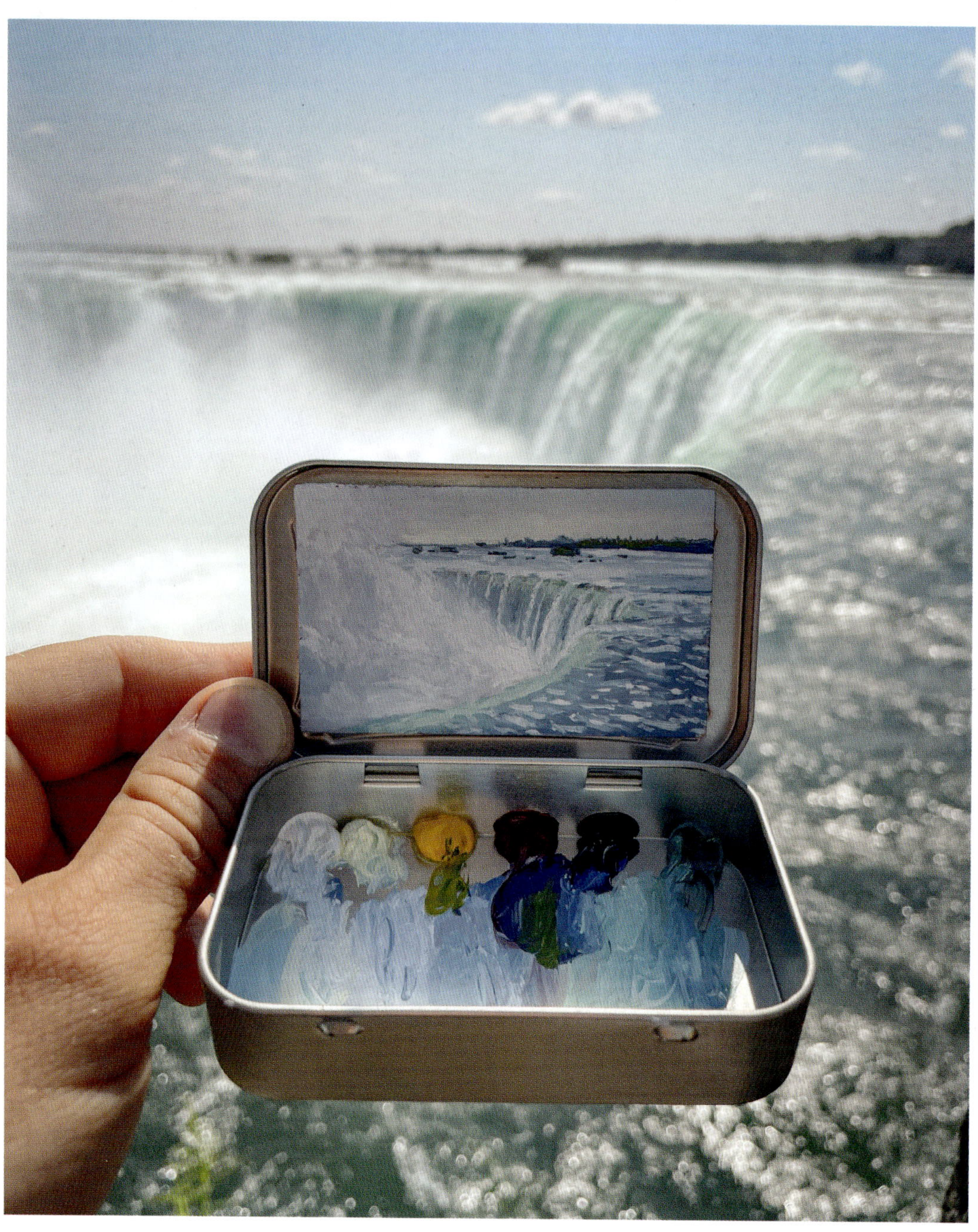

When visiting a busy tourist destination that is packed with people, I always have the urge to paint something. It would be nearly impossible to try plein air painting with a normal-sized setup without getting dirty looks from people, but mint tin painting is compact enough to be able to set up in a place like this, even for several hours, without being in anyone's way. Check out the gallery on pages 66-67 to see some more examples of paintings I created in crowded tourist destinations (perfect for mini painting).

Painting at destination spots is one of my favorite things to do. Meeting passersby is always fun and the painting is more than likely to sell, simply because so many people are familiar with the location. And how many people visit places as tourists and take lots of photos, but don't spend enough time to really soak the place in? Painting at a destination location really provides the chance to become immersed in thoughts about it as the light changes and as different people come and go.

In this exercise, I will be painting the beautiful turquoise-green water of Niagara Falls from the Canadian side, as well as from the American side (see sidebar on page 64). It was interesting to contrast the two locations while painting in different lighting conditions.

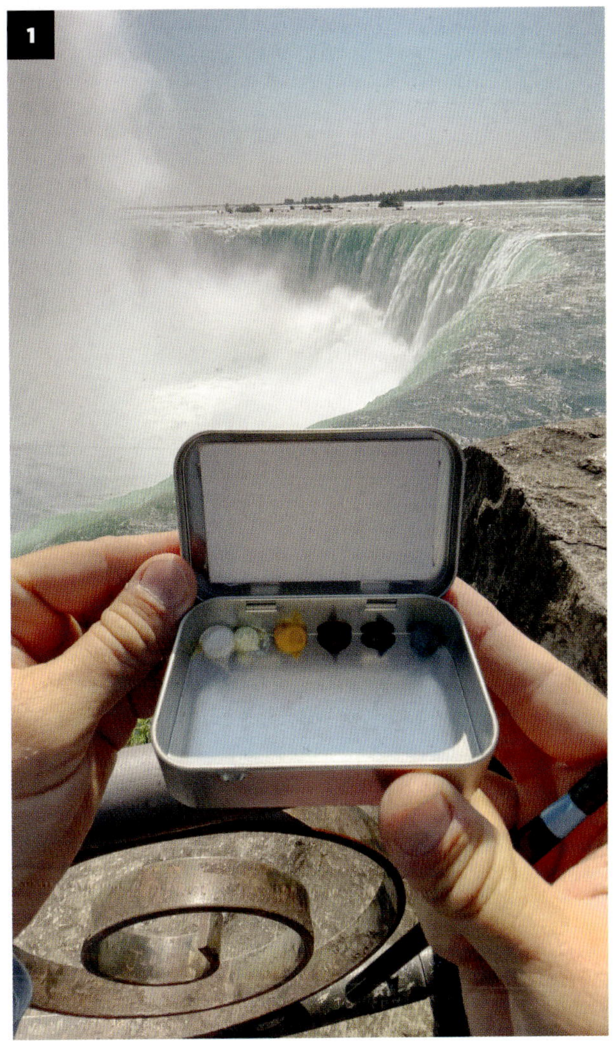

1. I'm on the Canadian side of Niagara Falls, painting with a different color palette than usual—Titanium White, Nickel Titanium Yellow Light, Chrome Yellow Deep, Permanent Madder Brown, Prussian Blue, and Cobalt Turquoise Light. What's not visible in this picture are the dozens and dozens of tourists who are packed shoulder to shoulder behind me and on either side along the railing to view the waterfall.

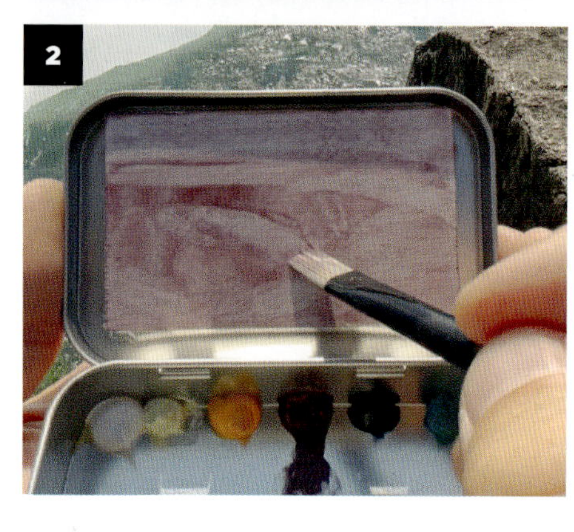

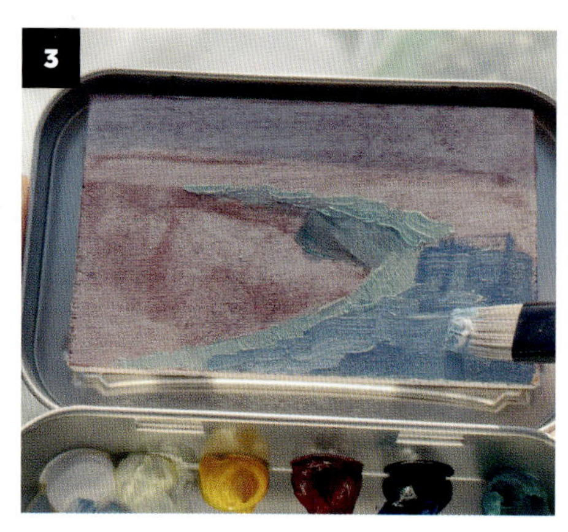

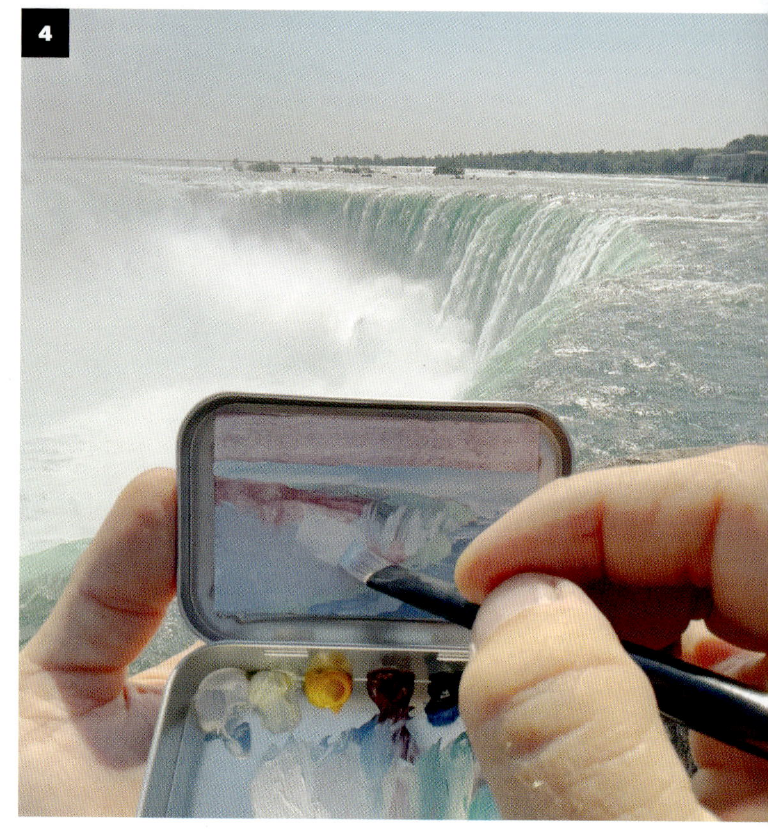

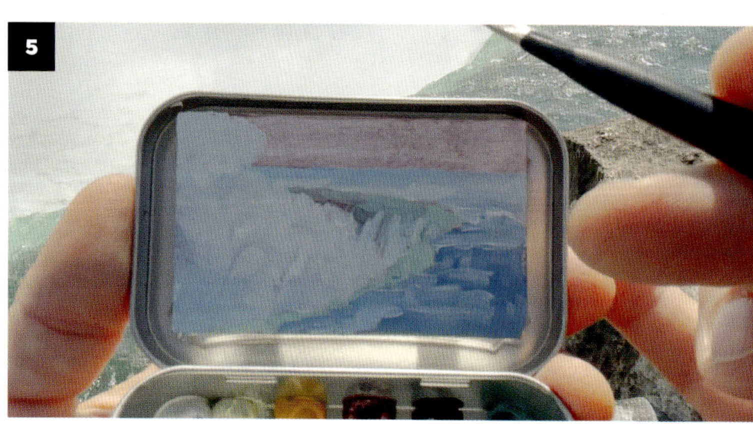

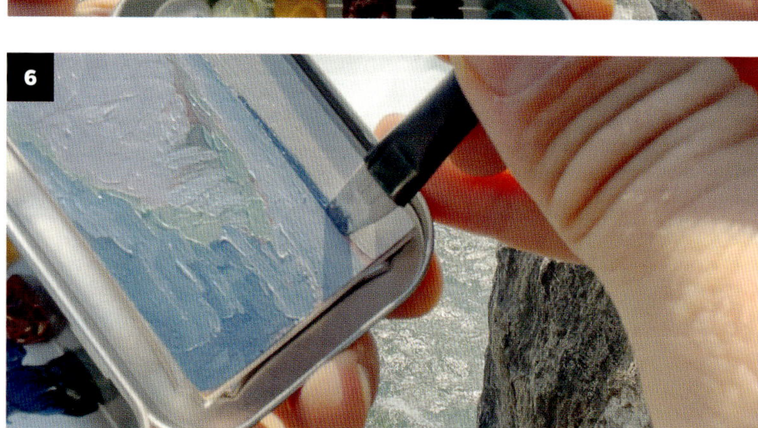

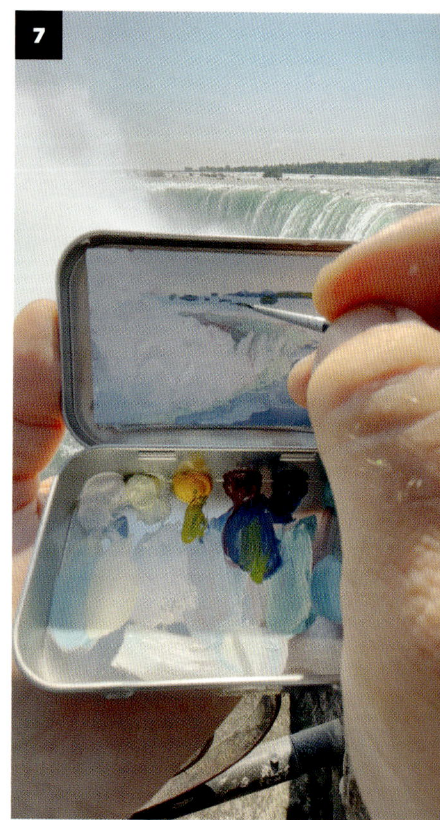

2. I've toned my whole surface with Permanent Madder Brown; my underpainting approximates where the values are, so I can quickly establish my composition. I want to paint the C shape of the Horseshoe Falls, with the mist rising up on the left side of my composition.

3. I'm beginning to paint the turquoise color of the water just after the waterfall drops, along with the deep blue of the water before the edge.

4. I have now blocked in a light blue gray for the mist coming up out of the abyss and the rest of the water in the river, leading up to the horizon. This includes the nuance of bright sunlight glaring off the edge of the water at the top of the waterfall on the other side of the curve. While painting that with white, I'm also hitting a few areas illuminated by the sun to the right of the waterfall, in the falling water itself, and on the top side of the mist.

5. The rest of the mist is now blocked in, which is nearly white toward the top. It is a sunny day today, with the sun high in the sky and slightly behind the waterfall, meaning that the mist and the far side of the waterfall are backlit.

6. I'm still using my large brush, but now I am using it on its side to edge the distant land upriver. Because of the atmospheric perspective, it is a deep blue color. Later, I will probably add a few highlights that are greener from the sun hitting the tops of the trees over there.

7. At this point, I'm switching to a small detail brush to paint all the islands in the river, because the whole thing is basically blocked in now.

8. There are some very bright highlights on the river directly below me, where the sun is reflecting brightly off the surface. Because it's so bright, I have no problem using pure white.

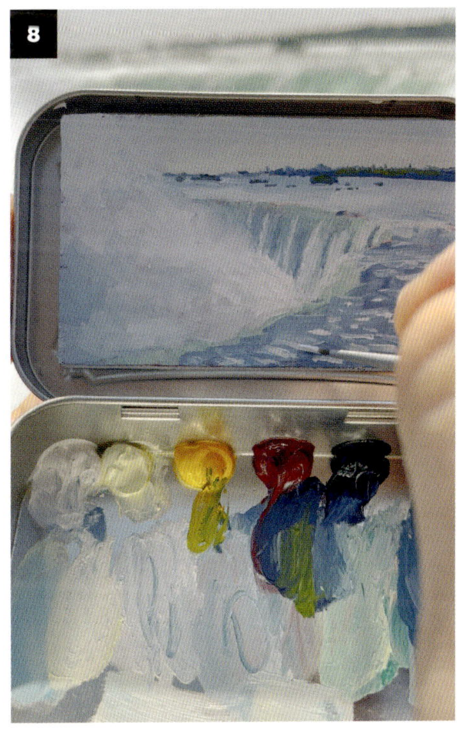

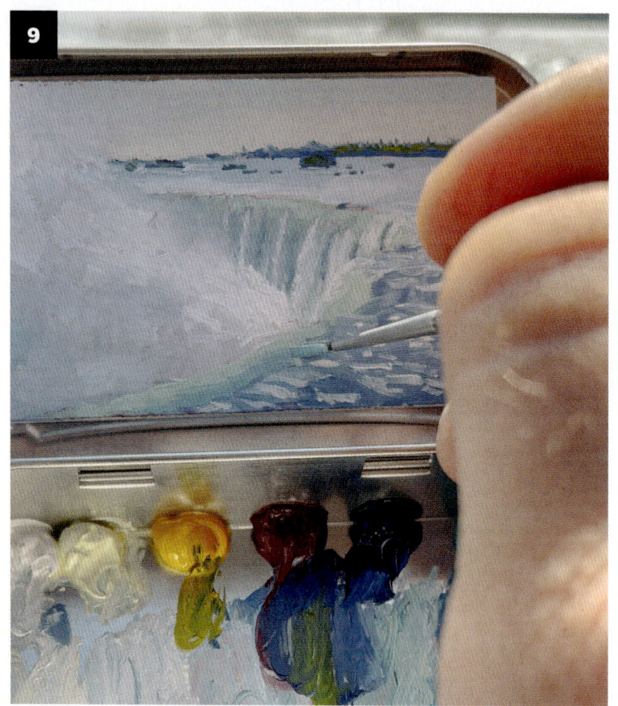

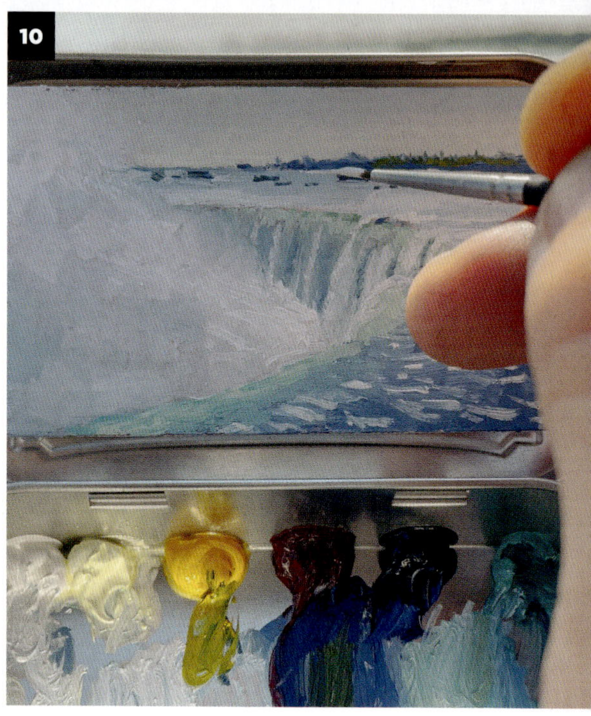

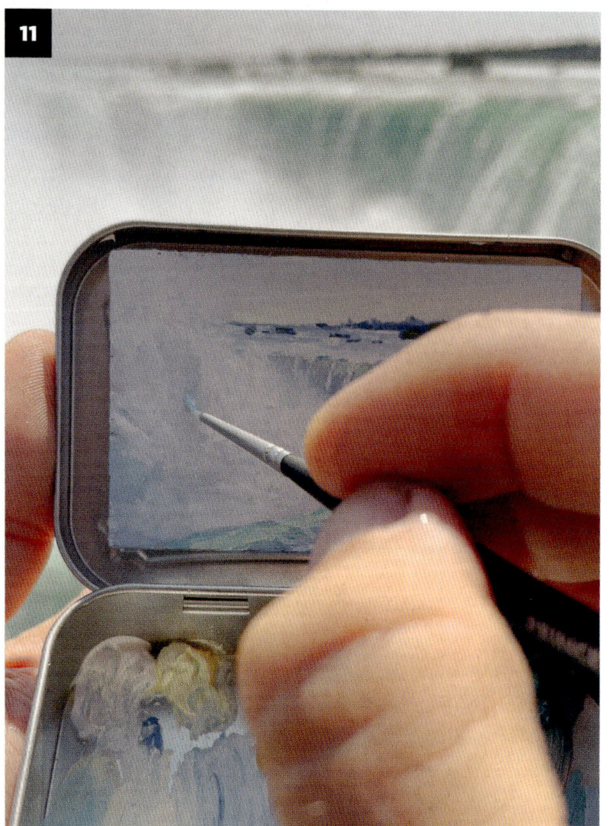

9. The edge of the waterfall has a nice turquoise color that I am trying to get right. It's a softer edge; because the light is refracting through the water, it is illuminated slightly from behind.

10. Finishing up final details on this piece, I'm noticing a distant shimmer off the water at the horizon, which I record with Titanium White paint.

11. The last thing I'm doing is adjusting the mist with my small brush, changing its opacity here and there. In this shot, I'm painting a touch of turquoise over the mist to make it look as if you can see a hint of the waterfall behind it.

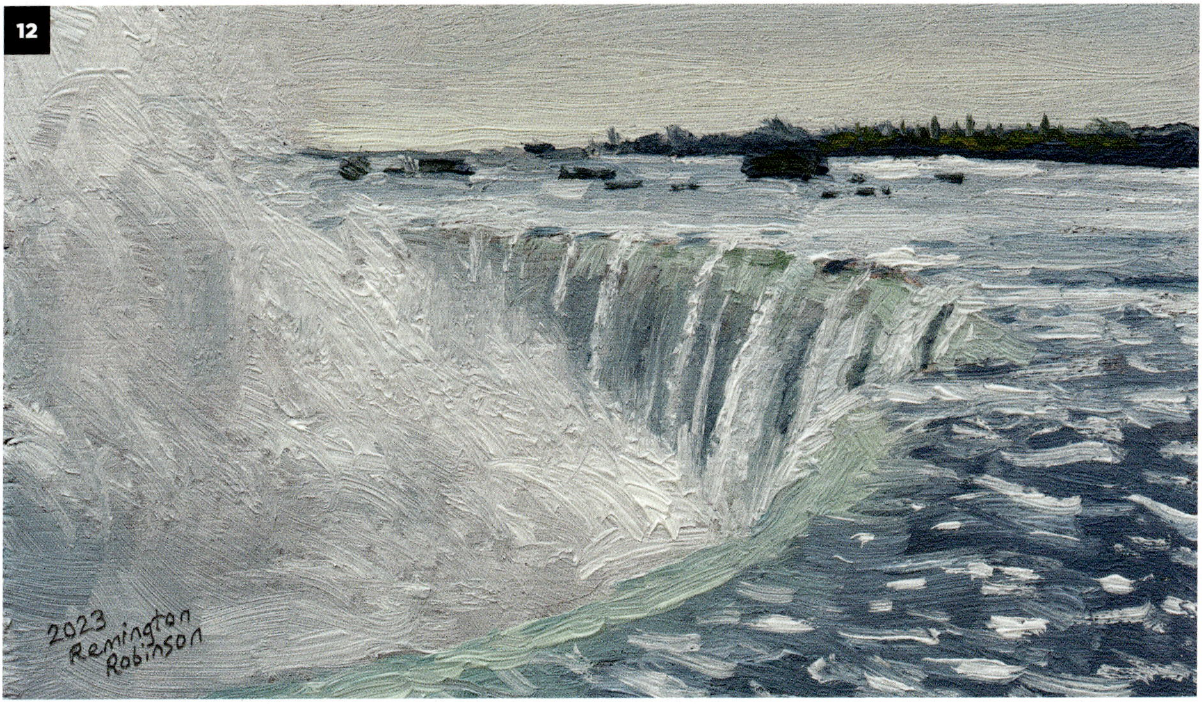

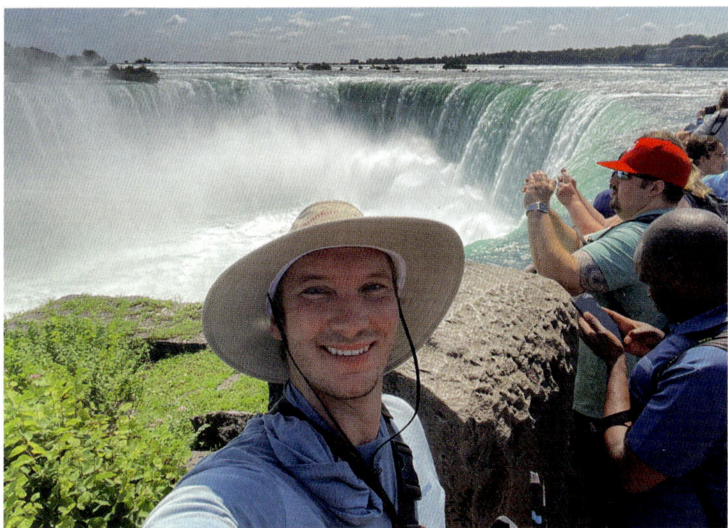

12. Here's a close-up of the finished painting.

After finishing the painting, I figured that I would also be a tourist and take a quick selfie.

THE AMERICAN SIDE OF NIAGARA FALLS

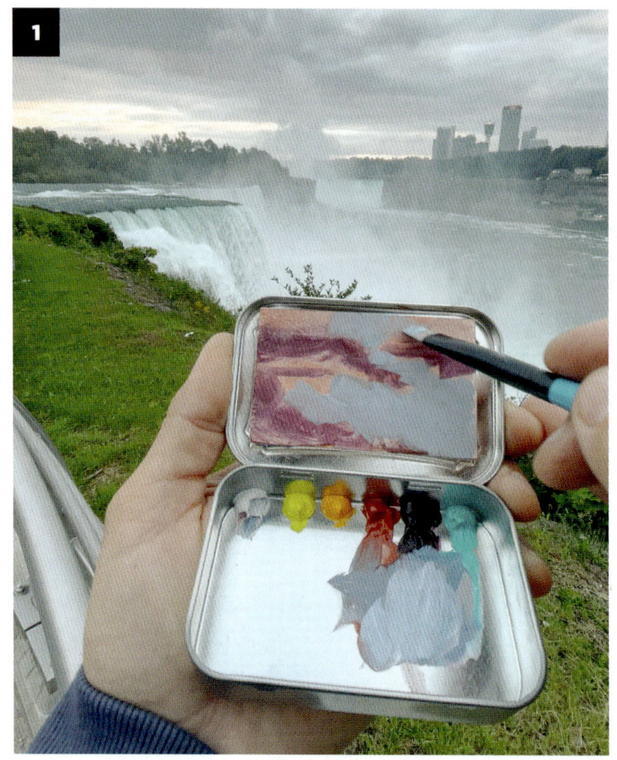

I have heard people say that the view on the Canadian side of Niagara Falls is better than on the American side, but as far as painting goes, I could argue against that opinion. If you are wanting to paint at Niagara Falls, I would recommend painting at the American side, because it is less crowded and the mist coming from all of the waterfalls is visible all in the same line of sight. While the view at the Canadian side is really spectacular, especially because of its close proximity to the waterfall, I wouldn't necessarily say that it is a better view overall; it's just different.

Speaking of the American side of Niagara Falls, let's go there for a moment, and see how it differs from the Canadian side.

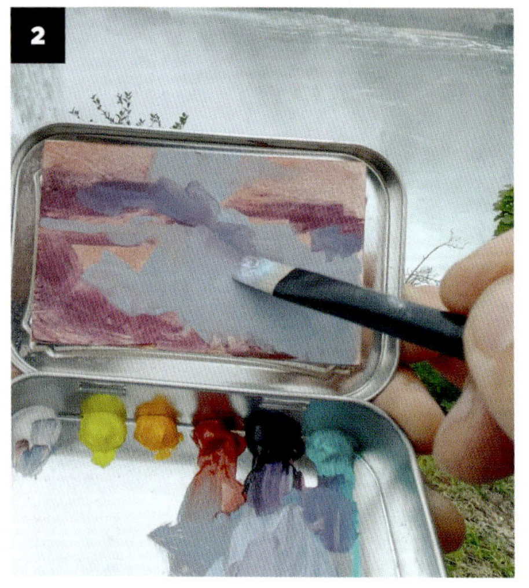

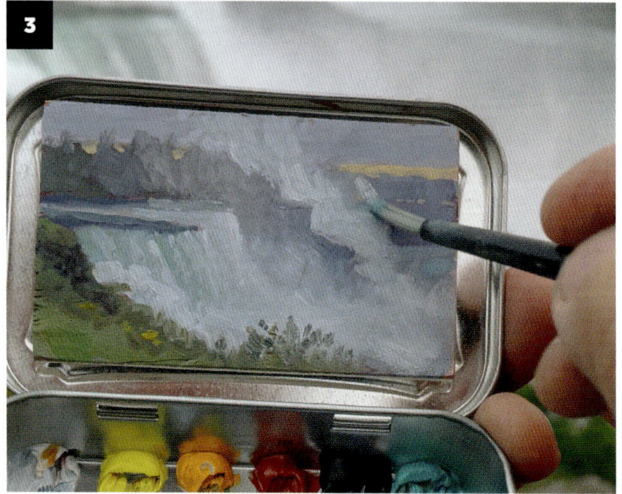

1. I'm over here at the American side of Niagara Falls on a cloudy day, and I'm just beginning to block in all of the mist. The view over here is nice because all that mist is stacked up on top of itself. There are also some tall buildings in the background. I'm not going to paint those this time, though.

I'm also noticing that there aren't as many people over here as on the Canadian side. It might be because it's a cloudy day, but I think it is because there are way more viewing opportunities on this side, so people are more spread out.

2. The abundance of mist visible from this side allows for more opportunity to blend paint and really try to achieve an effect of atmosphere. It's somewhat of a challenge, because the actual shape of the mist is naturally always changing, but this allows for a little bit of improvisation.

3. After blocking in everything, it's fun to tweak the mist by simply adding more light gray oil paint and blending it into what is already there.

4. Here you can see the finished painting on the American side of the falls.

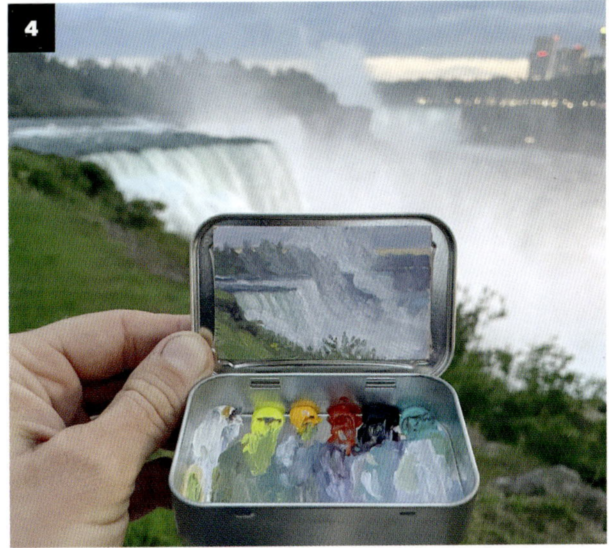

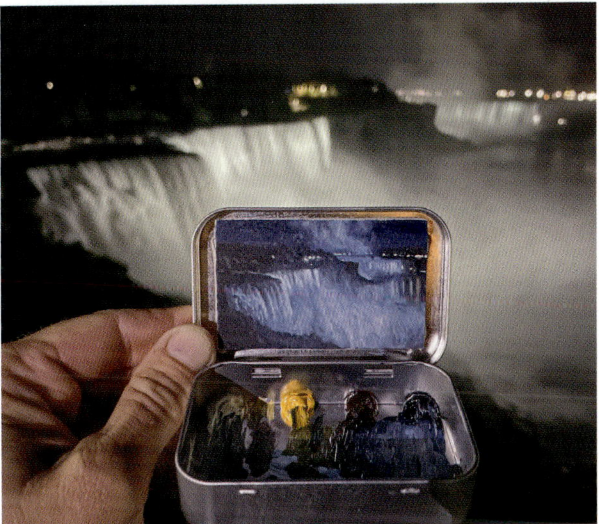

There's a nice overhang on the American side where I painted a nocturne, which was a real treat, because the waterfalls are all illuminated at night. I'm glad I brought my headlamp—there are no overhead lights there. A late-night fireworks show over the river concluded the evening for everyone while I was finishing up this painting.

GALLERY: PAINTINGS AT TOURIST DESTINATIONS

The following is a small selection of paintings made at busy tourist destinations around the world.

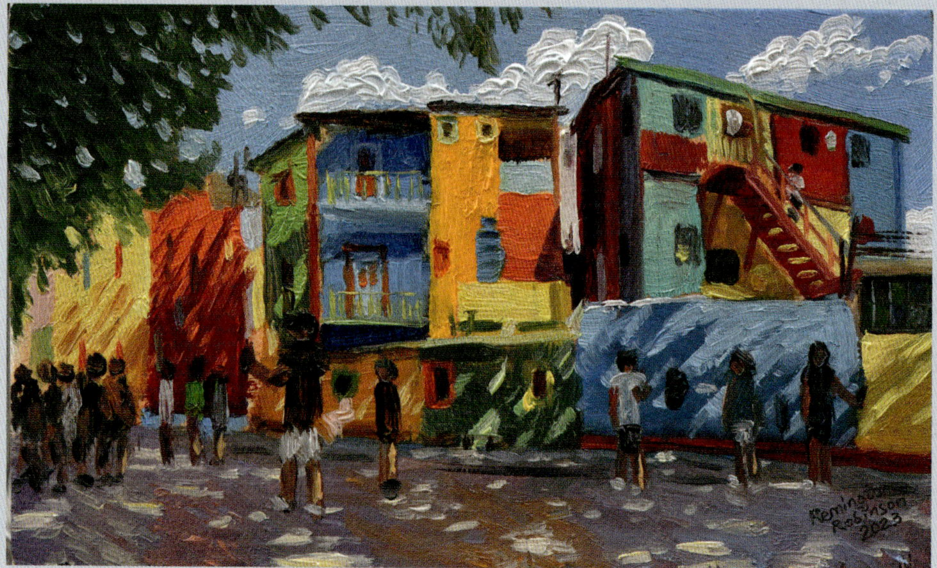

The La Boca neighborhood in Buenos Aires, Argentina, is a congested tourist area due to its numerous, beautifully colored buildings.

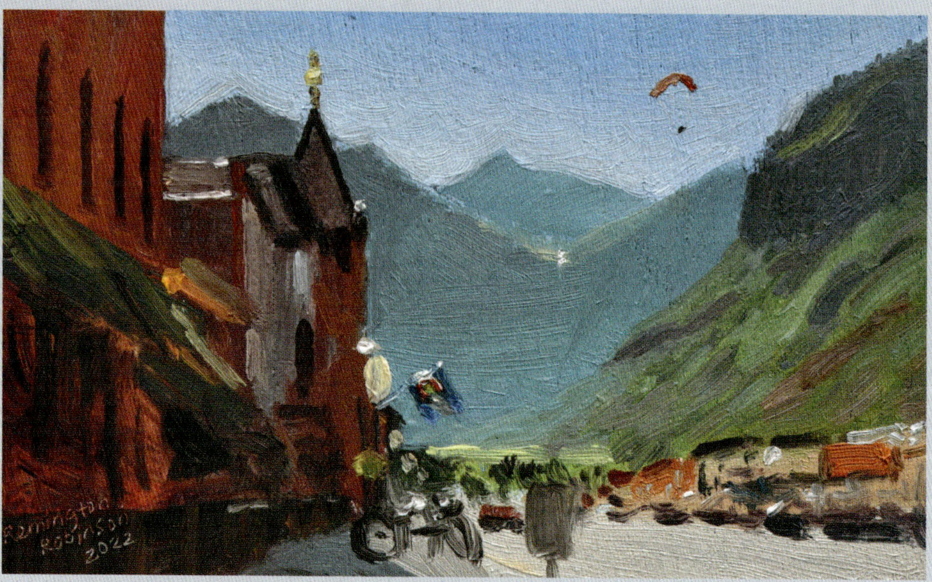

A paraglider over downtown Telluride, Colorado on a sunny summer morning. Due to recent rain, the air in the valley is backlit by the sun, producing a nice turquoise color in the distant atmosphere.

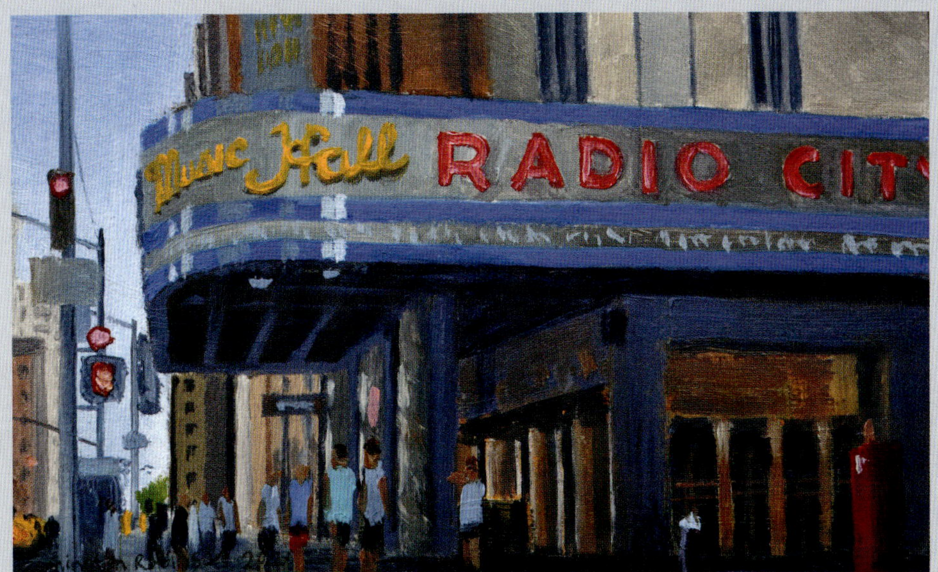

The whole city of New York feels like a tourist destination, as there are several tourist hotspots scattered throughout the city that are great painting locations. Radio City Music Hall is one of them, as one of the Big Apple's more notable cultural icons.

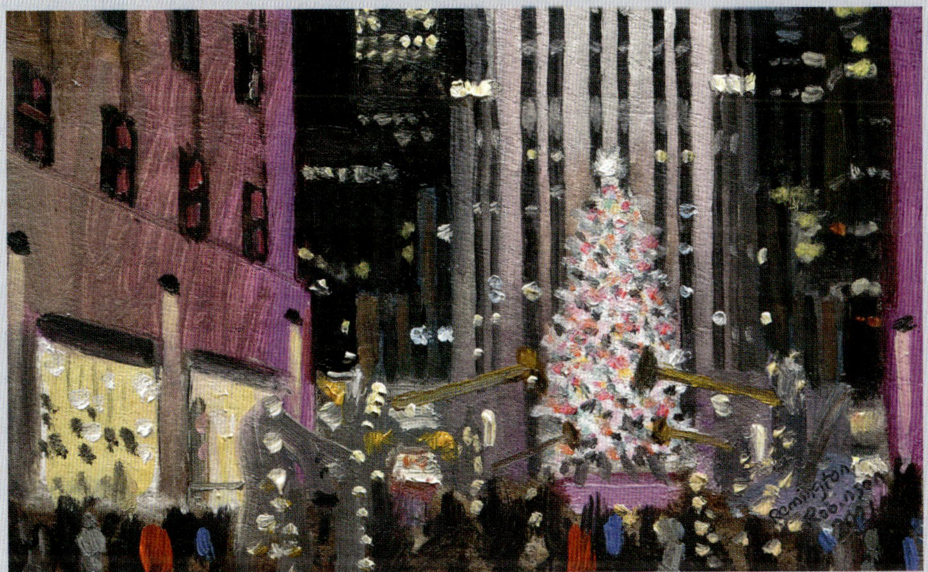

A very busy tourist destination in December is the Rockefeller Center in New York City. Indications of many people are very loosely painted on the bottom of the picture plane, with more tight detail focused on the structure of the buildings and the light reflecting off of them.

LINEAR PERSPECTIVE: DUMBO, NYC

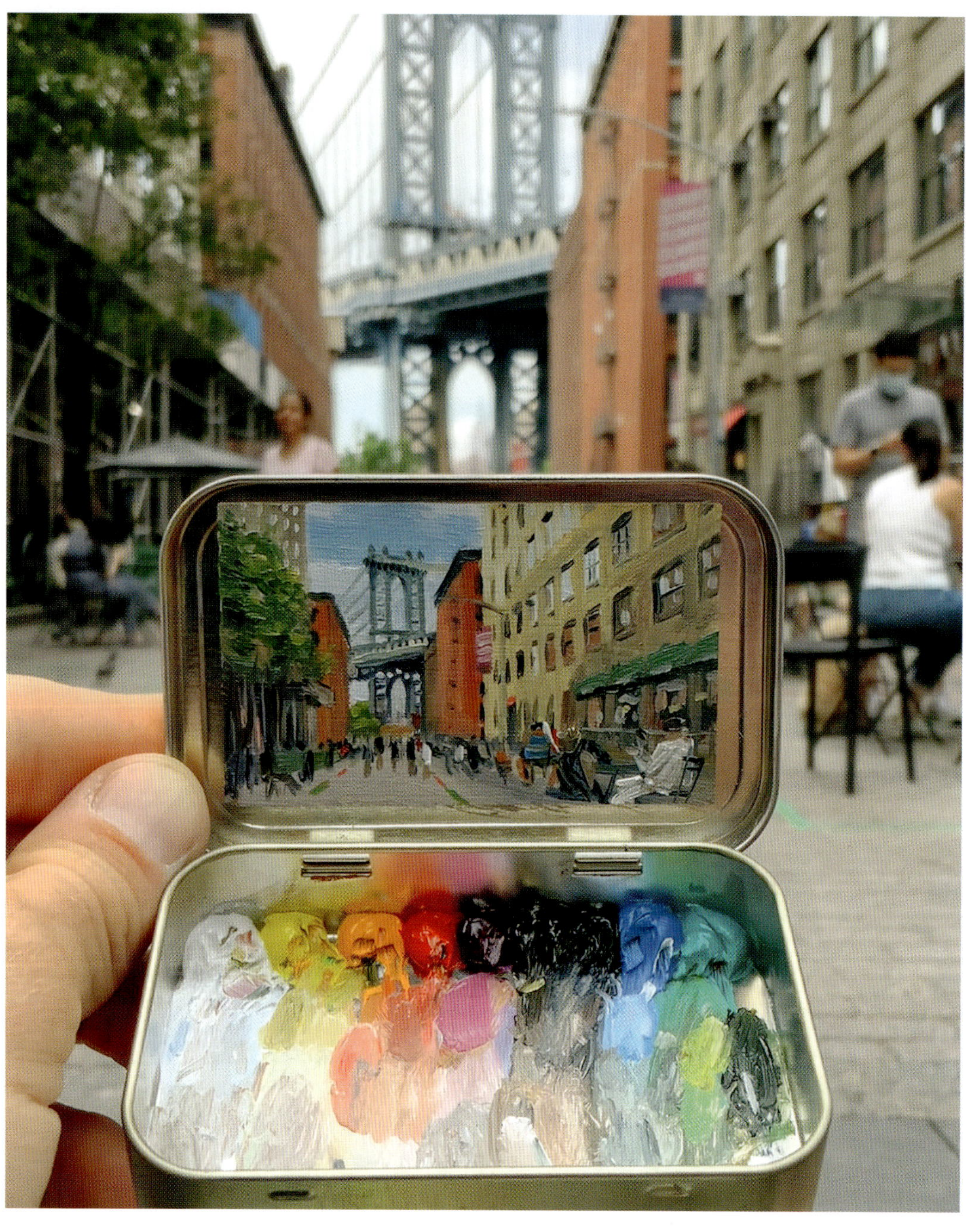

Many people who have explored New York City and ventured over to Brooklyn have stumbled upon this famous view of the Manhattan Bridge.

The primary focus of this painting is structure. One of the most important technical qualities of this painting is the one-point perspective, and another is that the verticals line up and are reasonably parallel to each other.

One trick to knowing exactly where the point of perspective should be on a straight, level street like this is simply the position of your own head in relation to the street. Because I was sitting in the middle of the street and my head was about 3 feet (1 meter) off the ground, I knew that my vanishing point was located directly down the street, in the middle, and slightly above the horizon. If I were standing, then it would be a little higher; if I were on the sidewalk, then the vanishing point would lead directly down the sidewalk.

The windows in this painting are not perfectly rendered, but I felt that the structure of the perspective was more important to make the painting look correct. I started the windows of the building on the right by indicating where they go by making light tick marks dotted carefully away from the vanishing point, signifying the top and bottom of each window, and then making sure they lined up vertically before adding color of some specific windows.

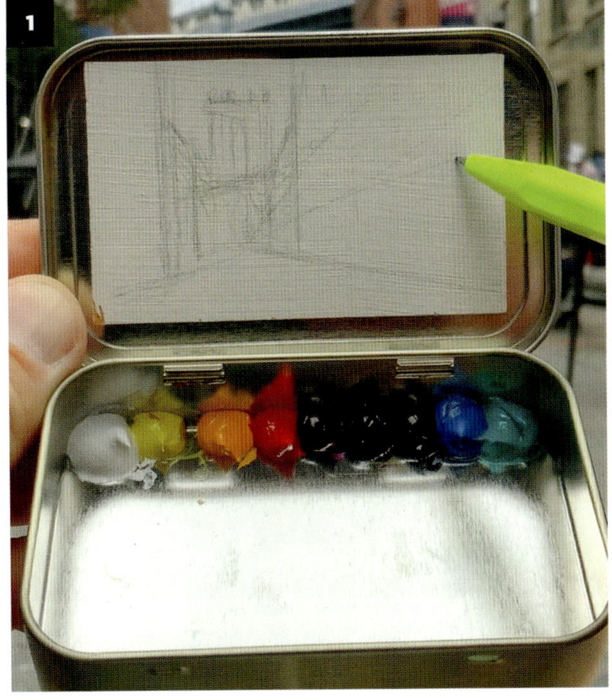

1. Before doing anything, I am imagining the composition for this painting. I decide to implement the classic "rule of thirds" in a few ways: the bridge, which is the focal point, will be located approximately in the upper-left intersection of that imaginary tic-tac-toe grid of thirds, and the vanishing point for my one-point perspective would be located on the lower-left intersection of thirds.

I begin the sketch for this painting with my vanishing point and a few lines of one-point perspective radiating out from it. The perspective lines will help the structure of the buildings be some-what accurate.

2. During the sketching process, I am closely observing everything I will be painting, which includes paying close attention to the value scale. What is the lightest thing and what is the darkest, and how does everything else in between relate in value? Here, I quickly note the darkest values with a light scribble.

Remember, you want to indicate where the darkest parts are, but don't want to make the pencil marks too dark. This is not a drawing and I want to get to painting as quickly as possible. Second, if there's too much graphite, the paint might not bind on that spot, and it can tint the paint gray.

3. The first paint color I am mixing is the light blue for the lower part of the sky. I start with Titanium White and add a little touch of Cerulean Blue. Typically, a blue sky gradient is lighter and greener as you look closer towards the horizon, and darker and more purple of a blue the higher you look. Cerulean Blue is similar to Phthalo Blue in that it is on the greener side as blues go, but it is a lot less concentrated and therefore has a lower tinting strength than Phthalo Blue.

As I paint, I am making my way around the bridge, not painting too thick, but using just enough paint to cover the surface. I'm not painting perfectly inside the lines, but only slightly overlapping them. Especially with this light color, I am doing my brushstrokes sparingly because I don't want the graphite to possibly tint my paint gray.

4. Now that the lower part of the sky is painted in, I mix the blue for the upper part

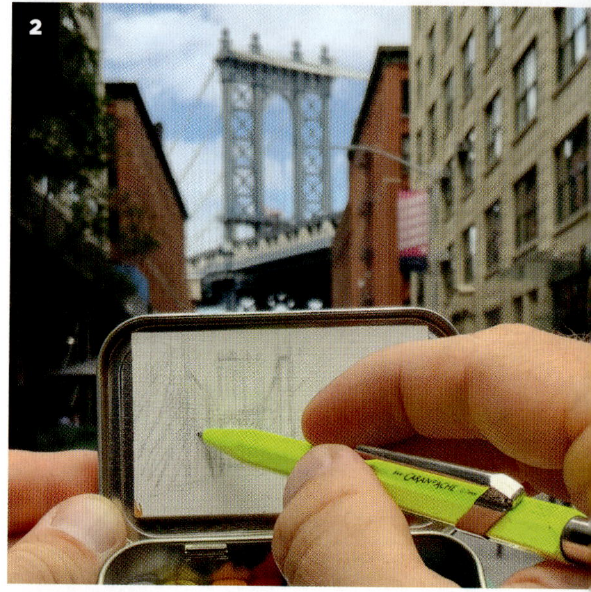

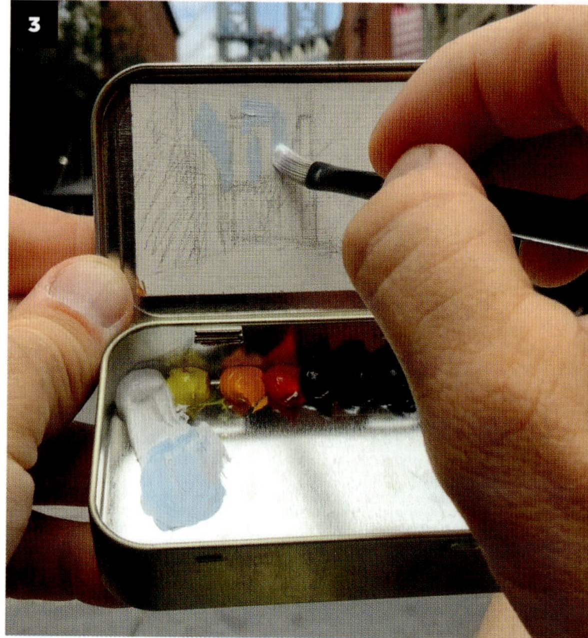

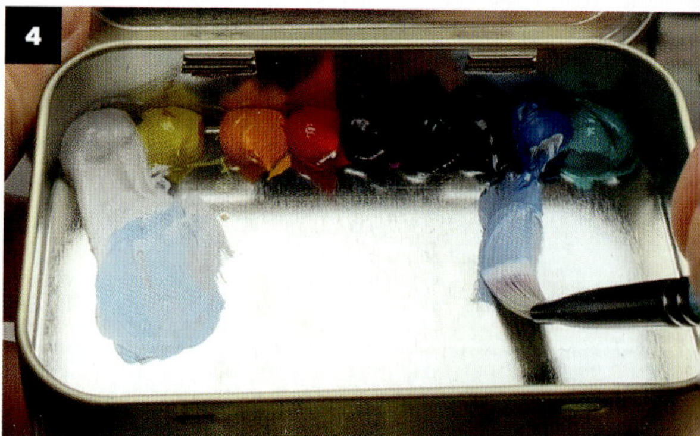

   MINI PLEIN AIR PAINTING

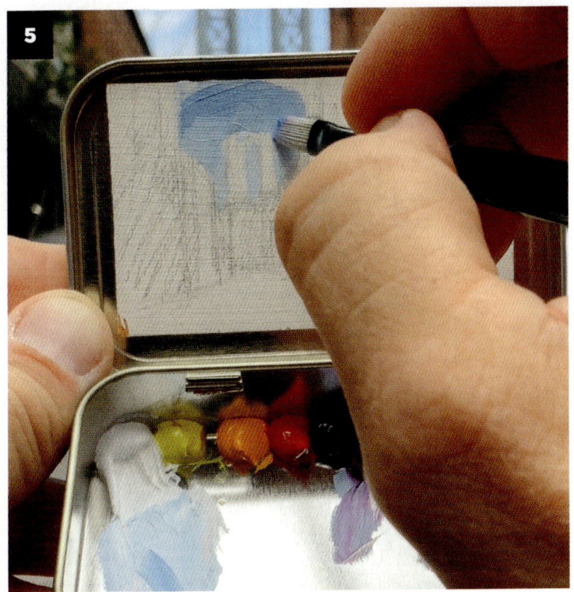

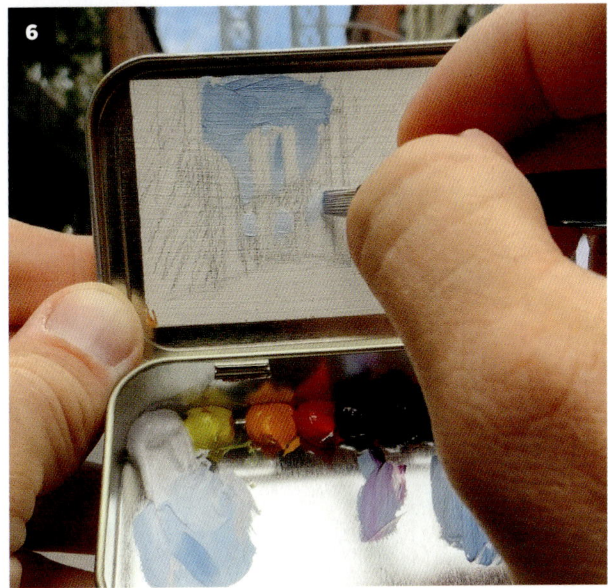

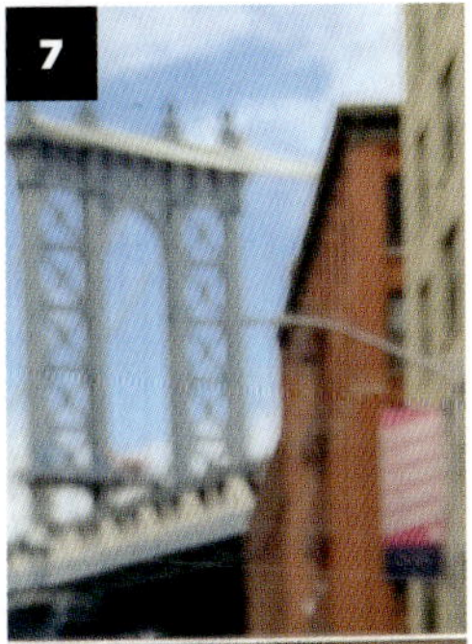

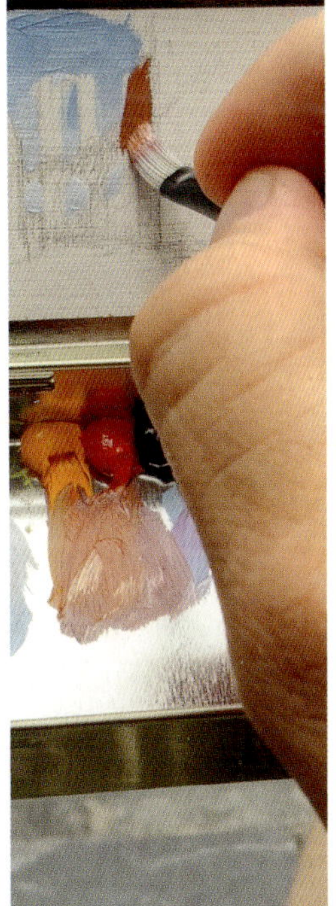

of the sky. This involves a bit more Cerulean Blue than the last mixture, plus a bit of Ultramarine Blue, which is a slightly more purple shade of blue.

5. I am dissatisfied with the strength of the violet-blue shade I am getting at the top of my sky, so I decide to dip into my magenta to crank up the darkness and intensify the violet tint of that blue. I don't add so much that the blue looks magenta.

To make the sky gradient go a little faster, I load the paint on my brush as an in-brush gradient (page 22).

6. Here, I am quickly dipping back in to that lightest blue to paint in the negative space of the sky behind the lower part of the bridge.

7. Now for the red brick building on the right of the bridge. I begin mixing this color with bright red, then add a dab of Cobalt Teal to mute the red. Then I add Cadmium Orange, plus a touch of white to lighten it up slightly. I realize that it needs more orange, so I add more to my mixture and lay in the color of the building. My application is not very clean, because I am just trying to get the right color down so far. I'll clean up the edges later.

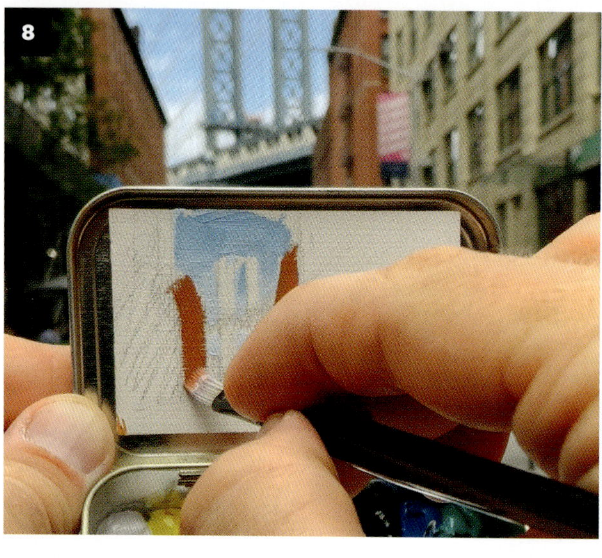

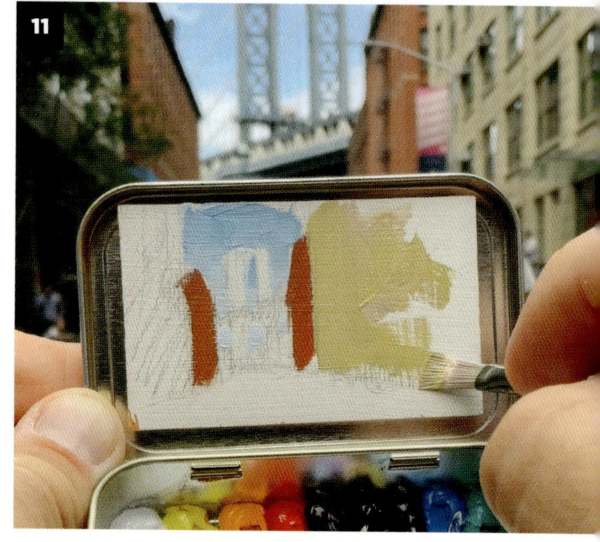

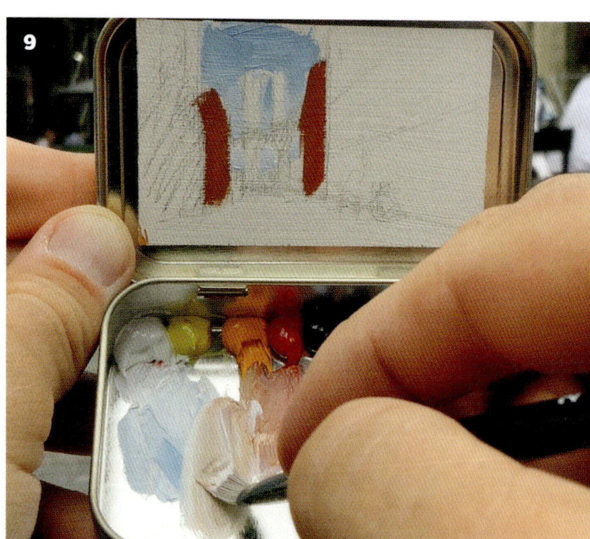

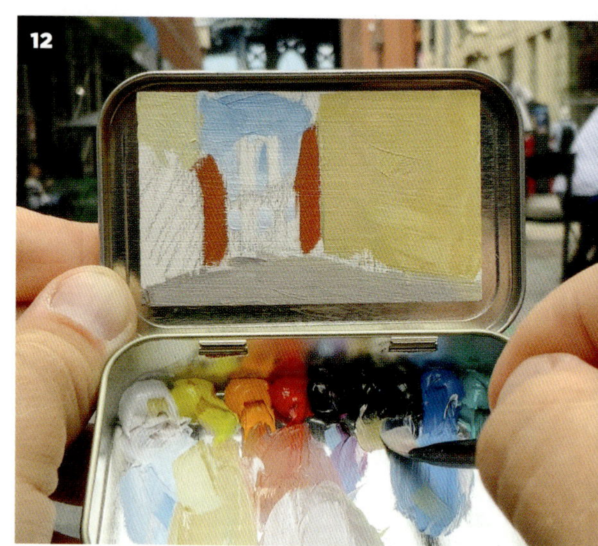

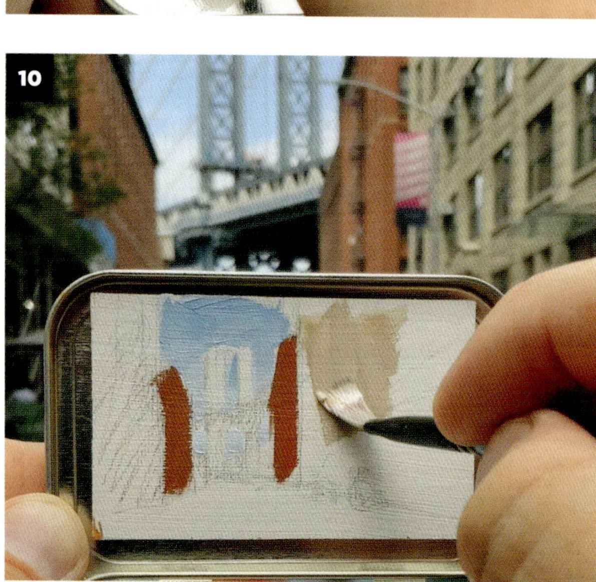

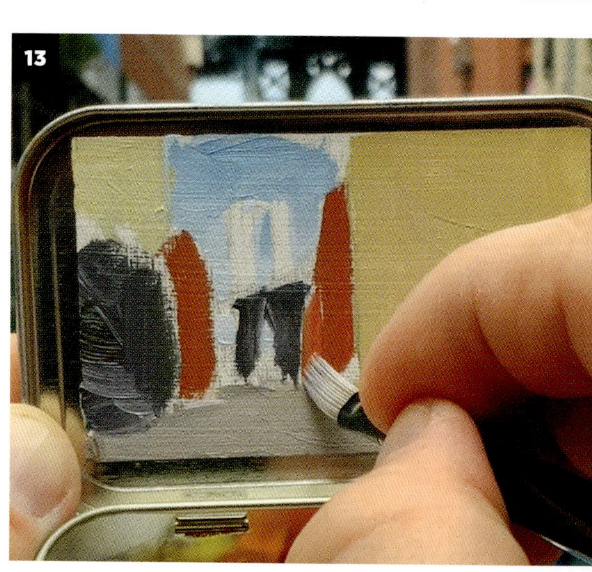

8. The red brick building to the left of the bridge is just about the same color as the one on the right, so I paint that color in. Upon closer inspection, the buildings are slightly different colors, so I decide to add some more red to my mixture for the building on the right and make another pass over it with my color before moving on.

9. Now I will mix the color for that large yellowish building on the right, which takes up nearly the entire right half of my painting. I begin mixing this color by swirling my brush around between the light blue of my sky and the orange-red next to it, and then add a little bit of Dioxazine Purple to mute it down.

10. After spreading a little of that pigment onto that area, I realize it is entirely the wrong color. That building has more yellow in it.

11. I add a liberal amount of Lemon Yellow to that mixture, plus a tiny bit more Dioxazine Purple to mute the yellow down.

This mixture looks more accurate to the building color. I fill it in, occasionally touching my brush into my mineral spirits to extend the color so it spreads over the whole building, and not minding if this new color mixes with the wrong color that's already there. After this, without washing my brush, I will dip it into the white so I can have a lighter version of the same color for the building in the upper left corner.

12. I've just blocked in the street, which is a warm gray color that looks purplish and slightly orange. To mix this, I didn't bother washing my brush from the previous yellow wall color. That final street color mixture is Titanium White, Ultramarine Blue, Bright Red, and Cadmium Orange.

13. For the dark gray, I mixed Ultramarine Blue, Cadmium Orange, and Magenta together. This color, left slightly unmixed to make it more interesting, was used to block in the left side as well as under the bridge in the distance.

Now that all the largest shapes are blocked in, I can narrow in on filling in smaller sections before detailing. I am dipping my brush back into that red brick color from earlier and altering it slightly so I can add another building I am now noticing further down the street.

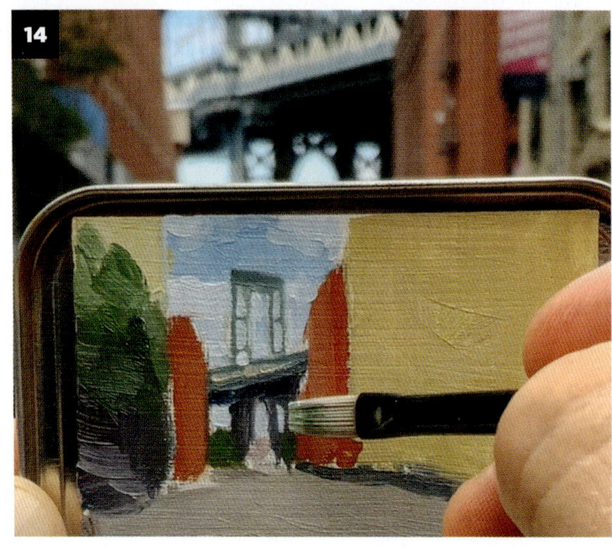

14

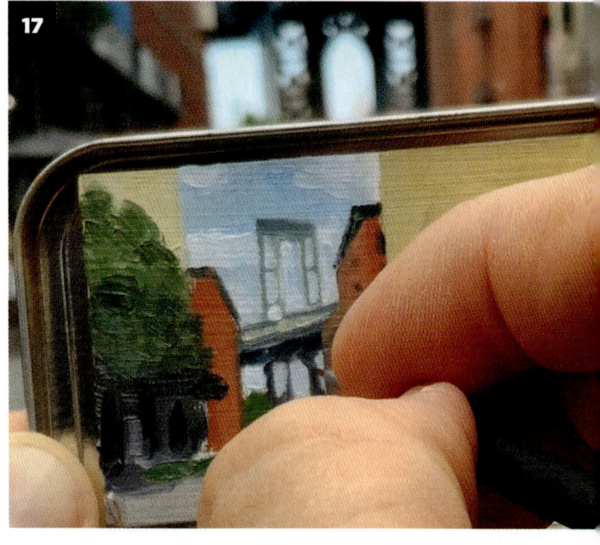

17

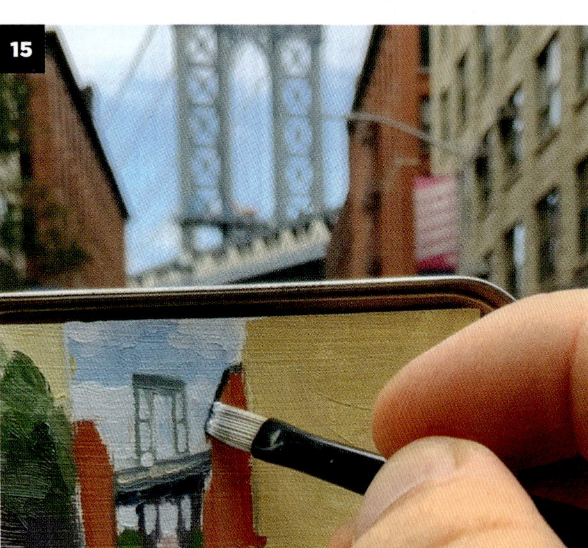

15

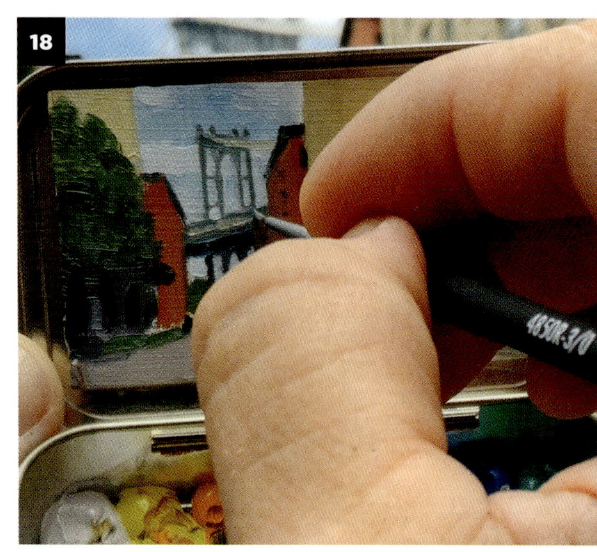

18
485MR-3/0

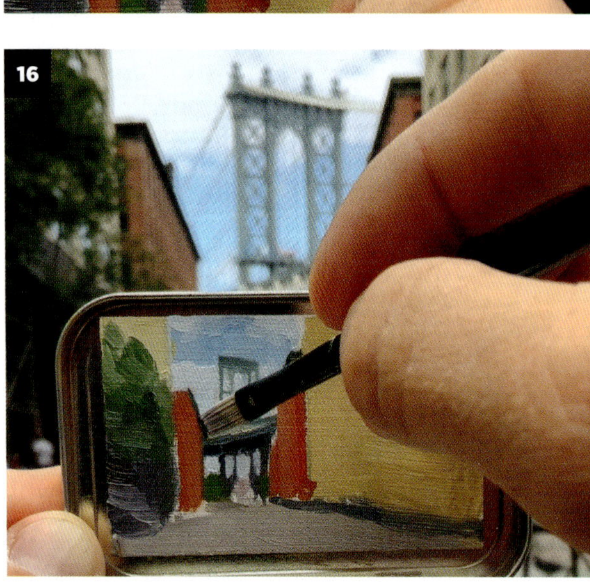

16

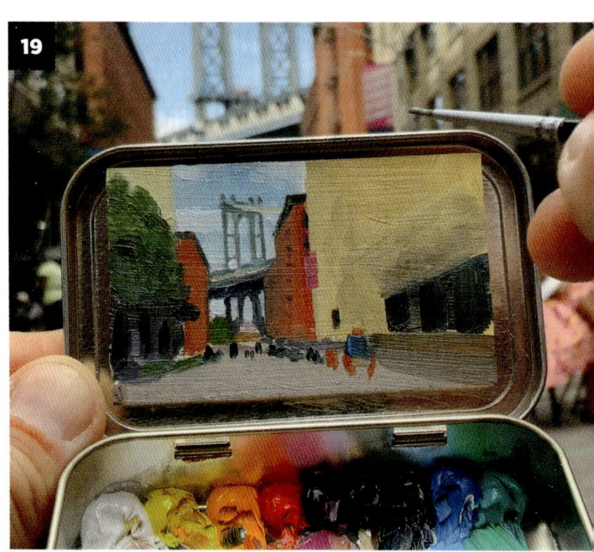

19

14. Skipping forward a bit here, and you can see that I painted the majority of the bridge in with a grayish blue-green tone, and am now working on painting in the negative spaces in between the trusses of the bridge. I mixed a green for the foliage on the left, and for the trees in the park at the end of the street below the bridge. I also painted some white clouds in the sky and started to build out the right side of the street with a gray streak where the yellow building meets the street.

15. I'm now edging the tops of the buildings with a dark gray that is close to black. This line and the next one are both painted with the vanishing point in mind, which is located at the bottom of the bridge trusses, halfway between the two buildings.

16. When I'm doing these edge sections, I can correct the inconsistencies that I had painted earlier when I sloppily laid down the color for the buildings. If you remember my brushstrokes when I initially painted the red of the building, they were not the exact shape of the building. I knew I could come back and overlap these dark building tops over those sloppy brushstrokes.

17. Now I am working with a small round brush and can skip around, building out details all around. I have a grayish-black color loaded onto my brush, and have started to put some dark details into the shaded area on the left, as well as some window details in the red building on the

right. In this picture, I am just starting to build out the understructure of the bridge.

18. Since I'm at the point where I feel ready to tackle the bridge, I am noticing more and more detail in it. The large suspension cables draping down off the top right of the bridge look stacked together as a golden tan streak from my vantage point, similar to the color I painted the large building on the right. Each suspension cable attaches to the top of the bridge at one of the four little structures that look like balls on top of a cube. Each one must be at least 10' to 15' (3 to 5 m) tall, but in my painting they will each manifest as a small gray tick mark made with that grayish blue-green mixture. Then I start rendering the bridge to make it look correct, including the archway in the middle.

19. As I continue detailing, I keep everything as simple as possible. If I add too much detail in any one place, that place will seem to have more emphasis on it. The main thing I want to emphasize in this painting is the Manhattan Bridge. Everything else is extra. I want it to look right, but at this stage I am reminding myself to stay focused and see this painting though to the finish line with efficiency. Part of this efficient way of working, besides not stressing out and toiling over perfection, is that if I have a color on my brush, to use that color in as many places on my painting as possible before switching colors.

20. I'm getting to the finish line here in this shot, with the final touches of the smaller negative spaces on the bridge. I've skipped all around and added details where I felt they were necessary, and omitted some that were unnecessary. Some details I feel are necessary to include without making them exactly perfect are: small lines to indicate the suspension cables draping down to the left, a streetlight, windows on the buildings, and people in the street. The people are painted in with a bunch of tick marks that represent pants and shirts.

The windows on the building on the right also follow the lines of the linear perspective. Their verticals all line up, and their spacing becomes tighter as they recede away.

21. Here's a close-up of the finished painting.

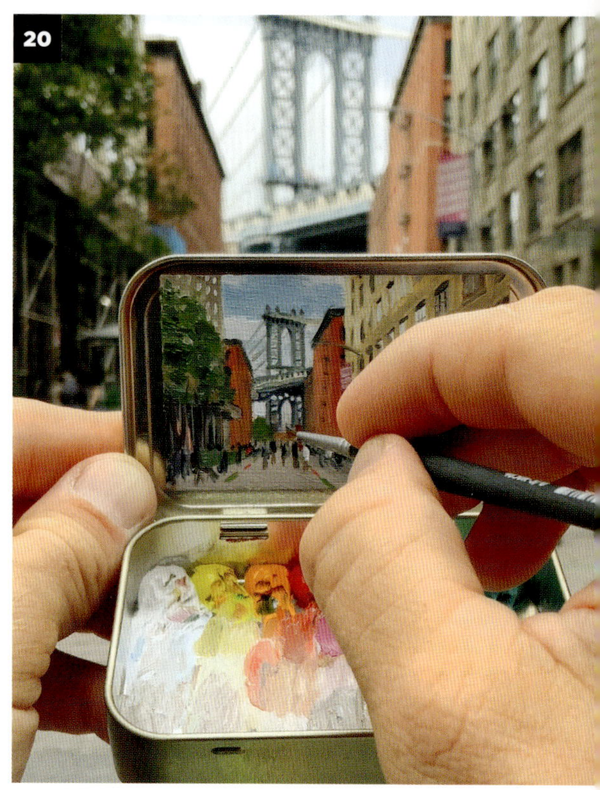

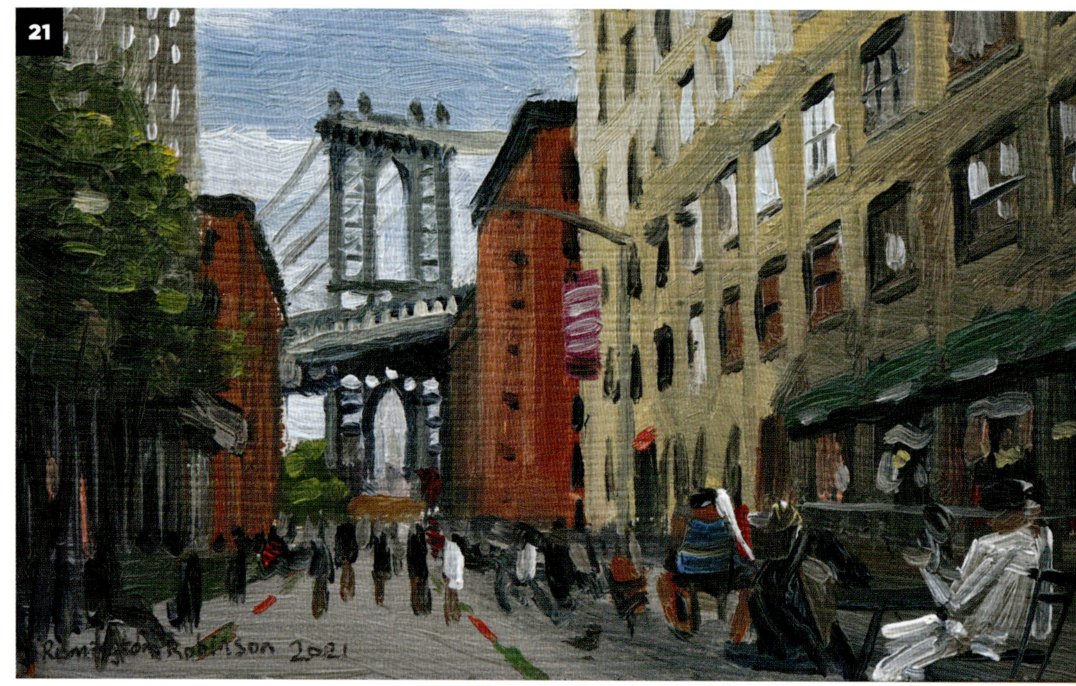

   MINI PLEIN AIR PAINTING

GALLERY: LINEAR PERSPECTIVE

The following is a small selection of paintings made using linear perspective.

Linear perspective was used to achieve the receding lines for the curb, sidewalk, fence, and house edged in this painting of red maples in autumn in my neighborhood in Boulder, Colorado. This painting is also an example of painting foliage.

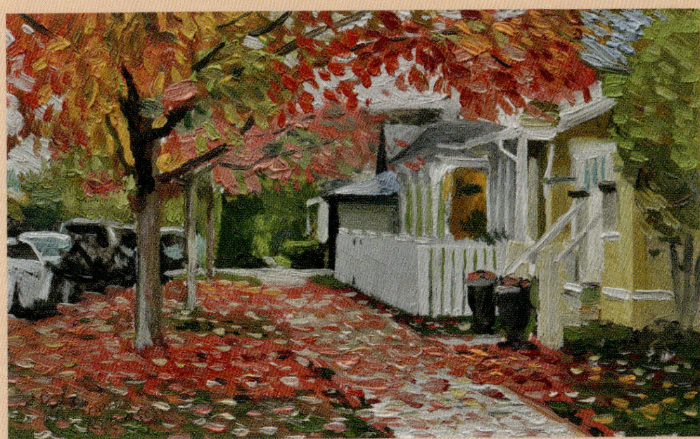

Lines of perspective were used to map out the initial structure of this parked pickup truck in Mazunte, Mexico.

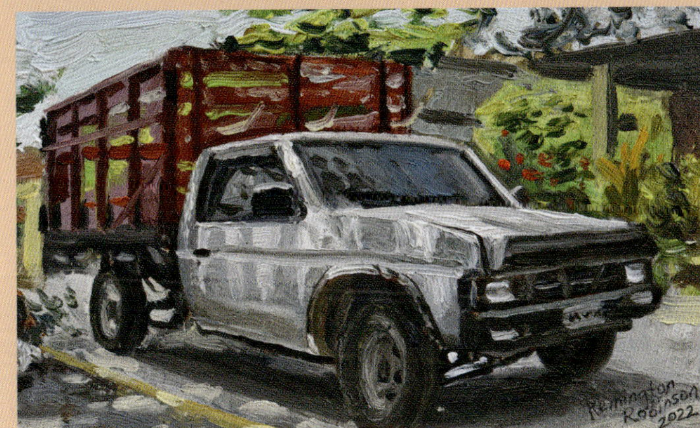

People walking on a promenade in Central Park, New York City. This scene employs the use of both linear and atmospheric perspective, and features moving subjects (page 122) as well as foliage (page 48).

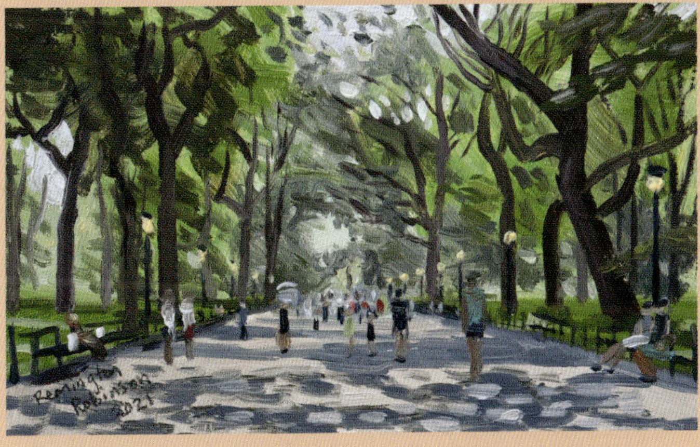

ATMOSPHERIC PERSPECTIVE: BACKLIT YELLOW ASPENS IN THE ROCKY MOUNTAINS

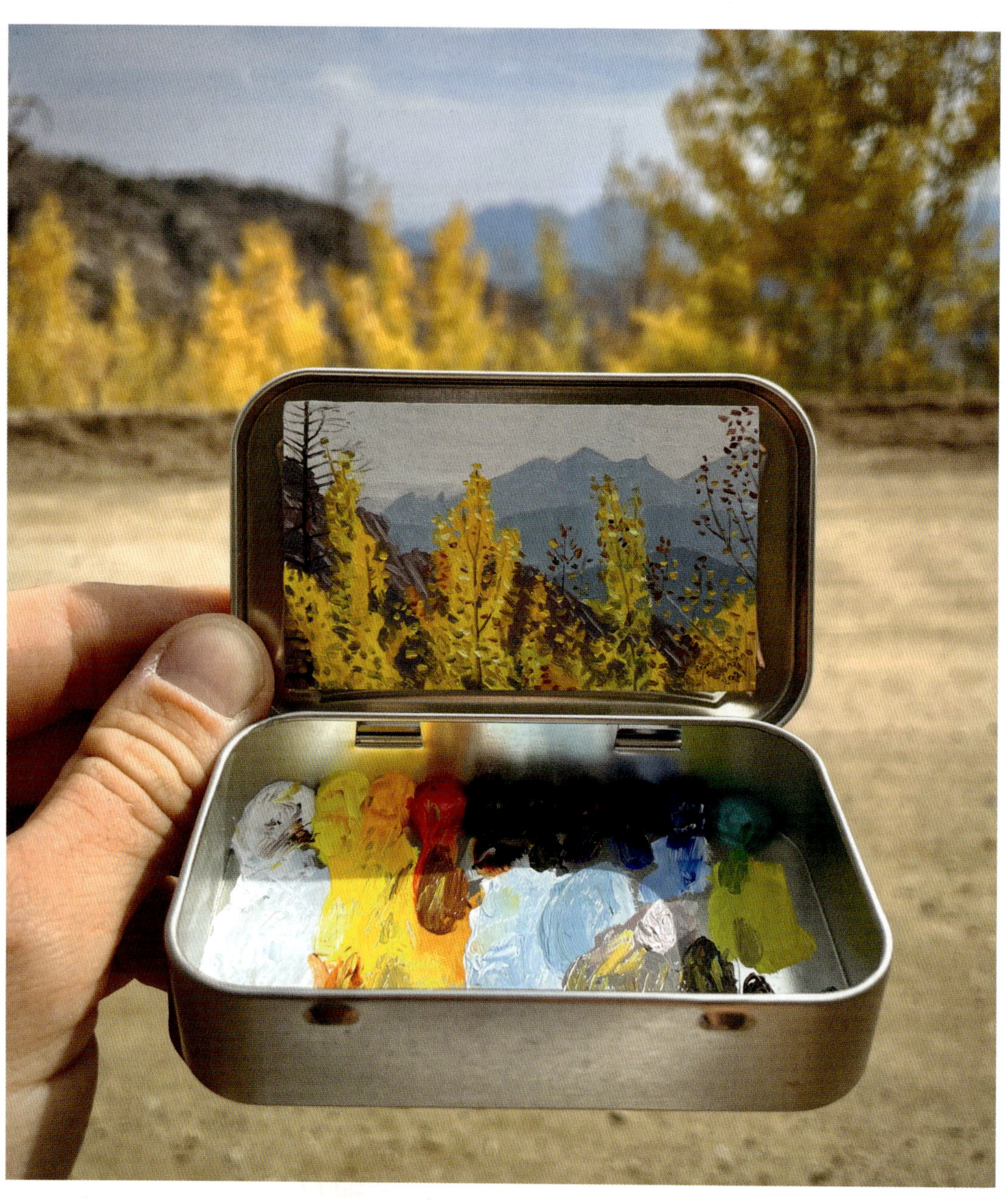

Atmospheric perspective is a fairly basic concept: it's the influence that the atmosphere has on color in between the viewer and a distant object. Some people refer to atmospheric perspective as "aerial perspective."

The general rule, in terms of color, is that objects typically become lighter and bluer the further away they are, hence the term "distance bluing" that is sometimes used. Distant landmarks—mountains, trees, buildings, even distant clouds close to the horizon—usually can be observed with some atmospheric perspective influencing them.

Distance bluing is a good starting point. However, this rule has exceptions; depending on different factors of climate, distant objects can appear to be different colors. In some situations, the color can be a very saturated blue, while in others, objects can look completely gray, purple blue, or even blue green. During sunrise or sunset, faraway objects can be a more intense blue or purple, and the objects closer to the sun can look yellow, orange, or even red. In rain, snow, or fog, subtle forms of gray usually prevail. Smog can make things gray, blue gray, or a warm orange gray. Wildfire smoke can make things look all sorts of colors—gray, gray blue, orange, or brownish. See the sidebar at on page 80 for visuals on how these elements can affect atmospheric perspective.

To take the idea of atmospheric perspective even further, the direction of direct sunlight also plays a role in how the atmosphere looks. When the sun is lighting a scene directly, that scene will tend to have less atmospheric depth than if it the same scene is backlit.

For example, imagine you are looking west, and there are distant mountains in that direction. When they are directly lit by the morning sun coming from the east, they have less atmospheric depth than they do in the late afternoon, when they are backlit by the sun. One rule here is that the brighter the light is, the more it cuts through the atmosphere.

In the late afternoon, the setting sun behind the same mountains will cause the face of the mountains to be in shadow. All of that sunlight is filtering through the atmosphere, which colors and lightens those shadow areas based on the color of the sunlight and whatever the composition of the atmosphere is like that day.

Those are the two opposites of direct lighting. All other angles of direct sunlight proportionally influence atmospheric perspective as a combination of those two concepts. In cloudy conditions, the sunlight is diffused by the clouds, flooding the entire landscape with overhead light.

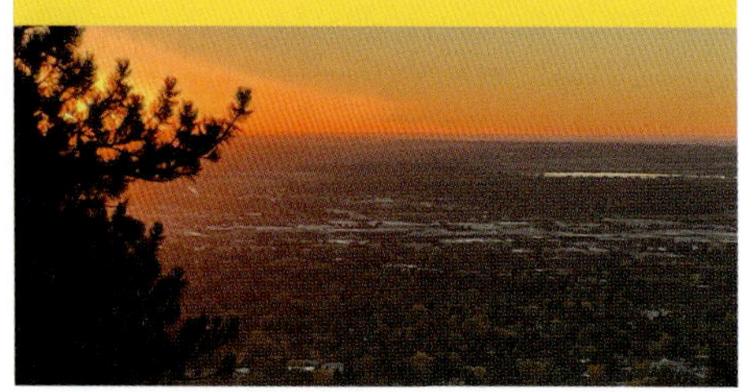

All shadows in this case are soft, as opposed to the relatively definite shadows created by direct light.

With atmospheric perspective, all values get lighter at a distance, but the dark areas are more noticeably affected. Lighter areas cut through the atmosphere more. Because the dark areas are more affected by the distance bluing of the atmosphere, contrast between light and dark areas—detail—is lost over distance. In painting, this means that one can intentionally leave out detail at greater distances to enhance the effect of atmospheric perspective. Check out the gallery on page 87 to see some more examples of paintings that show atmospheric perspective.

When the subject is back-lit, another term for this is "contre-jour," which is French for "against daylight."

As sunlight passes through the atmosphere during this low-humidity Colorado sunrise, nearly all colors are visible over the entire landscape: the sky contains red, orange, yellow, and green, while the land below is orange, red, purple, blue, and green.

The weird orange light in this image is due to wildfire smoke at sunset.

WEATHER AND SUNLIGHT EFFECTS ON ATMOSPHERIC PERSPECTIVE

Take a look at all the ways weather and the way sunlight changes through the day can affect atmospheric perspective.

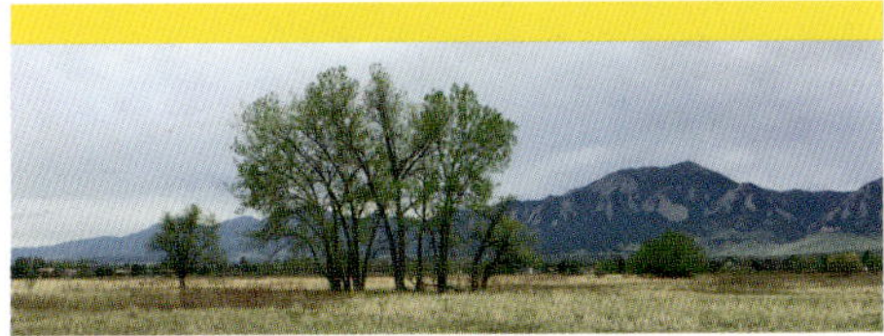

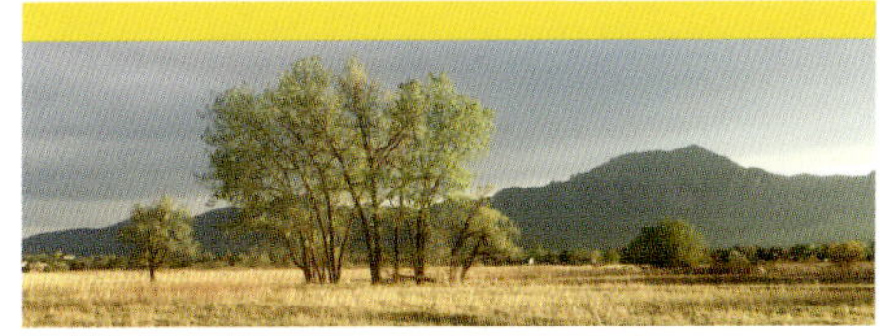

Notice how the mountains are a more saturated blue on the right, and become lighter blue as they recede away to the left.

An hour after the previous image, the mountains are lighter on the right side because the sun is shining across the land-scape from that side. In this particular case, the atmosphere is slightly green looking—a combination of the distance bluing and the yellow golden-hour sunlight.

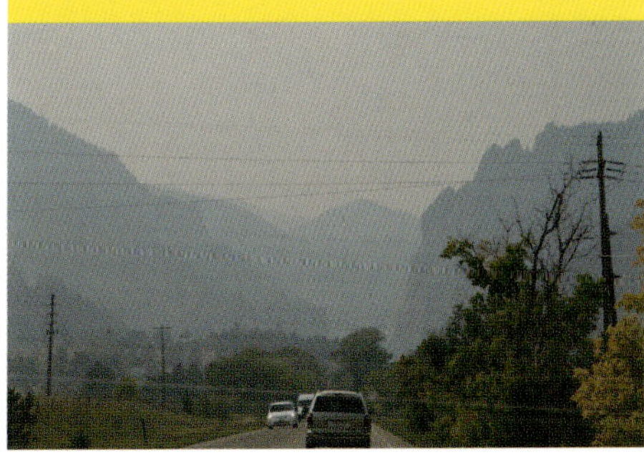

During this sunrise in Mazunte, Mexico, the sun only became visible several minutes after it rose over the horizon. The high humidity from the ocean likely played the biggest role in obscuring its light. Other factors contributing to this atmospheric condition could possibly have been pollu-tion and smoke from fire.

Wildfire smoke during the day can create its own atmospheric perspective, as seen on these mountains, which are a dirty blue-green-gray. The sky just above the mountains is cloudless, but the blue sky is obscured by gray smoke, with a brownish tint closer to the horizon.

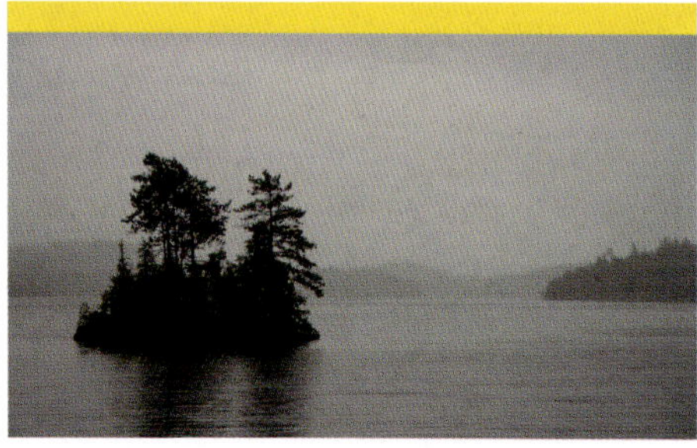

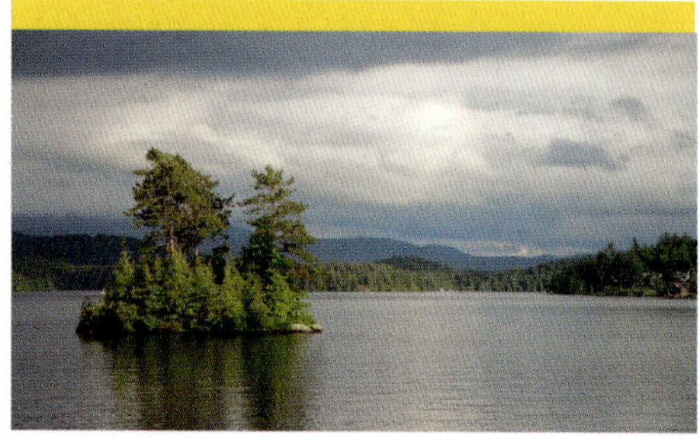

Distant detail is lost in the rain, and the edges of these hills are blurred by the rain.

The same scene on a different day shows the distant mountains as blue, while the trees across the lake are not too much lighter than trees in the foreground, due to direct sunlight.

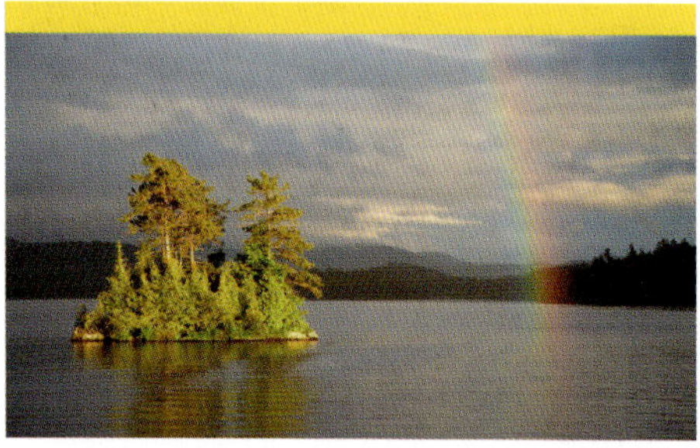

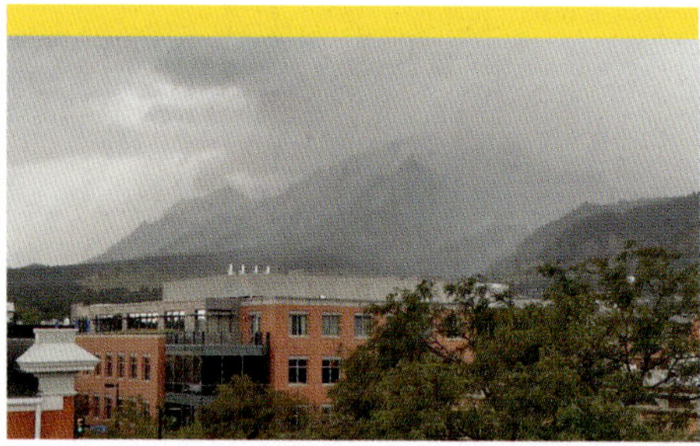

In yet another view of the same scene, rainbows create their own atmospheric perspective effect—everything inside the rainbow is lighter, with a more pronounced atmospheric perspective than is outside of the rainbow. Notice how the orange-yellow golden-hour sunlight is affecting the color of the distant mountains.

With rain, each individual droplet creates its own lensing effect, so all of the trillions of little raindrops put together can make the background slightly blurry. This concept can be translated in painting by making edges slightly soft if the distant objects are affected by rain.

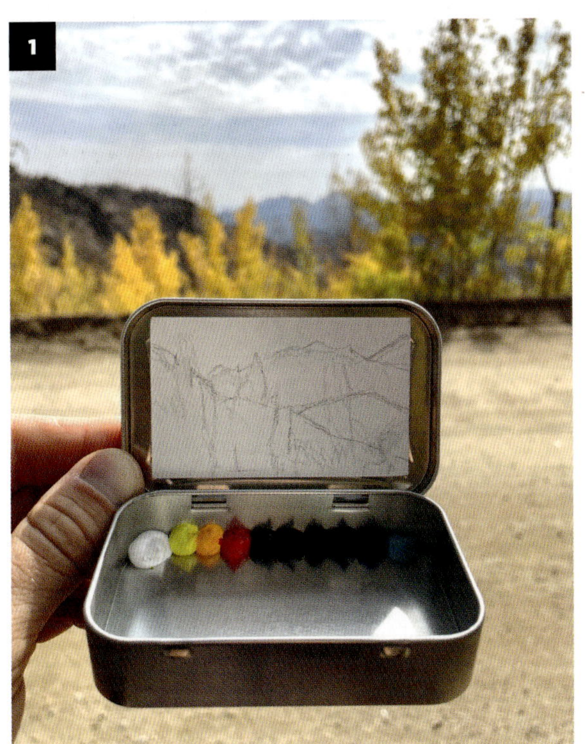

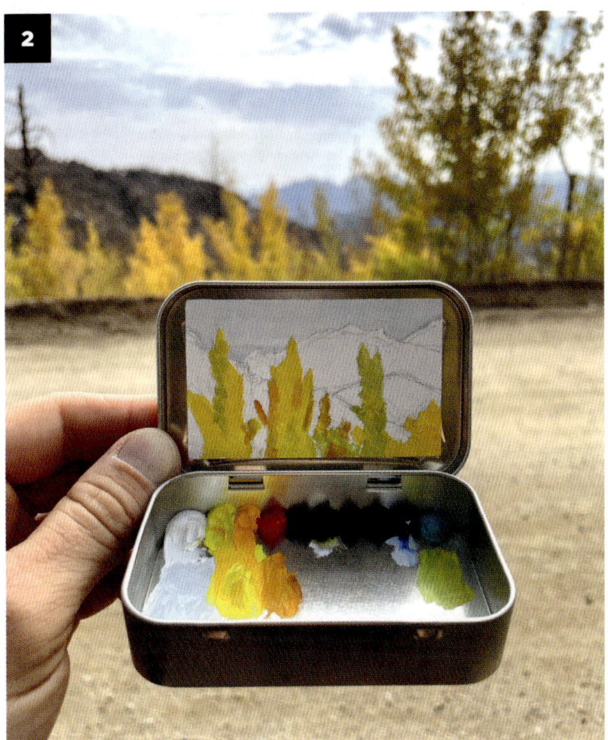

1. In this project, the mountains I am painting are lit from behind, as I was painting in late morning, looking east and southeast. This first step shows my pencil sketch for the painting. I chose to delineate some of the mountain layers and the yellow tree shapes. Take note of the use of the rule of thirds: the horizon of mountains is roughly on the line of the upper third, and the Flatirons are visible on the last layer of mountains, located approximately at the intersection of the upper and left third lines. Also, the two most prominent yellow aspens fall approximately on the left and right vertical third lines.

2. The first paint I put down is a very light gray for the most distant atmosphere beyond the mountains, including a vague indication of the horizon, which is shown with a slightly darker tone of gray with a touch of blue. Even though atmospheric perspective is the purpose of this demonstration, the main subject of this particular painting are those saturated yellow aspens. So, before doing anything else, I fill in the yellow trees because the high chroma and saturation of that yellow is crucial to maintain. Yellow can easily become contaminated and muddied by other colors, so it must be treated with care and cannot be painted over-top of other colors if saturation and color purity is the objective.

After painting the yellow, I add some other basic color-blocking nuances to the yellow trees before moving on to the rest of the painting.

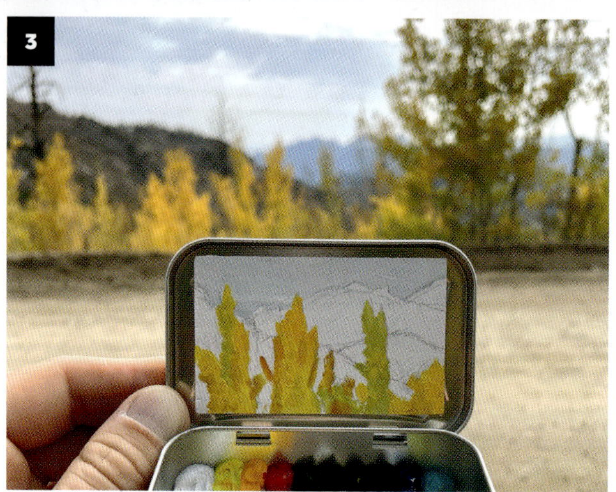

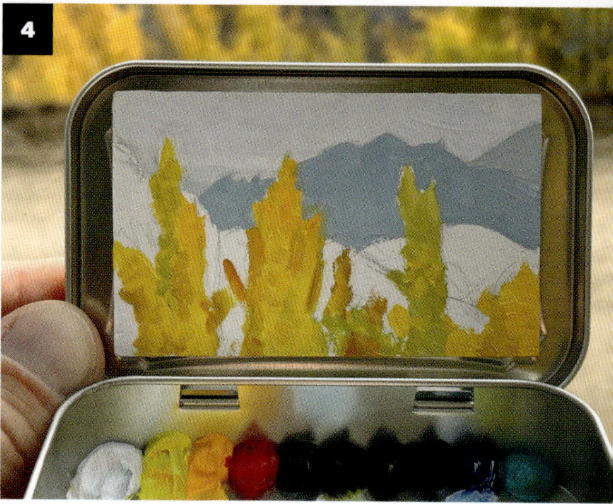

3. Speaking of color nuance, there is just a hint more in this image than the last one. Can you spot it? It's in the yellow of the trees. I tinted it slightly more orange in several places.

4. Now for painting the mountain layers. It is a very light value, so I begin with white. I then use the smallest corner of my flat brush (or the end of the tip, if it's a round brush) to slightly and incrementally, ever so carefully, tint it until I reach the mixture I want. For this mixture, I use a small amount of Cobalt Blue and a smaller amount of Raw Umber to mute it down, plus a little touch of Dioxazine Purple.

The blue I am seeing in the atmosphere, on location, is not completely saturated. But if you look at the mountains in this photo versus my painting of the mountains, you might notice that the mountains look more saturated. I am just trying to paint what I am seeing. The camera often picks up colors differently than they are perceived by the human eye, and if you are looking at this photo right now, you are not seeing the "real" mountains, but a photographic image of them.

5. As I keep painting the layers of mountains, I make sure to stay consistent with the colors I am introducing into my color mixture, but incrementally increasing each color as I go. I am always building on the same mixture, but not mixing all of my color mixture together for each new color, because I need to see the colors together on my palette before applying them to the painting.

This new, closer mountain layer builds on the same colors as the layers behind it as a darker gray-blue shade. Besides there being less white in this mix, this color mixture is the same as the previous layers of mountains, except for one thing: there is a slight amount of green in the mix. This is because it is closer and the green of the trees is starting to show through the atmosphere.

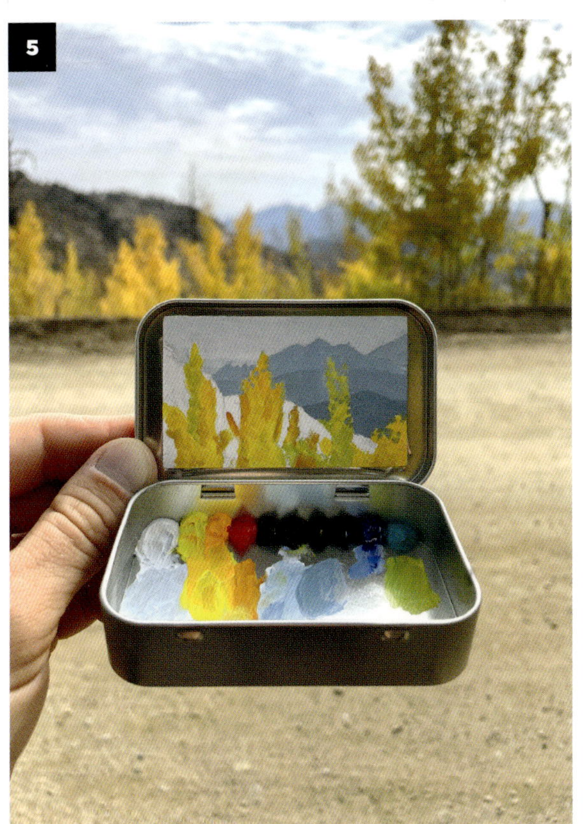

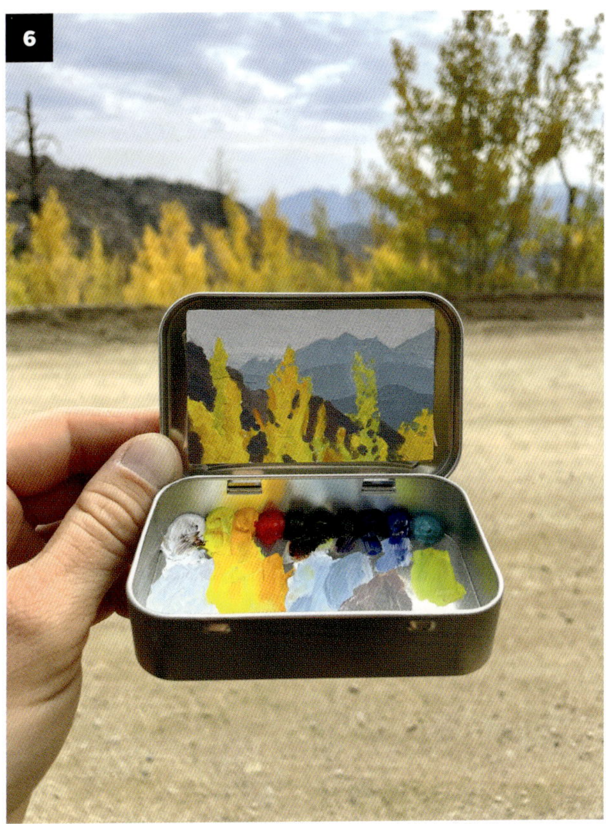

With each of these mountain layers, I am taking extra care to paint around those areas of yellow to preserve them as best as I can. You can also see that after I have filled in the mountain shades, I have begun using each of those shades and painting a few areas of negative space in the trees where the mountain is visible in openings between the leaves.

6. The last area that needed to be blocked in was the mountainside just beyond the yellow aspens. This provides nice value contrast and color contrast to the other elements in the painting and breaks up the composition nicely.

It is dark, but it will not be the darkest dark in the final painting. That darkest value will be reserved for some tree branches and dark leaf details in the foreground among the yellow aspens. The brown hillside is affected by atmospheric perspective in a mild way, because after all, it is also at a distance. The shadow areas are the main thing to look at in this case, and these are just slightly blue and a tad lighter than similar shadows in the foreground.

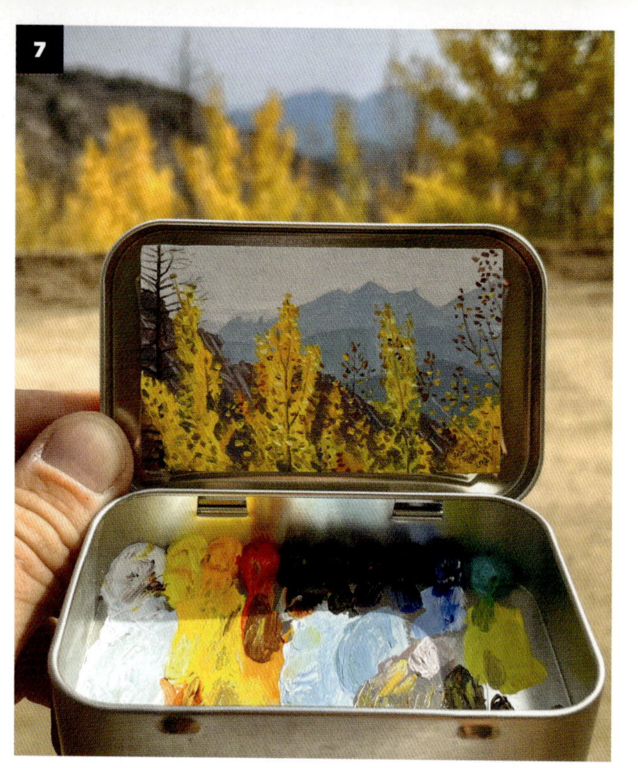

7. For the final step of the process, use a very thin detail brush. The dark mountainside from the previous step is finished with a few selected rock highlights. Compositionally, the painting is flanked by two dark trees that hold everything in—the dead conifer on the far-left side and the sparse aspen on the far right with dark brown, dead leaves (painted with Burnt Sienna, a nice warm brown). Other final branch and leaf details in the foreground are sprinkled throughout the yellow aspens with restraint, so as not to overwhelm the overall yellow look of the trees.

8. Here's a close-up of the finished painting.

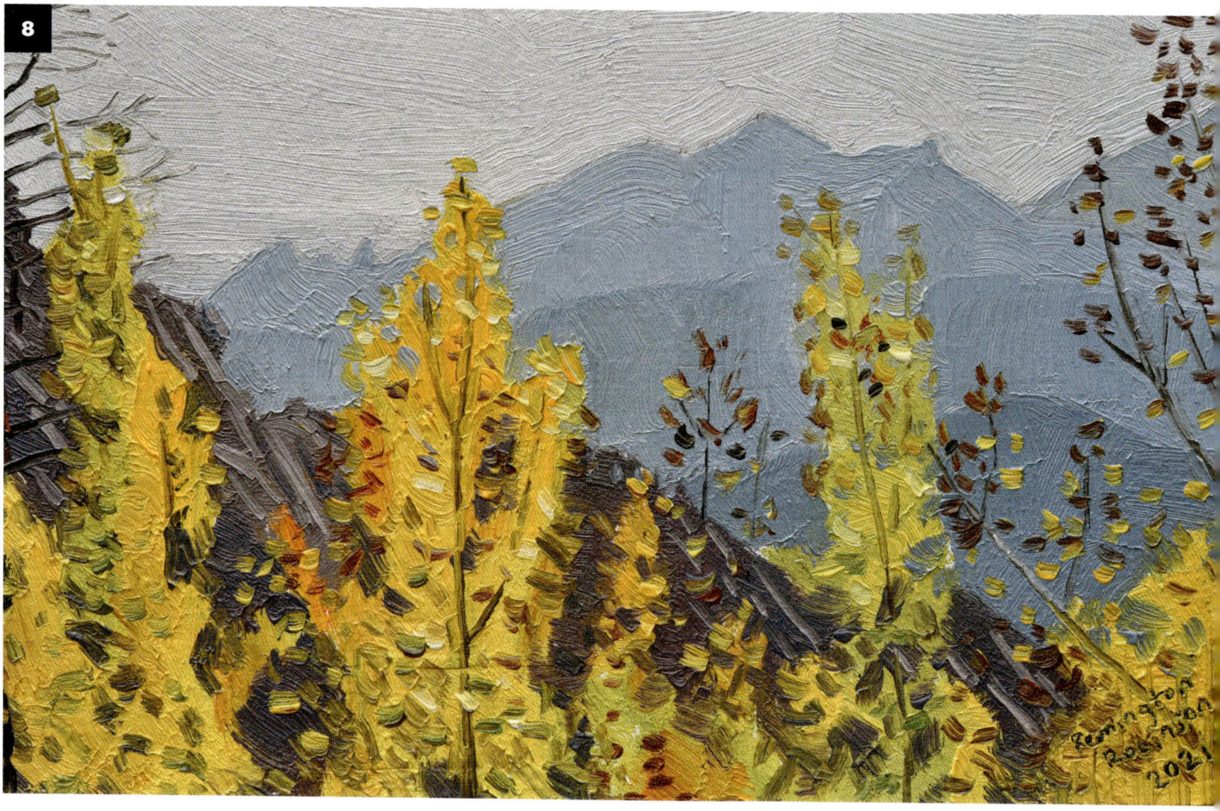

The following is a small selection of paintings made using atmospheric perspective.

The view of the atmosphere from the vantage point of an airplane over Wyoming makes it possible to really get a good look at the depth of the atmosphere all the way to the horizon, whereby the actual horizon line is often completely obscured.

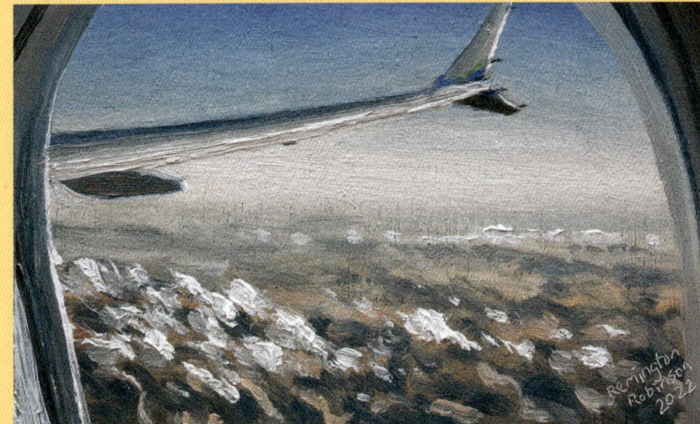

An example of both atmospheric and linear perspective in downtown Chagrin Falls, Ohio. The darkest darks are all in the foreground. The farther back in space you look, the dark values get lighter.

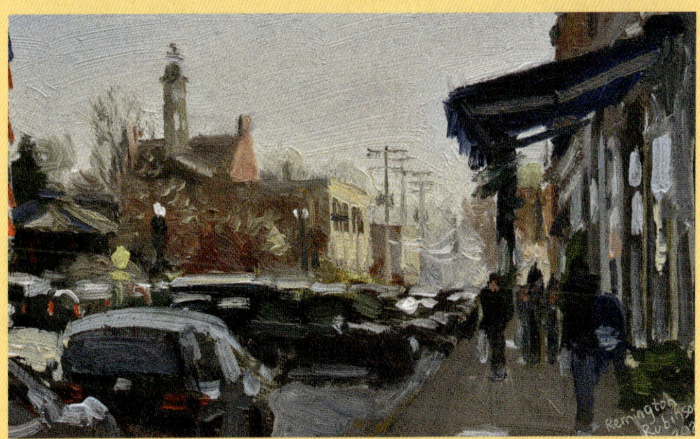

This view of the setting sun over Kanazawa, Japan offered the possibility of accentuating the painting with lots of color, particularly the orange, yellow and purple contre-jour (against the sun) in the clouds and buildings.

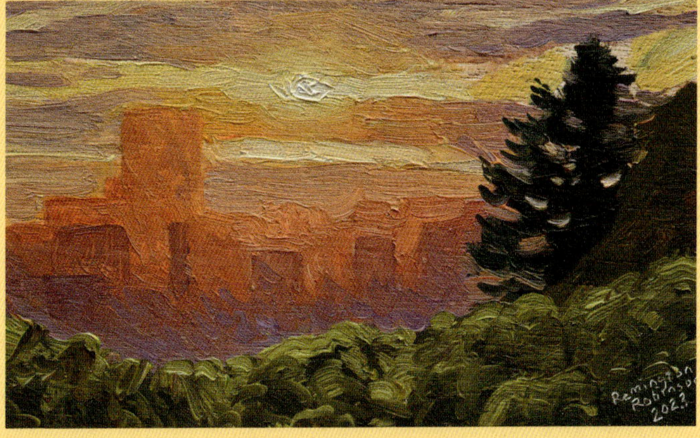

SNOW:
KEYSTONE, COLORADO

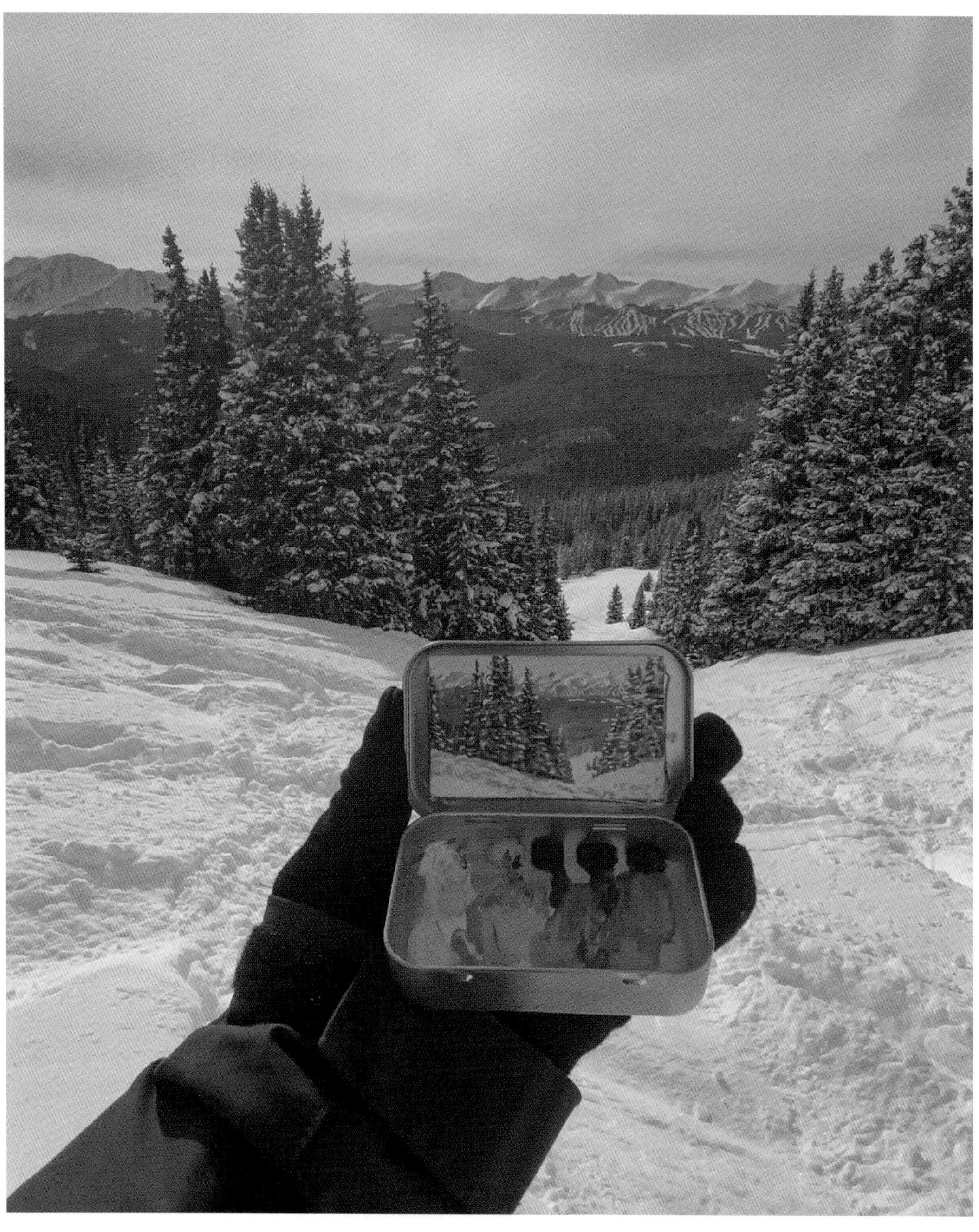

There are breathtaking mountain vistas to see while snowboarding. Since I started painting miniatures, I have often brought my supplies with me to the ski resort in case I wanted to paint something. It all fits well in my large snowboard jacket, and is not noticeable. Many times, I've gone to the resort by myself and spent the majority of the day painting. Other times, I went with friends and let them know that I wanted to paint something and they should take a few runs without me. That's exactly what happened on this particular day at Keystone Resort in Colorado.

Besides the fact that this tutorial shows that you can paint small even on the ski slope, the greater purpose for this exercise is to talk a little bit about painting snow. The main thing about painting a blanket of white snow is that the snow is almost never completely white. Often, it is a combination of gray and blue, but it can contain other colors in various circumstances. I have seen turquoise in the shadows of some snow. And we've all seen snow that is stained brown because of particulate that either settles on the surface of the snow or became part of the snow itself as it was forming. When painting snow, pure white should be saved for the absolute brightest highlights. I like to start with off-white and work my way up to pure white during the course of the painting. White paint becomes easily contaminated, and you can use this quality to your advantage.

By starting off with a paint color that is just off-white, with a light gray or light blue, and gradually easing more and more white into the mixture while you paint, it is possible to achieve a lot of subtlety within the whites overall. Check out the gallery on page 98 to see some more examples of snow paintings.

Also, when painting in the cold, there are a couple points to keep in mind. Oil paint does not freeze in cold weather; it might slow down somewhat in its workability. However, if it is snowing and the snow gets into the paint, it melts, and that water refreezes in the paint, eventually rendering the paint unworkable until it is brought into a warmer environment where it can thaw.

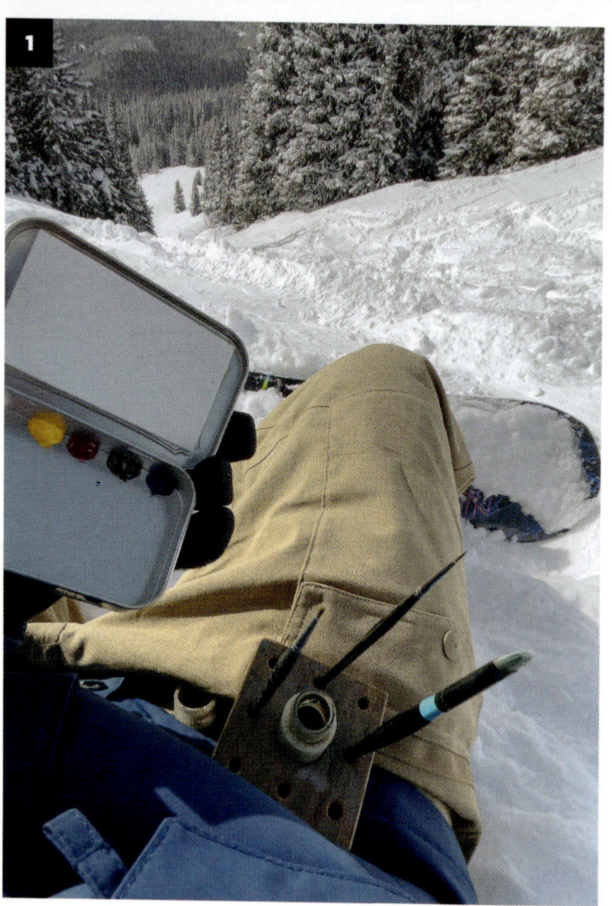

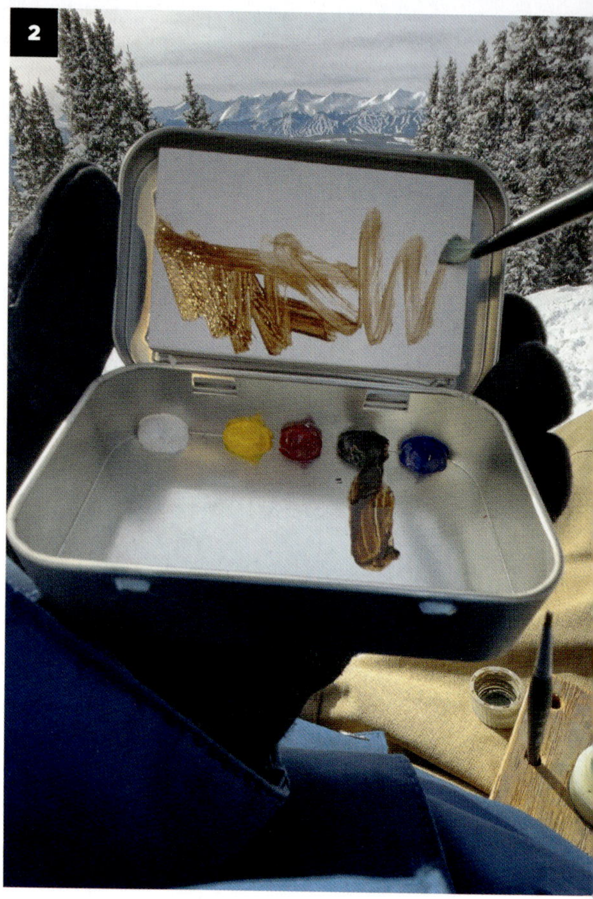

1. I've found a spot in the Keystone back bowls where I want to paint, and I've simply sat down in the snow without even removing my snowboard from my feet. The deep snow turns into a nice form-fitting chair, and the cozy warmth of my outerwear means that I am perfectly content painting for an hour or so in what would otherwise be a fairly uncomfortable spot.

My palette this time is Titanium White, Cadmium Yellow Light, Alizarin Crimson, Burnt Umber, and Ultramarine Blue.

These are alkyd oils, which I like to use when my mint tin will be rattling around in my pocket for a while before I get to paint. The alkyds stay in one place on the metal tin, in contrast with regular oils, which tend to slowly slide around the metal tray if they are freshly applied before being taken on a bumpy ride. My odorless mineral spirits container sits on my lap, wedged into the wood block I made to hold it with three brushes. I do have a paper towel in my jacket pocket in case I need to wipe my brush between colors—but that is staying put in my pocket, because if it blows away, I may never find it in the snow.

MINI PLEIN AIR PAINTING

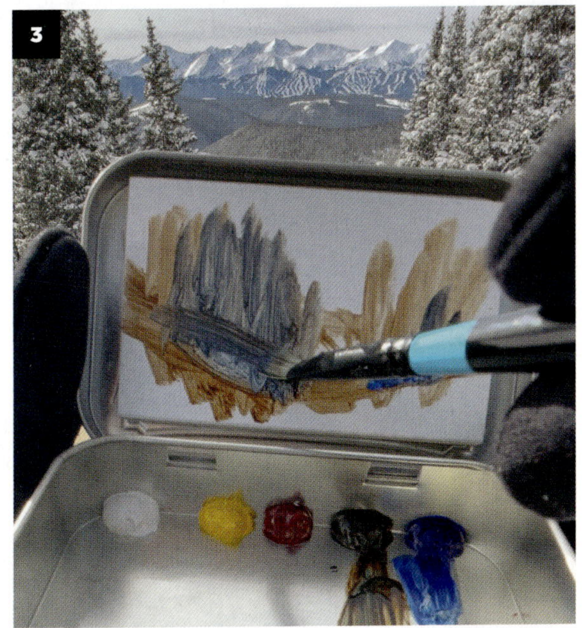

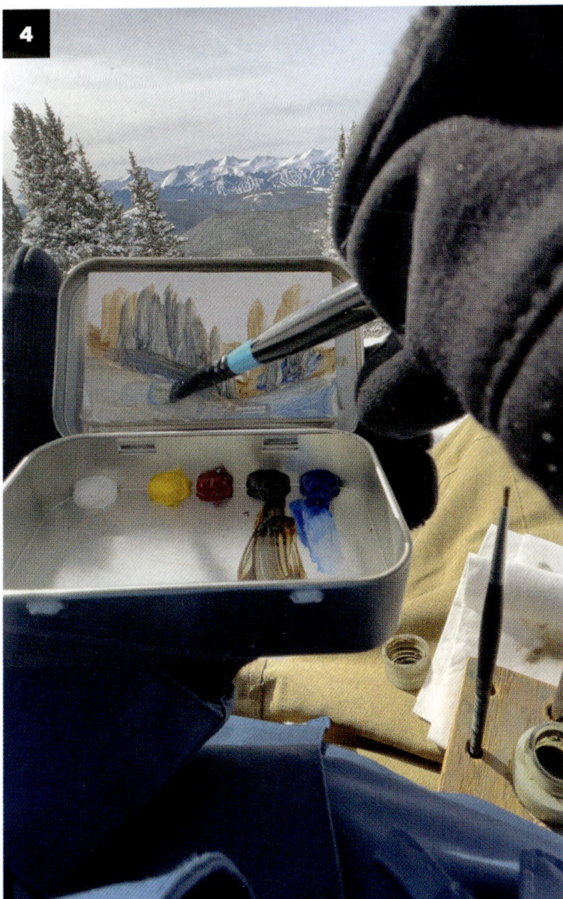

2. I'm starting off with some loose sketching in Burnt Umber to get a feel for the layout.

3. I've decided on a composition where the stand of trees on my right goes out of frame, and the full stand of trees on the left is fully visible. I also want some of the peaks in the distance on the far left to be visible.

Using the rule of thirds as a loose compositional guide, I want the horizon roughly to follow the top one-third horizontal line. My aim is also to make the ski slope I am going down land on or near the bottom right third, and the Breckenridge Resort, which is visible on the mountains in the distance, land on the top right third.

4. I am now covering the bottom area, where the snow will go, with a light wash of gray and blue.

5. Next, I have decided to block in the distant mountains. They are fairly blue due to the atmospheric perspective.

6. Continuing with the blocking, the mountains in the middle ground are greener because they are closer. Normally, they would also be darker than the mountains further away, except for the fact that they have a light dusting of snow on them, which lightens their value considerably.

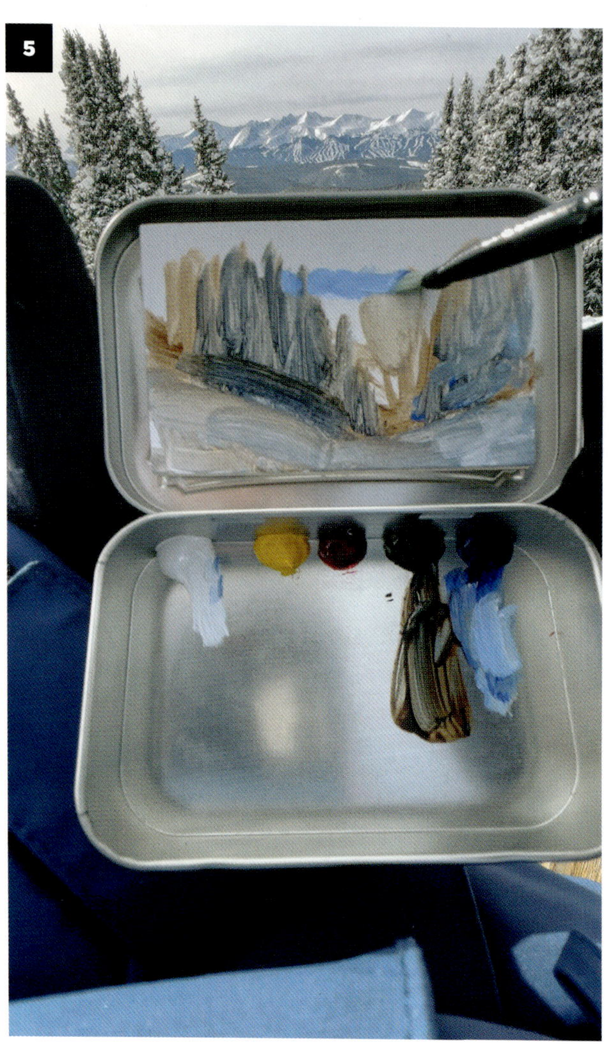

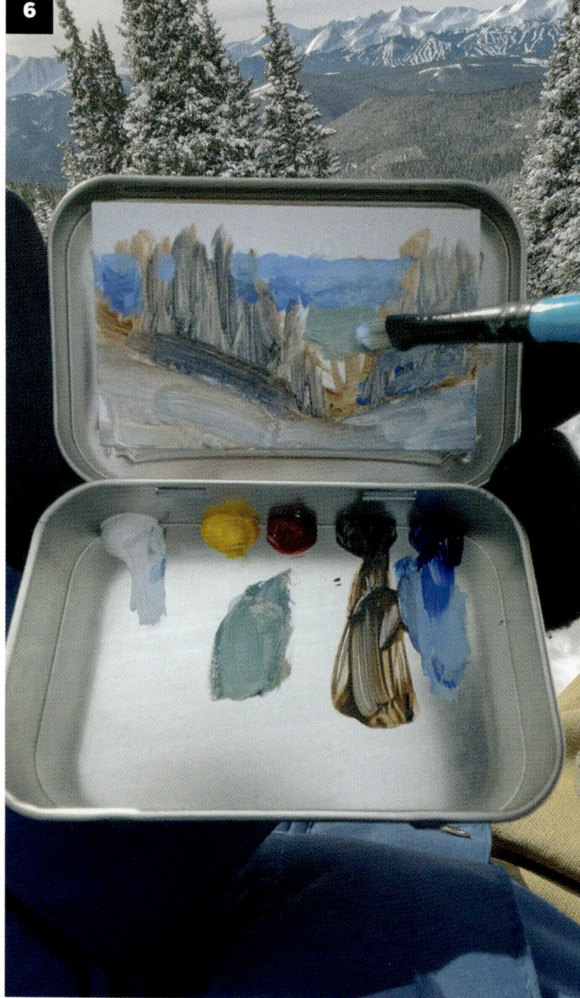

7. Now I'm blocking in the area where the clusters of pine trees in the foreground are located. This is a fairly dark mixture of Burnt Umber and Ultramarine Blue, emphasizing the blue, with a small touch of Cadmium Yellow Light. This produces a dark brownish green.

8. Now I'm beginning to block in the white for the snow. I've dipped my brush—which is still contaminated with other colors—into the Titanium White. As I paint, this white will begin to be affected by the unclean brush and the tinted underpainting, which is exactly what I want.

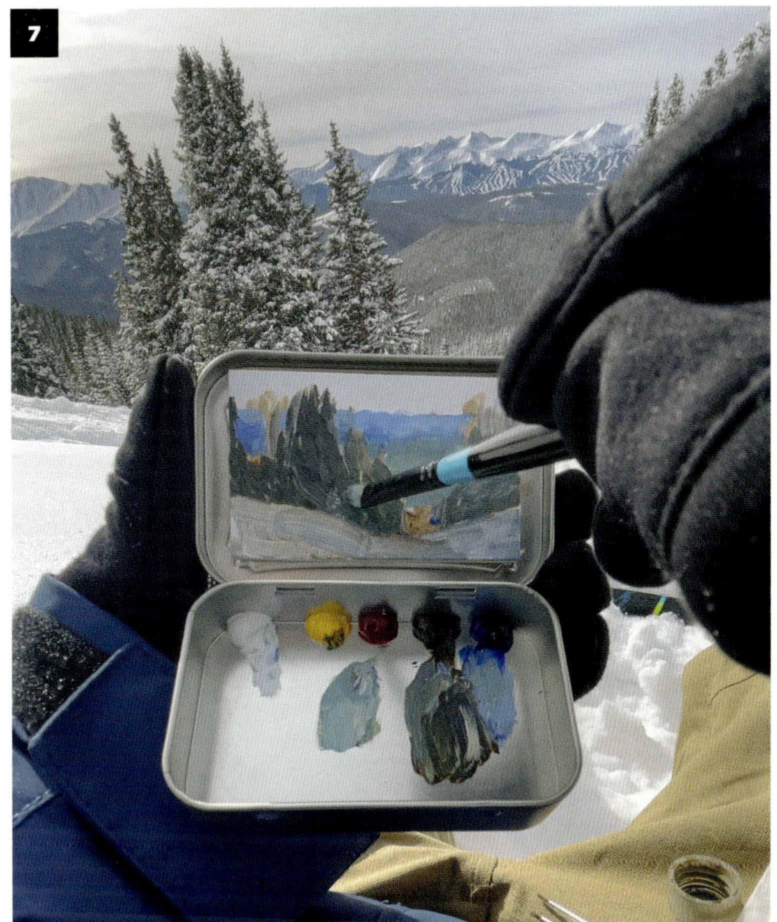

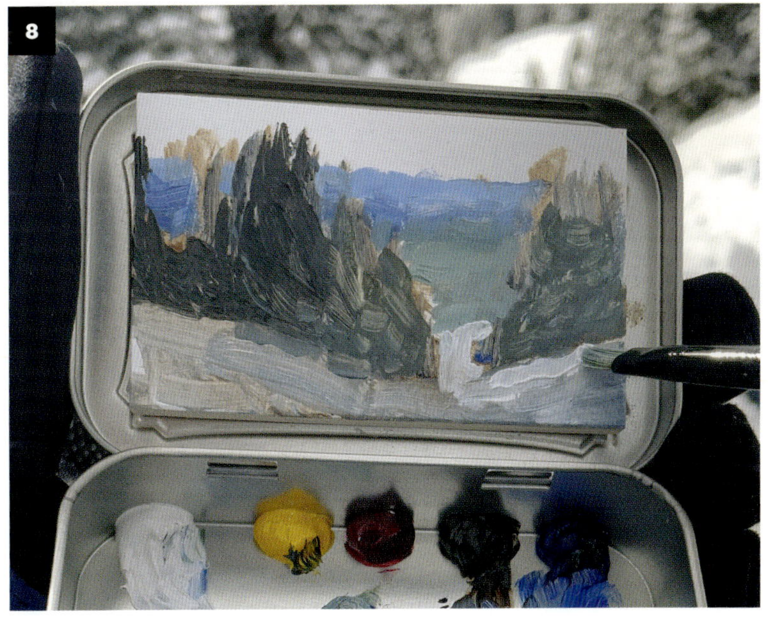

9. As I continue to block in my less-than-pure white, I start to take note of the different textures that are in the snow.

10. I still need to paint the sky in, but I can do that without washing my brush. All that white pigment has gotten into the bristles and diluted the impurity of the brush, so now the bristles are filled with a very light gray, which happens to be perfect for the sky today.

I even add a little bit of blue to one side of my flat brush to produce a mild in-brush gradient (page 22) for the sky color, even though it's overcast.

11. I mix a light bluish gray for the distant mountain peaks that are covered in snow, knowing that I can later paint highlights over them.

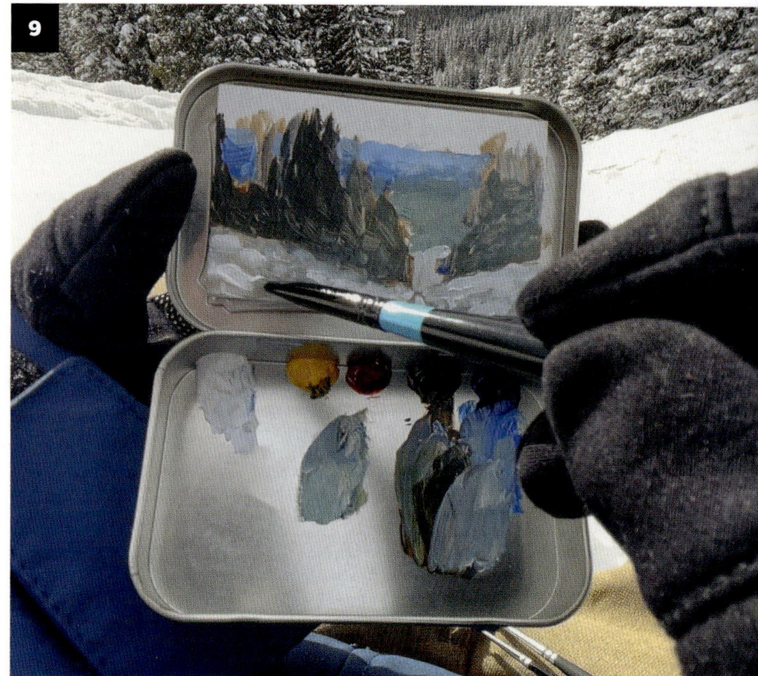

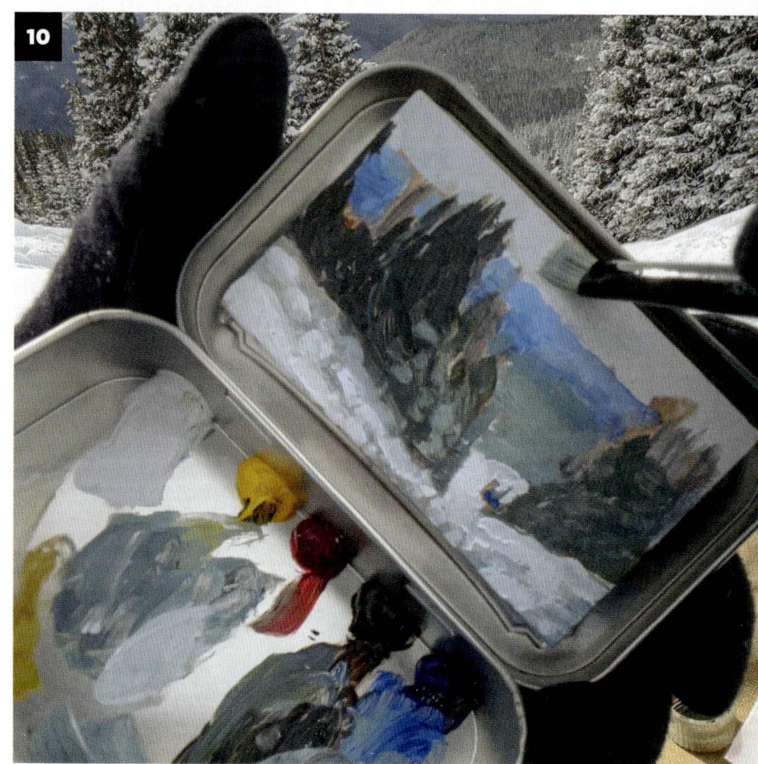

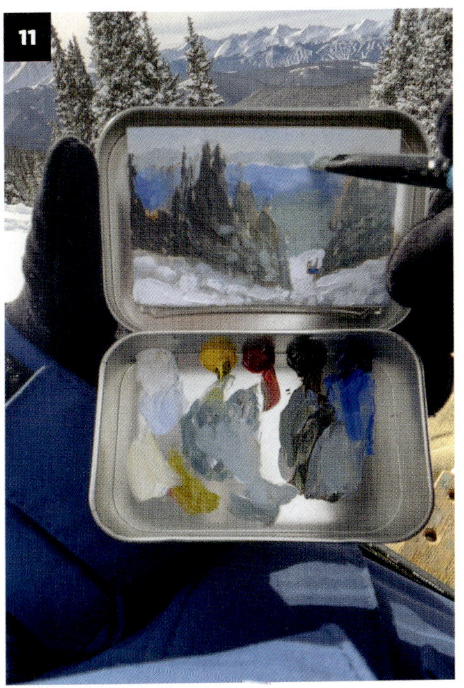

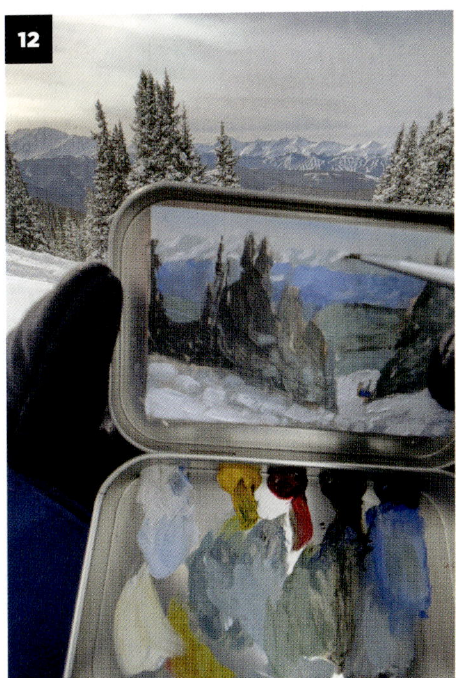

12. Here, I'm painting the highlights on those distant peaks. It's mid-winter, so even though it's the middle of the day, the sun is low in the sky and the light is coming from the south, off to the left in this picture. Any time you are painting, it is crucial to know where the light is coming from.

13. I've mixed a light greenish gray for the shaded snow on my side of the trees, and I am now loosely painting some of those larger snow clumps where that color exists. Later, with my smaller brush, I will make a pass over all of the trees with another color to finish that snow.

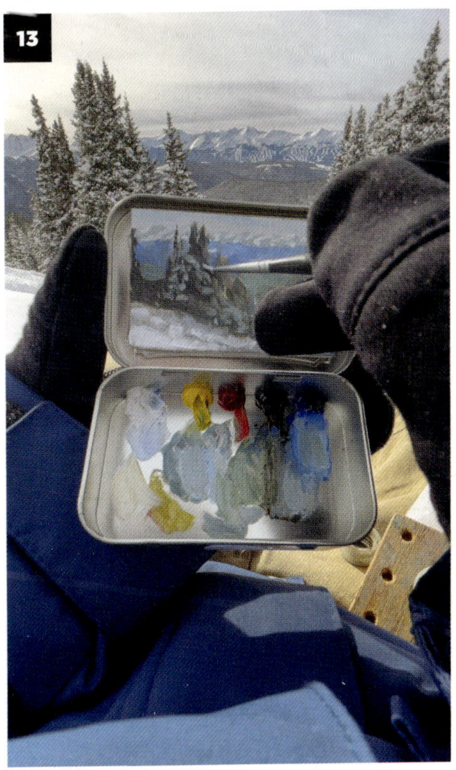

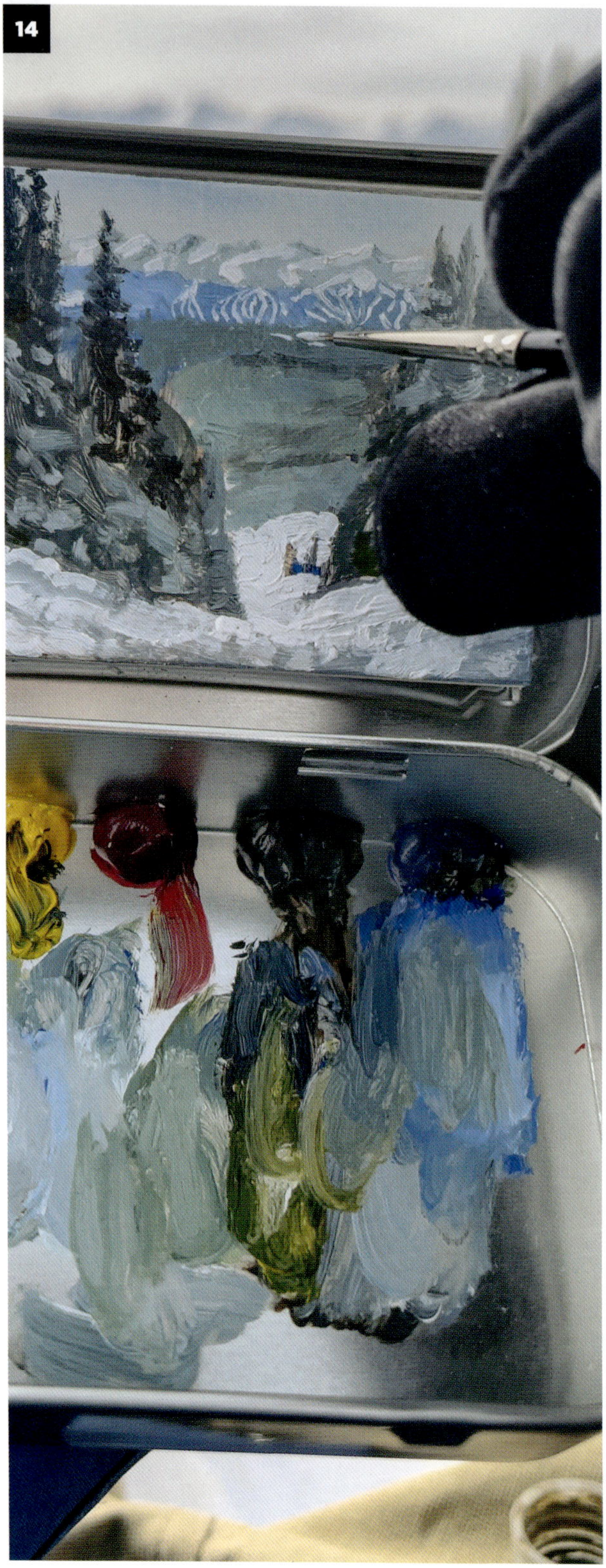

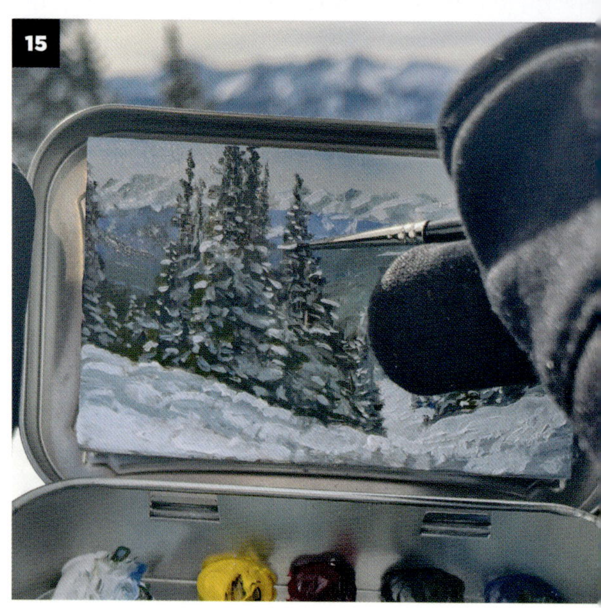

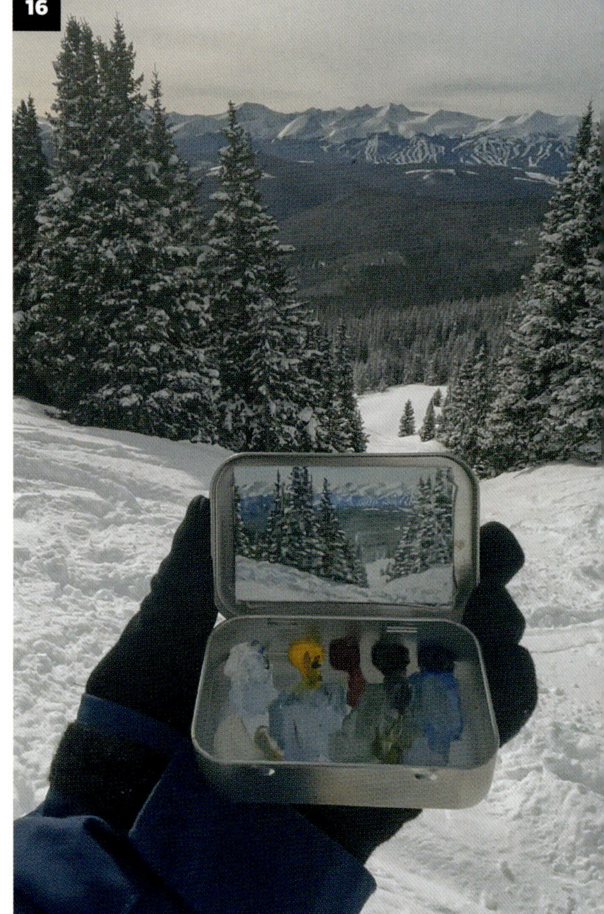

14. I'm ready to do fine detail now, and I've been getting antsy to paint those ski runs at Breckenridge. I'm trying to get them as close to accurate as I can, because I know that there are a lot of people who will recognize Breckenridge if they see it.

15. The last thing that needs to be done is to skip around the trees in the foreground with the snow color, which is basically fairly light gray with some white highlights.

16. And here's the final painting, which means I can put this back in my pocket and get snowboarding so I can go find my friends!

17. Here's a close-up of the finished painting.

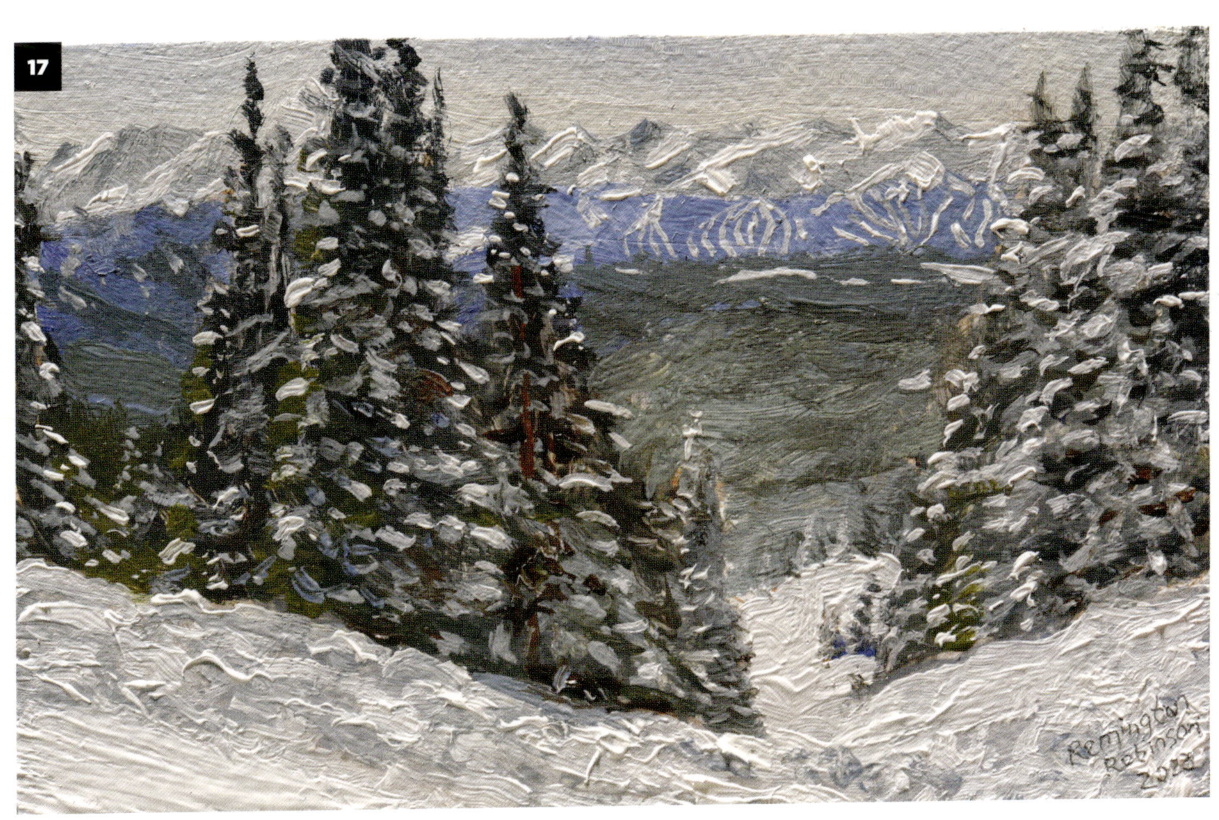

GALLERY: SNOW

The following is a small selection of paintings made in snowy weather conditions.

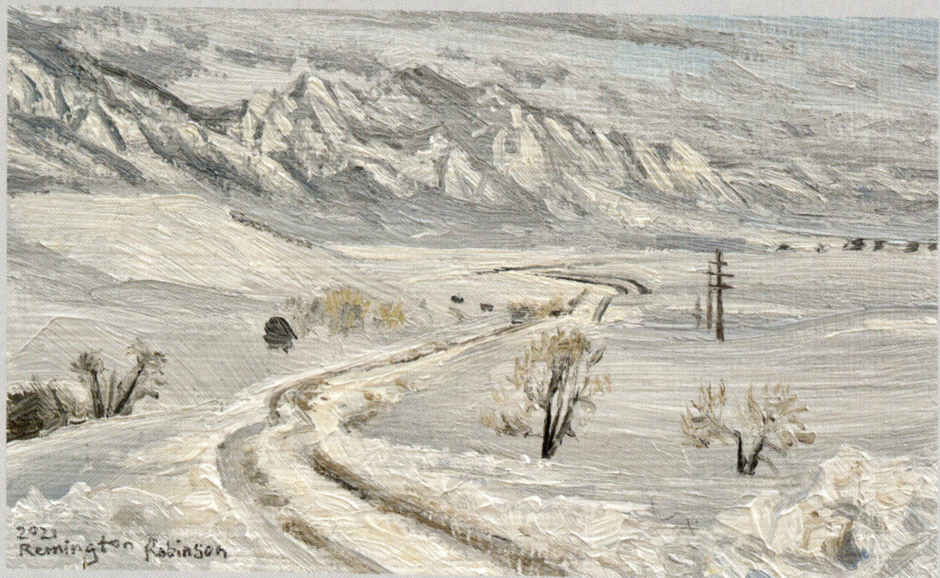

This snowy scene, on the front range of Colorado just south of Boulder, is characterized by lots of subtlety in the whites. Most of this painting is either light gray, or light blue, and the forms of the snow drifts are indicated by subtle changes in that light value.

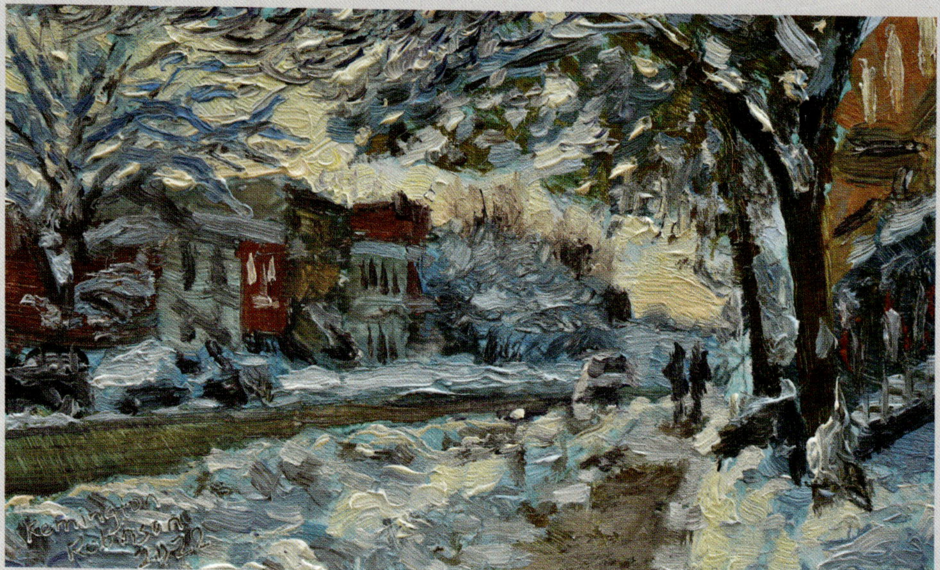

In this snowy scene in Montreal, Canada, there are lots of colors in the snow. The highlights are light yellow-orange, while the shadows are turquoise, blue, purple, and brown. The underpainting of this was done in Cobalt Turquoise Light, just for fun.

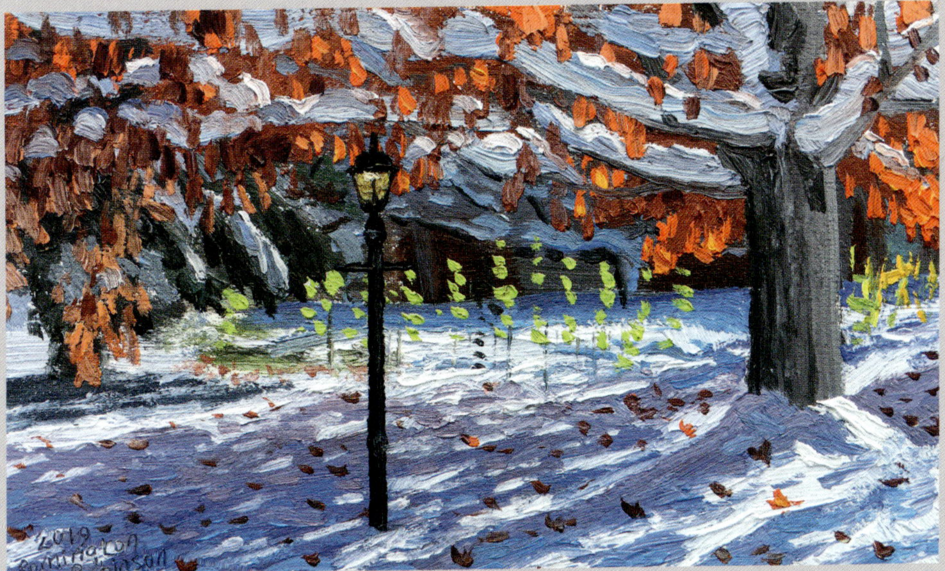

The reflective quality of the snow can produce exciting opportunities to paint. After an early snowstorm in autumn, the sun came out and the red leaves of this backlit maple tree cast their red light down onto the blue shadow, making it purple.

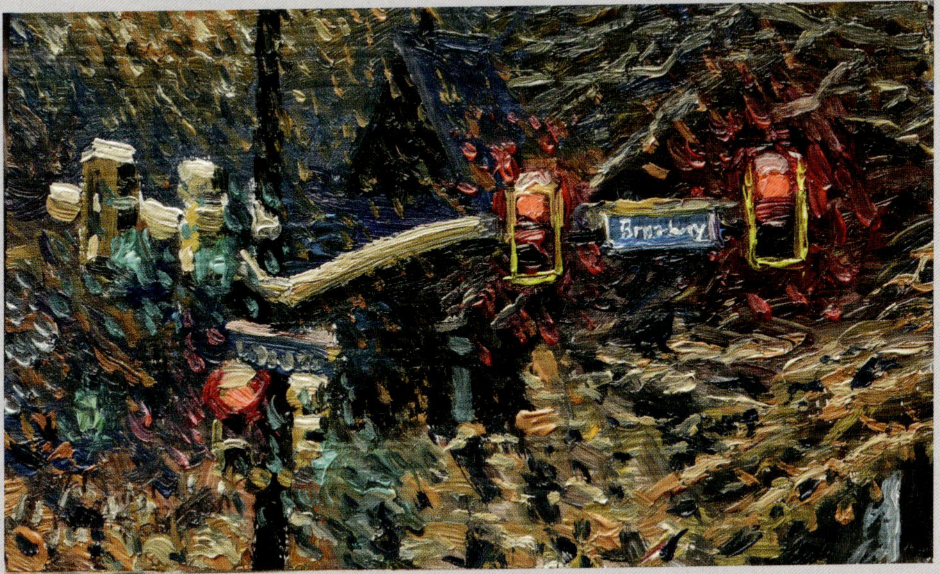

Snowy nights are one of my favorite times to paint because of the way the light reflects off of the snow. This traffic light was painted during a heavy snowstorm. Even though we know the snow is white, at night it picks up light from all the different colored light sources.

NOCTURNE: CITY LIGHTS AND WATER REFLECTIONS IN TOKYO

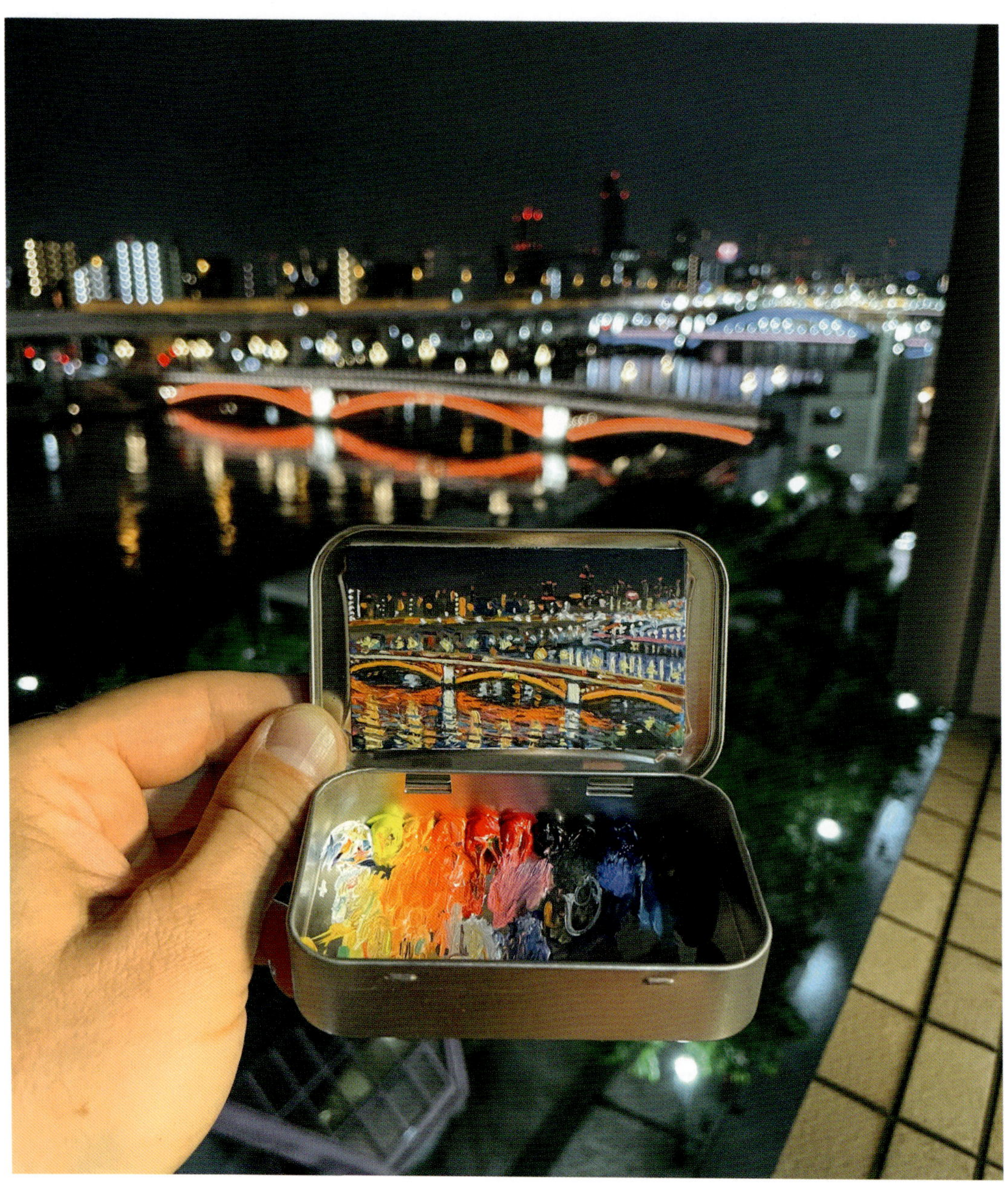

Painting nocturnes (i.e., painting at night) is all about using lots of pure color. Particularly in urban environments, there can be lots of brightly colored lights that reflect off the landscape, and areas with less light are places to paint with full-strength pigment (not diluted with white). If you can find the time to go out and paint at night, it can be extremely rewarding. Check out the gallery on page 107 to see some more examples of nocturnes.

When preparing to go out to paint a nocturne, I always bring a headlamp. Mine has a dim setting, which preserves the battery life. The most important thing, though, about having a dim setting on a headlamp, is that you can notice more color nuance in the landscape because your eyes don't have to continually adjust between a bright painting and the dark landscape.

This particular tutorial from Tokyo is yet another instance where having a small setup was beneficial. Traveling to a place like Japan is easier with a smaller painting kit, and its compact size makes it easy to work on a small balcony outside a small hotel room like this.

This painting is just as much about painting the water reflections as it is about painting at night. Reflections on water at night can be particularly fun to paint—whether it is on a body of water or on a wet road—because the color of the light is carried into the landscape in ways that are not possible during the day.

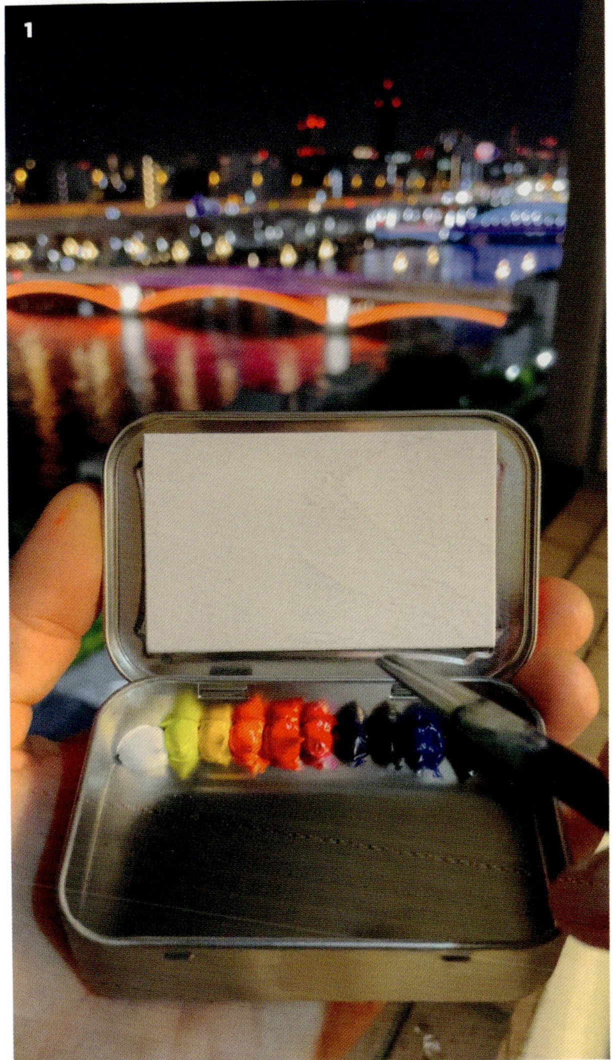

1. Nearly every color is represented in the lights down below, overlooking the Sumida River in Tokyo. I have plenty of color in my palette for the occasion—probably more than I need, actually—Titanium White, Cadmium Lemon, Cadmium Yellow Medium, Pyrrole Orange, Bright Red, Quinacridone Opera, Dioxazine Purple, Sepia, Cobalt Blue, French Ultramarine, and Phthalo Blue.

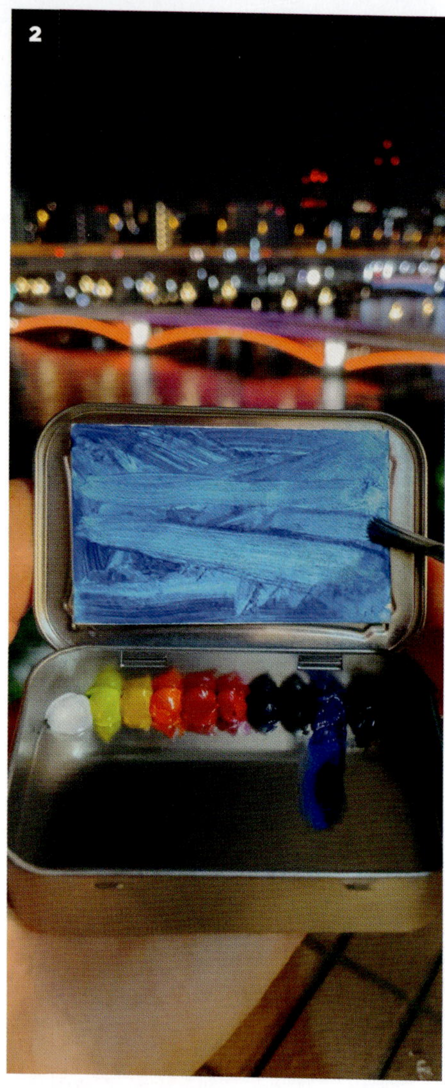

2. I am choosing to start my underpainting with Cobalt Blue. Blue is a nice cool tone that goes with shadows and nighttime. I miss a spot while painting, the blue will show through and the missed spot will not be noticeable.

3. I mix Sepia with Cobalt Blue so that I can start building up my dark values.

4. This underpainting in black and blue is basically just a loose sketch done in paint. I'm trying to preserve the areas where my light values are going to go by not putting too much pigment in those places, so that the underpainting won't compete with the paint that will go there.

5. I'm finding my lightest light values and indicating those.

6. Now for the exciting part! I'm beginning to put some color down. Even though I'm using a small brush, I con-sider this to be part of the blocking-in stage because I am establishing the location of the most prominent light structures—the pink and orange lights on the bridge in the foreground, with the water reflections, as well as the orange strip of light along the highway on the top third.

7. I've gone back to using a larger brush—a medium-sized round—where I am painting the glow of the night sky. There's more red on the horizon. I paint that first and even out the gradient where it shifts to dark blue at the top.

8. I've blocked in a warm tan midtone for the distant sky-line, and I'm now filling the bridge in with various colors.

9. There are several yellow lights on the bridge, and because the water has ripples in it, part of each individual ripple is reflecting the light directly above it. This can be simplified by painting a vertical streak of color for each light reflection.

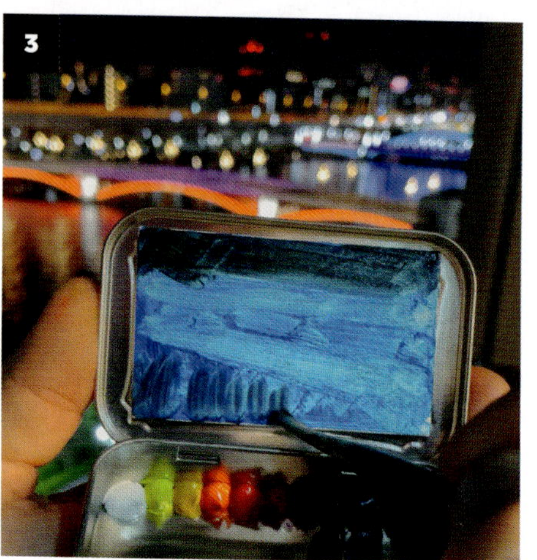

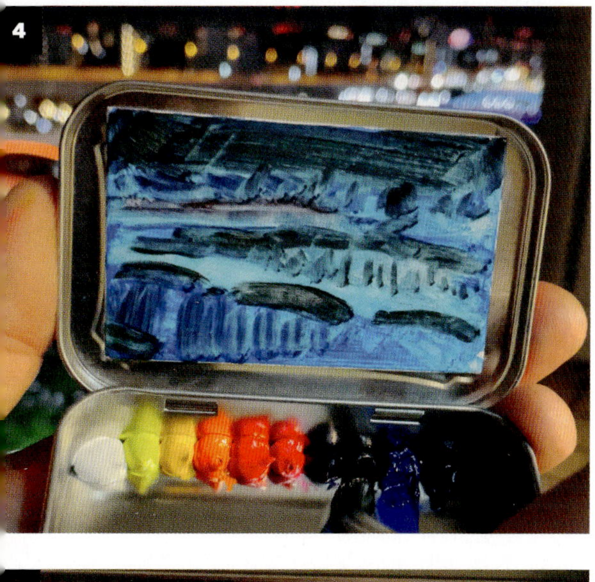
4

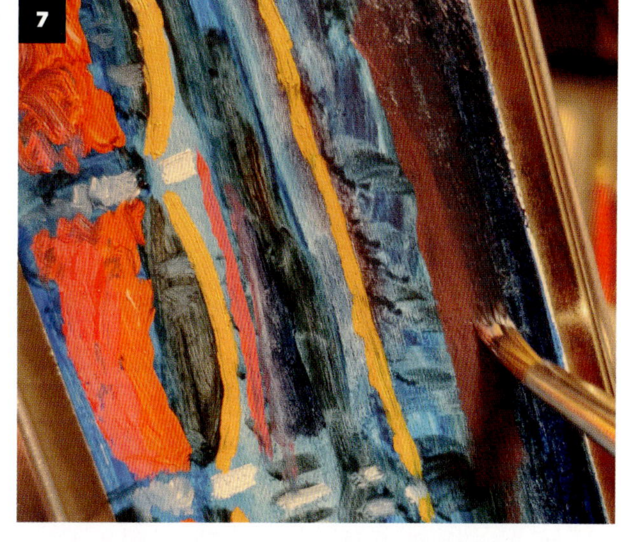
7

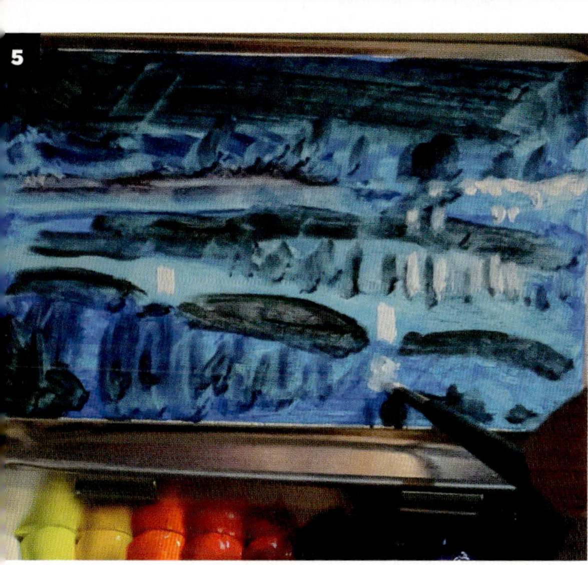
5

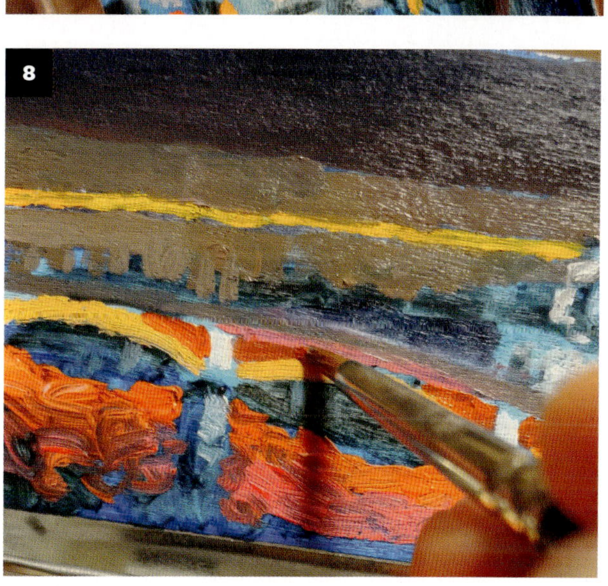
8

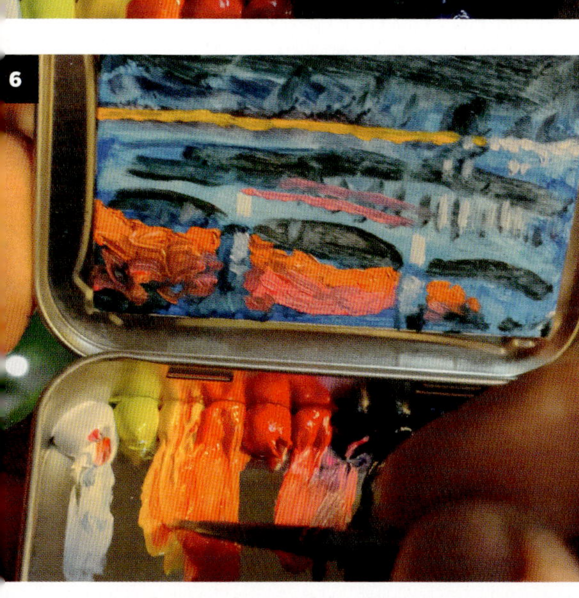
6

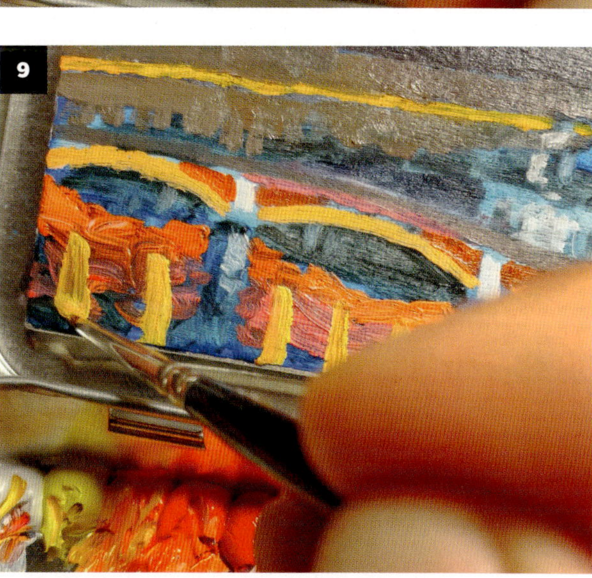
9

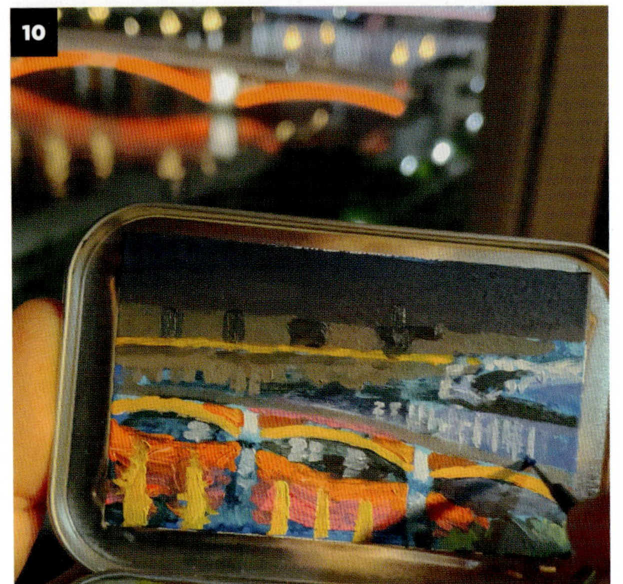

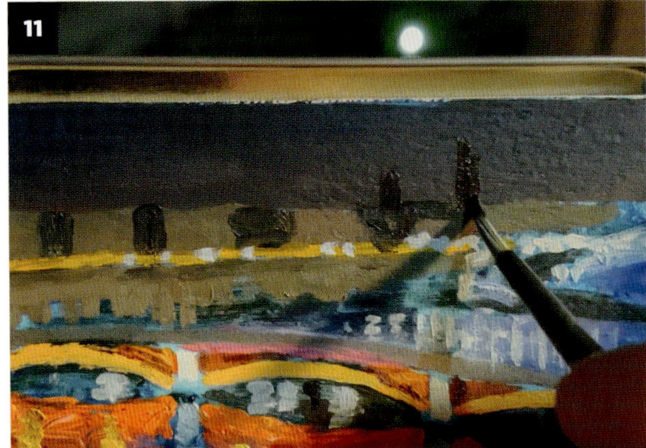

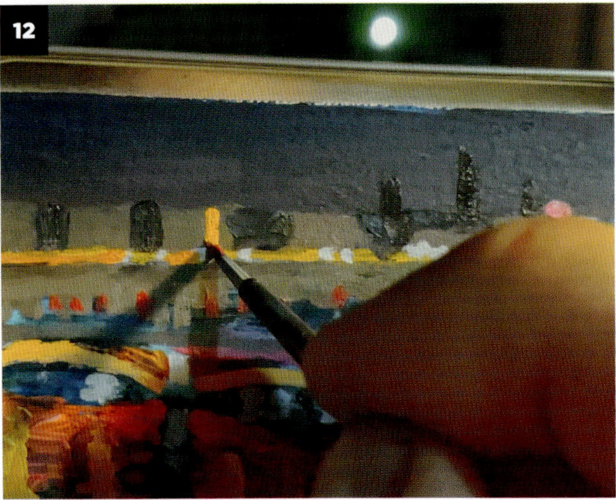

10. With a smaller brush, the same vertical streak technique can be applied to the other bridge lights reflecting off the water in the distance.

11. Now that there's a sufficient middle level of detail in the bottom half of my painting, I notice that the top needs more attention again. I continue blocking in different dark values for the buildings on the skyline.

12. Now I'm adding more detail to the top. When I'm painting, I like to skip around different areas of the painting as I go, so that I can build everything up in an even way. One reason is that the blocking-in stage usually takes less time than the detailing part, which means I can quickly record all of the basic visuals before any unexpected changes occur. For example, with nocturnes, lights get turned off if you work too late into the night. Another reason is that, if I have to leave for some reason, then at least I have a painting that is partially finished to the same stage, instead of a painting that is fully finished in one area, with nothing finished in another spot. Yet another reason is that I like balance and when something feels off, I like to go in and fix it right away.

13. I'm at the stage where I can switch to my fine detailing brush. On this bridge, there's a line of lights so close together that I can simply paint a long, thin line. This color is white mixed with a touch of Cadmium Yellow Medium. At this point, I'm also noticing that the roadway on the bridge is going to need some work for the bridge to look correct. I keep this as a mental note for later.

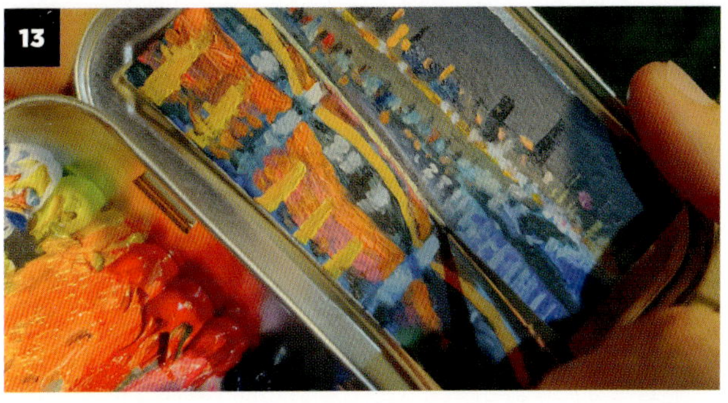

14. I've turned my attention to the water reflection of the bridge in the foreground. I'm being selective about how many horizontal strokes I paint in because I want to preserve the vertical strokes I painted earlier. I find the difference in direction of brushstrokes interesting in the final product.

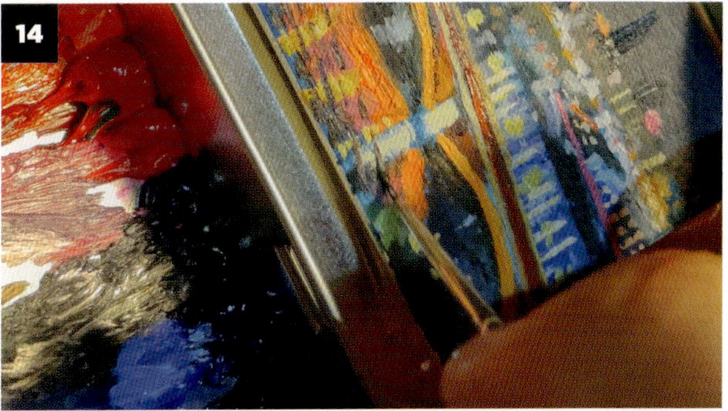

15. The color I'm working with here is a bright red, which I am adding all over this painting. I was just painting the taillights from cars on the bridge in the foreground, and now I am dotting a few lights on the cityscape on the horizon.

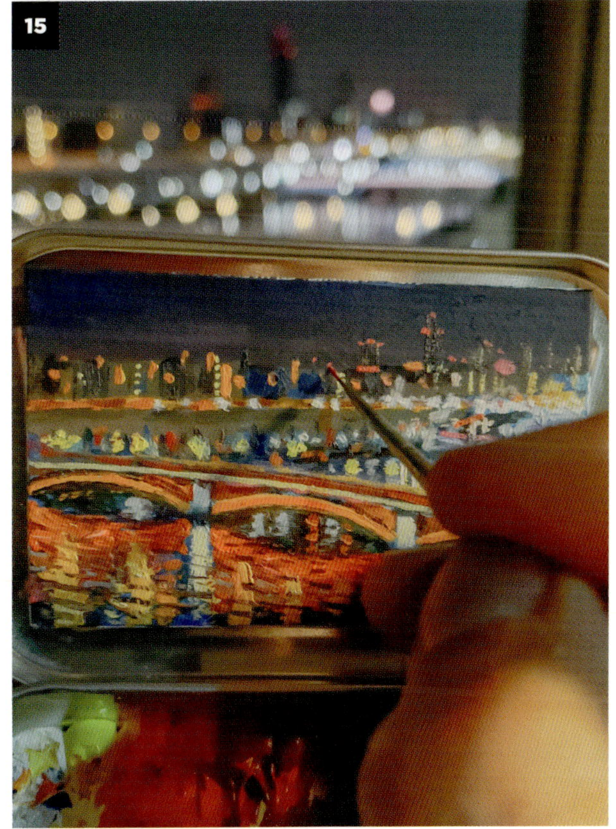

Plein air painting is all about efficiency—if you have the wherewithal to notice the same color in several different places, it's a good idea to paint them all at once to save time.

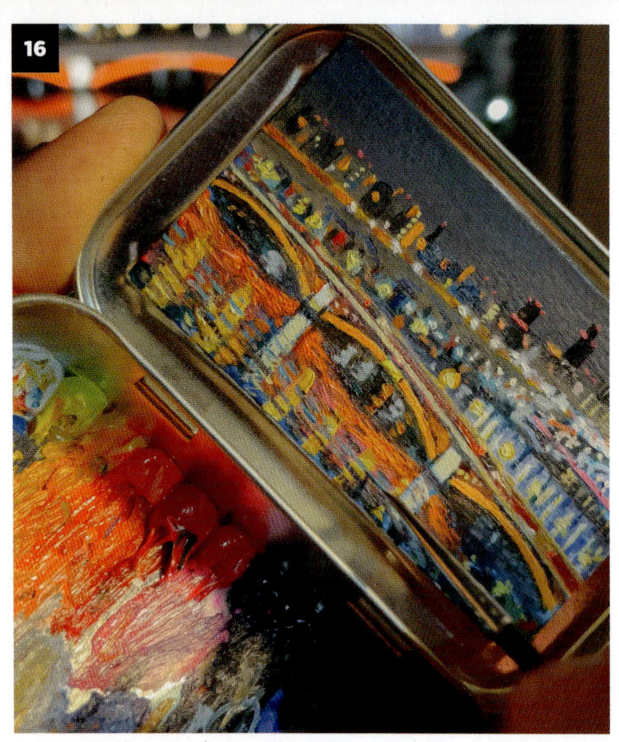

16. Now that everything is basically painted in, I notice one last detail to add. There is a blue glow around a lot of the lights, and that color is also reflected in the water.

17. This is the finished painting, which was actually painted over the course of two nights because about halfway into painting on the first night, the lights of all the bridges suddenly turned off.

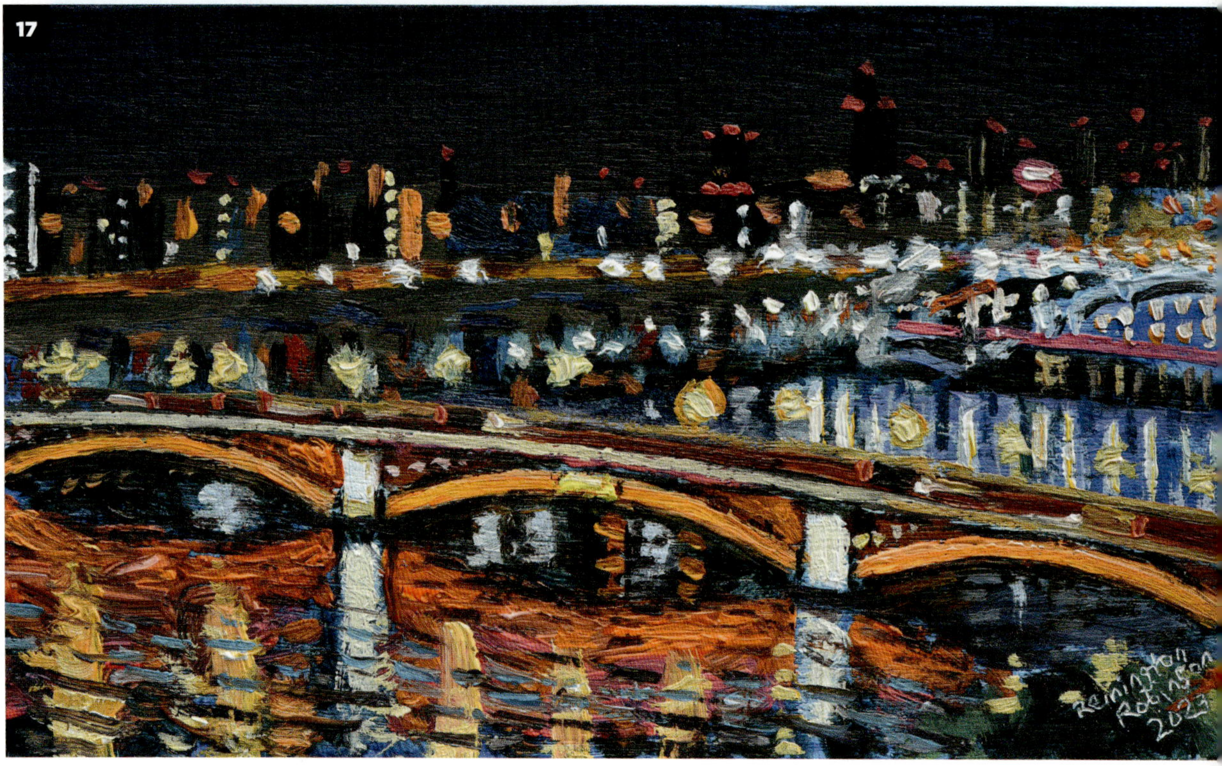

GALLERY: NOCTURNE PAINTINGS

The following is a small selection of paintings made at night.

A view of the American side of Niagara Falls at night from the Niagara Falls Observation Tower. Both waterfalls are illuminated at night by large lights located across the river. Painting all that mist at night is a fun experience if you don't mind all the tourists.

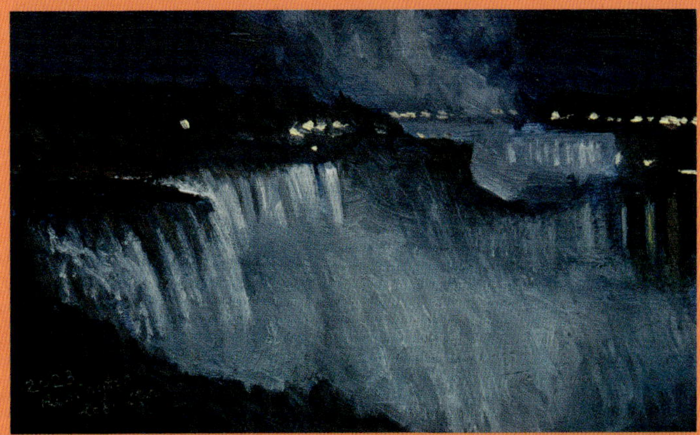

The Parroquia is a picturesque cathedral in the busy city center of San Miguel de Allende, Mexico. Zooming in tightly on a section of this ornate cathedral made for an exciting nighttime painting experience, especially with all the light reflecting within the structure.

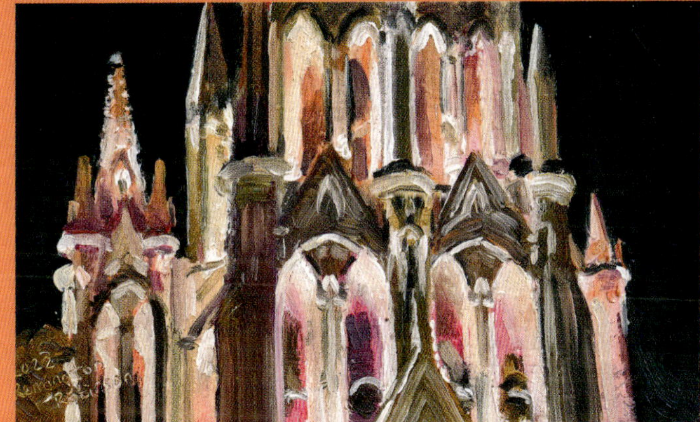

A car parked at a scenic overlook on Highway 93 in Boulder, Colorado, painted from inside my car. The headlights of my car and the other car act as the two primary light sources on the ground, the grass, and the tree. The deep blue twilight was really fun to paint!

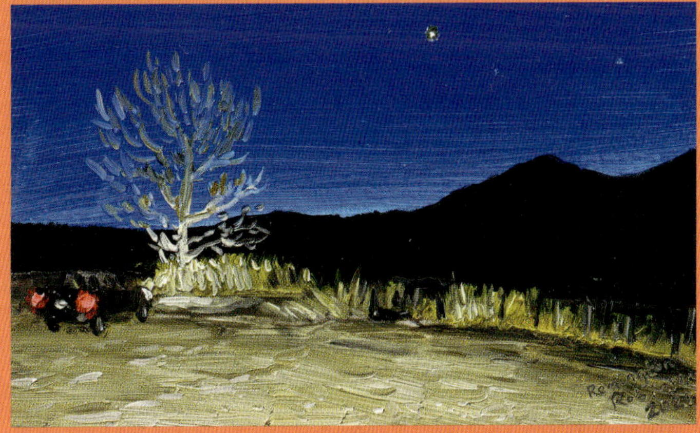

ODD COLOR PALETTES: BOULDER FLATIRONS

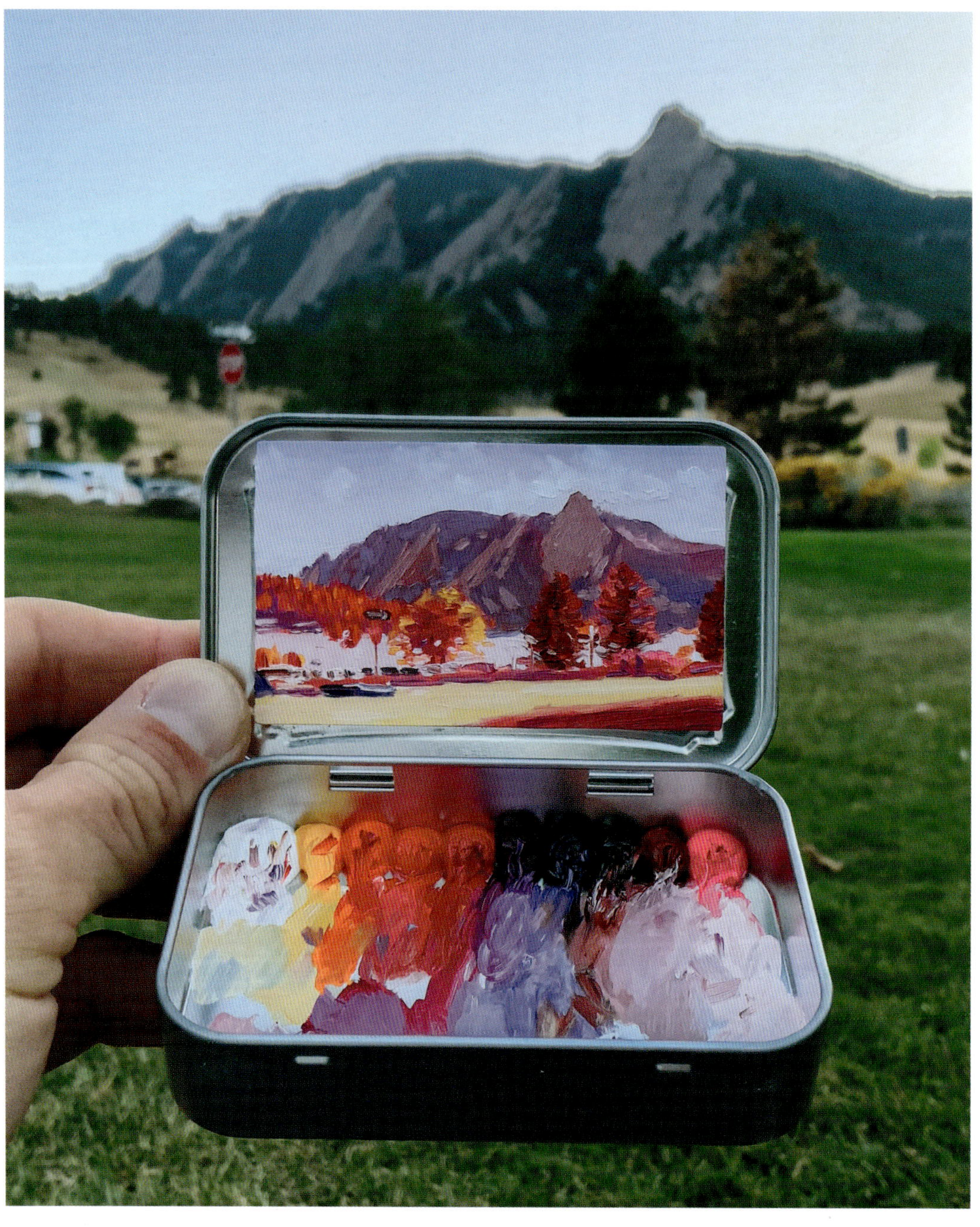

Sometimes, deciding what to paint isn't even about painting a particular subject: it's about using an interesting color palette, and letting that guide what you decide to paint. I really recommend going out and trying at least one painting with an unconventional color palette. This is one of those challenges that might have you squirming in your seat while you're doing it, but when it's done, it might be your favorite piece. A small-format painting is perfect for this type of thing because it lets you try out different ideas without a huge time commitment. Plus, the squirming part won't last as long!

This painting of the Flatirons in Boulder, Colorado is an exercise in color theory. I made up a rule this time, which is that every single color in my palette is either a version of red or at least contains red. Since green is the opposite of red on the color wheel, that means there is absolutely no green. But then again, there is also no true yellow or true blue. If you mix red with yellow, you get orange, and if you mix red with blue, you get purple. So, by that logic, the furthest that my color palette goes toward yellow is Cadmium Yellow Medium, which is a yellow orange, and the furthest it goes toward blue is Dioxazine Purple. Check out the gallery on page 114 to see some more examples of paintings with odd color palettes.

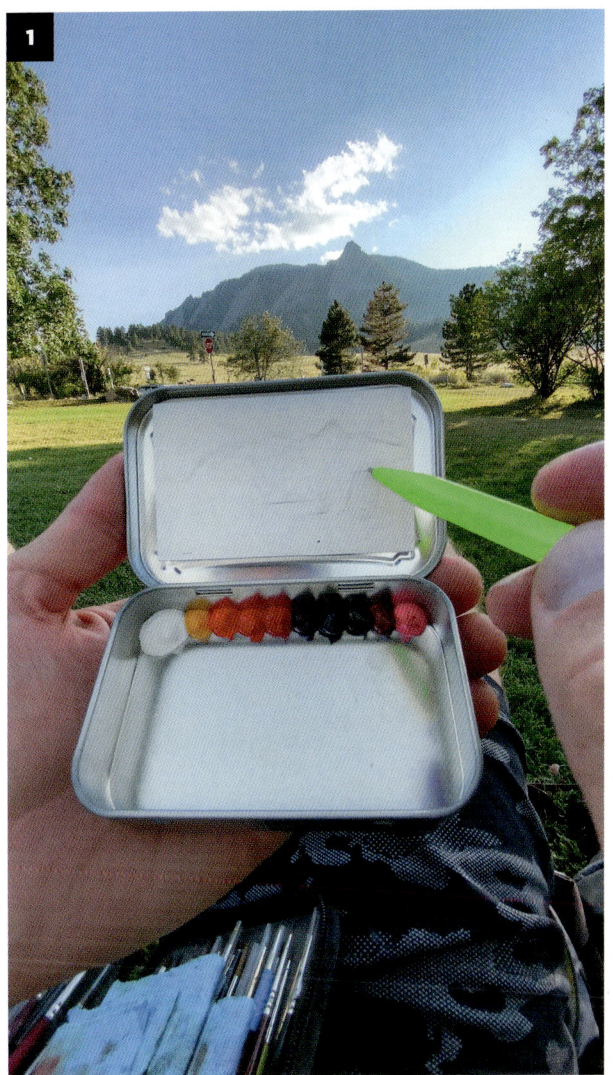

1. I start this one out in pencil by noting where the skyline is going to be on the top third horizontal plane. I'm also taking note of where various trees will be placed with a loose gestural sketch. You can see that my palette here has a few oranges, a few reds, some purples, and some pinks , plus Titanium White on the far left.

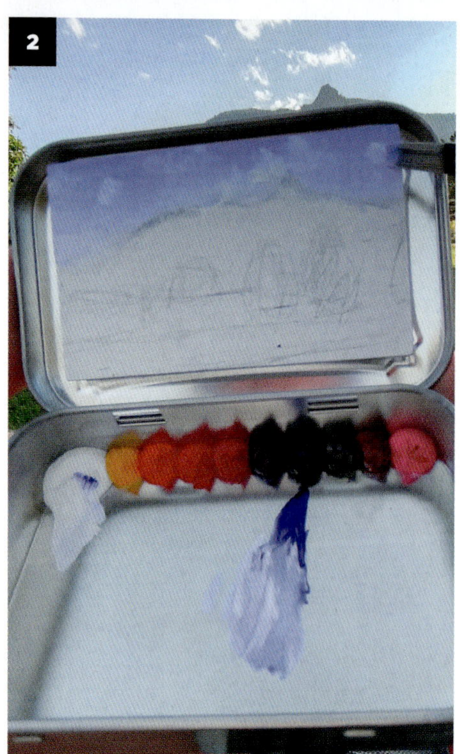

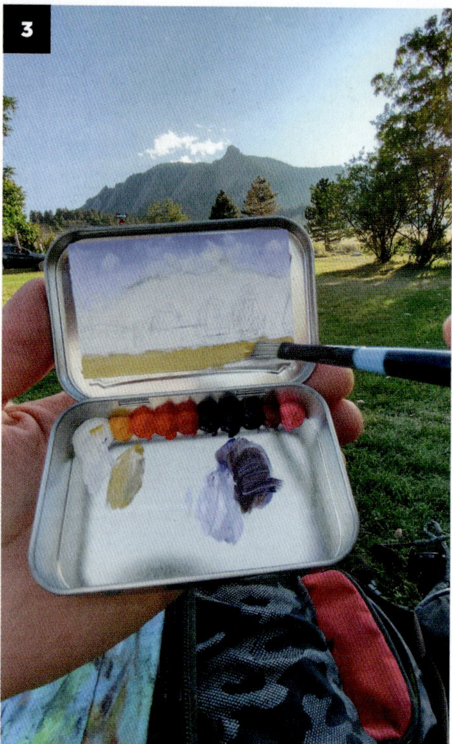

2. Since the closest color I have to blue is Dioxazine Purple, the beautiful blue sky today is now going to be purple in my painting. Weird! I might as well dab some white clouds in there while I'm at it, because I've been noticing that they are going away, and I want clouds in my painting.

3. Next, I'm blocking in the sun-drenched green grass as a light yellow orange, mixed with Cadmium Yellow Medium and Titanium White, because that will be the closest color I can mix to what I am seeing in the grass. I know the colors are, of course, not going to be correct in the final painting, but one thing I am especially doubling down on is ensuring that the values are at least correct.

4. I've run into a little problem. I can't mix green with "blue" and "yellow," because my blue is purple, and my yellow is orange. If I mix those together to try to make green, it will probably just turn out a muddy brown or gray. I don't want it to look like that. Instead, the darker green colors, such as in the trees, are going to be painted red. I've also blocked in a light pink color for the more-golden grasses further up in the park toward the mountains.

To account for the atmospheric perspective, I will tint my mountains a little bit more purple, while trying to stick to the accurate value of my real-life subject (see next page). I will also mix more white on the right side to account for the glow from the sunlight that is flooding the atmosphere on that side.

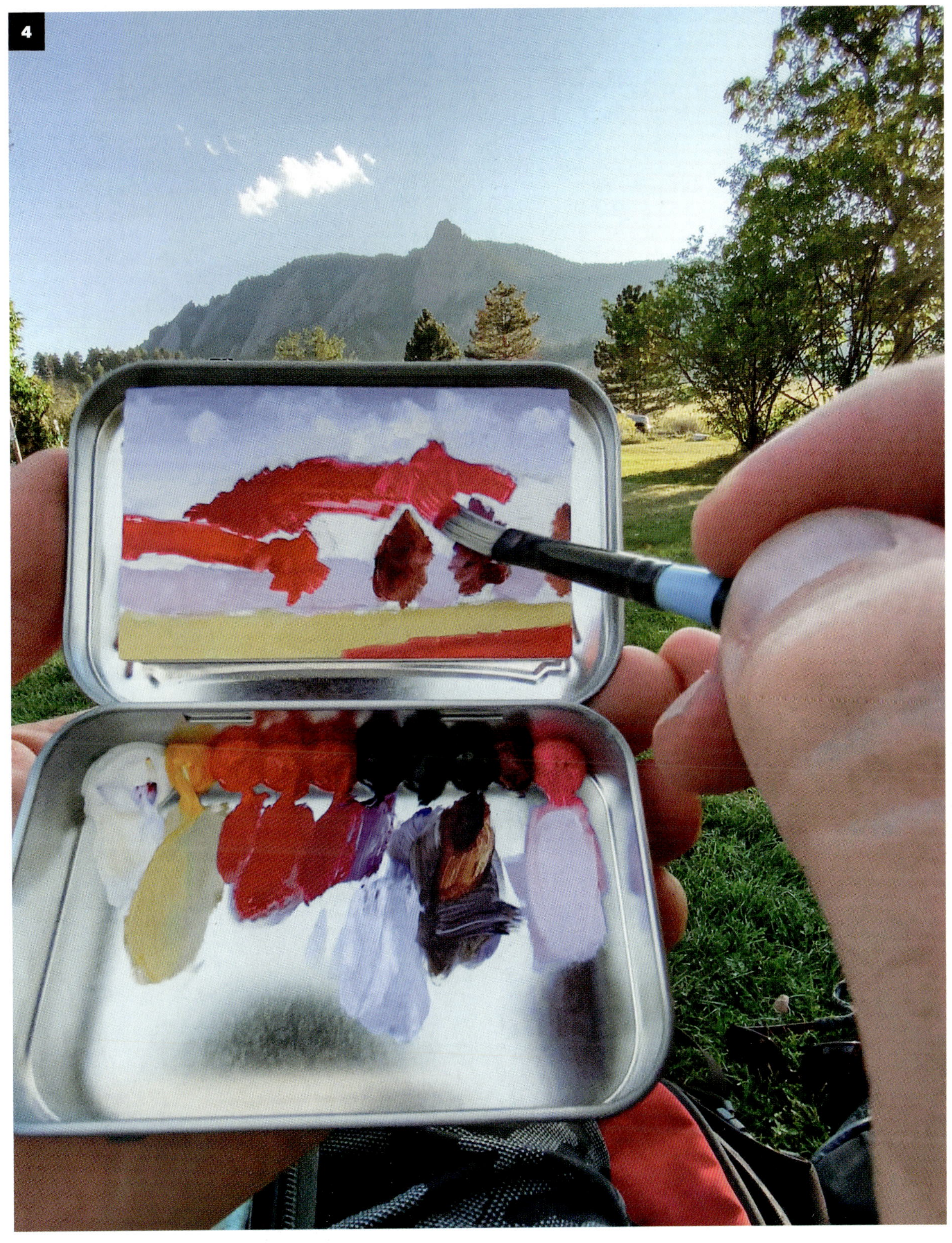

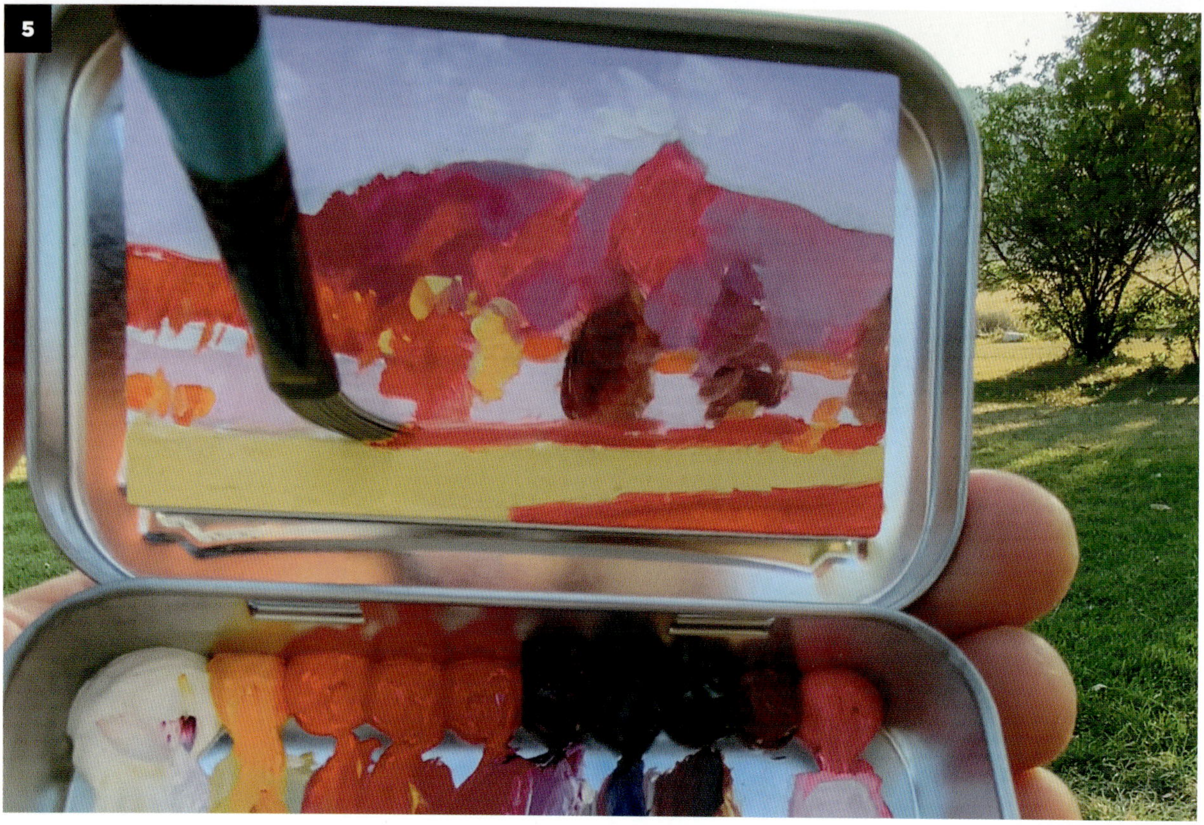

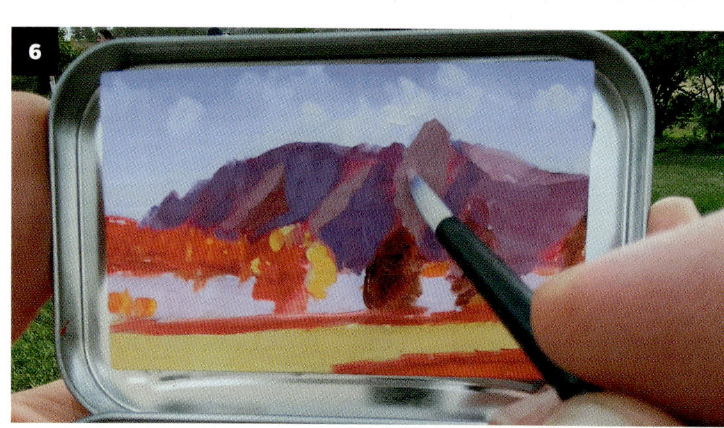

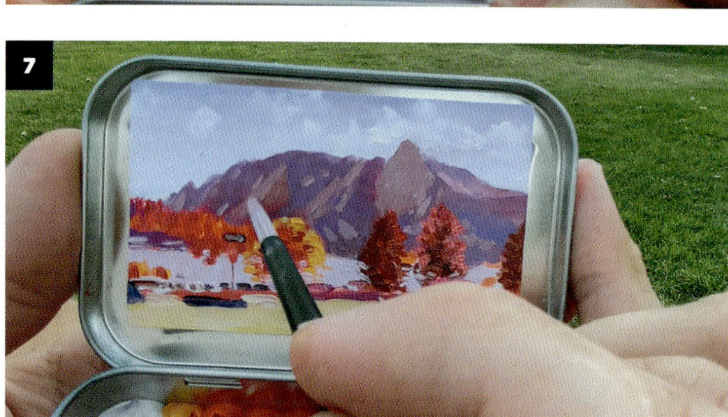

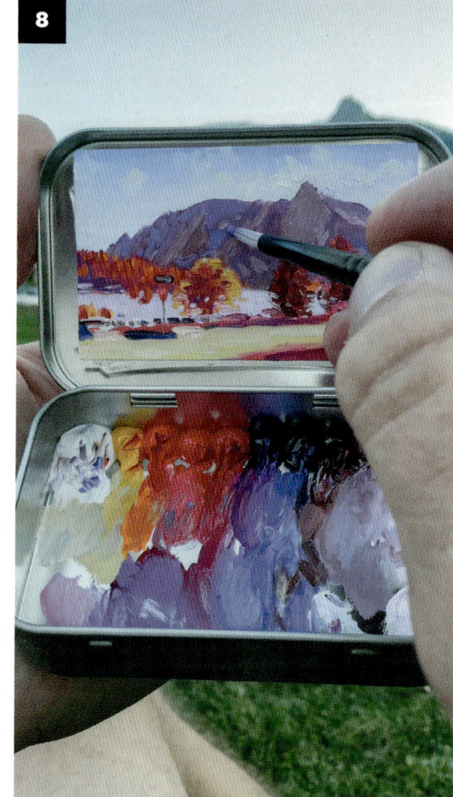

5. It feels very unnatural to paint red where there clearly isn't any, but I have to keep going. Some dark green shrubs and shadows of trees are located in this approximate area, which I am indicating with a long brush pull across the entire bottom third of my painting, at a slight angle down to the left.

I also noticed that the green foliage on the right side of the tree in the middle is lit up by the sun, and looks similar to the bright green color of the grass in the foreground. Therefore, that part also gets the light yellow orange. Now I'm really squirming in my seat!

6. Probably the only thing I can paint in its true-to-life color are the rocks of the Flatirons. As I begin working on finalizing the color nuances throughout my painting, I block these in with their correct color. I've also added some pink to the right side of the mountain that is getting hit with sunlight.

7. Now that everything is basically blocked in, I skip around the whole painting to start adding smaller missing details, as well as other little tweaks to color nuances.

8. Keeping with the idea of ensuring that my values are all correct, I go back into the distant trees on the mountain and tweak their color to a lighter but still saturated purple, boosting that effect of atmospheric perspective.

9. What was a slightly uncomfortable process turned into an exciting painting that I'm really happy about. Had I been working larger, it's possible that I would've given up halfway through the painting. But seeing it through on this small scale quickly shows the possibility of what it would look like on a larger scale, since this took less than two hours to paint.

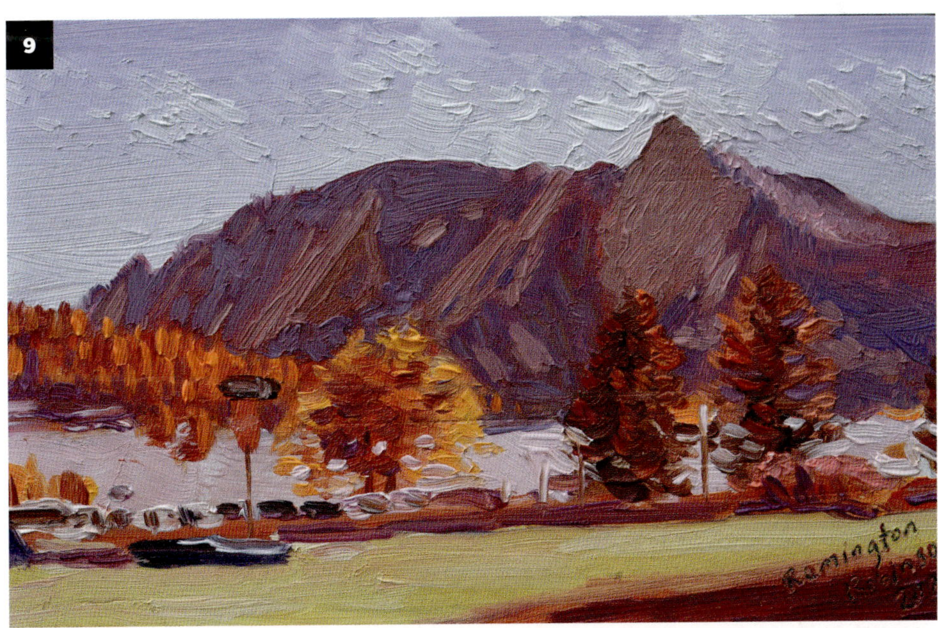

GALLERY: ODD COLOR PALETTES

The following is a small selection of paintings made with unconventional color palettes.

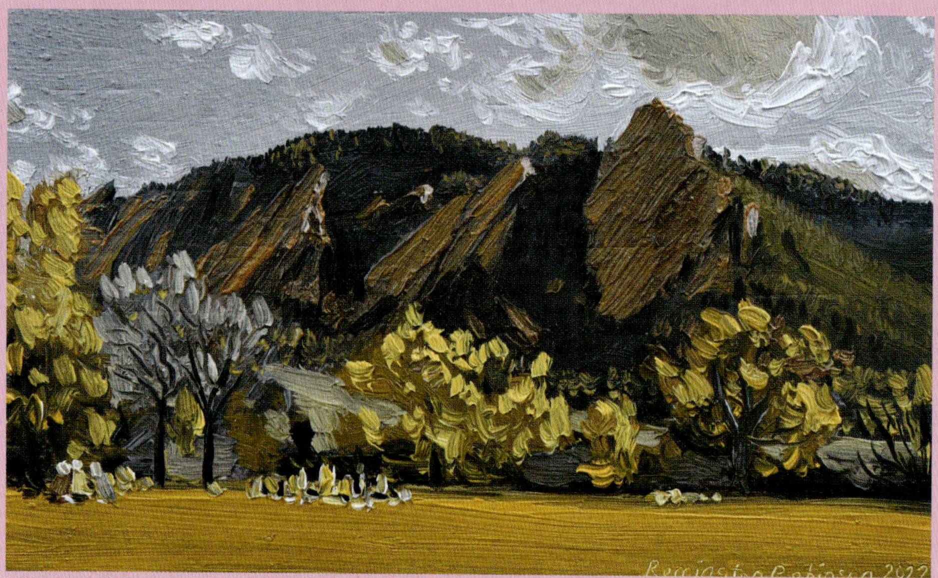

Here's another painting of the Flatirons in an alternative color palette, this time using Chrome Yellow Deep, Renaissance Gold, and Ivory Black. This color palette was inspired by the school colors of the University of Colorado, which are black and gold.

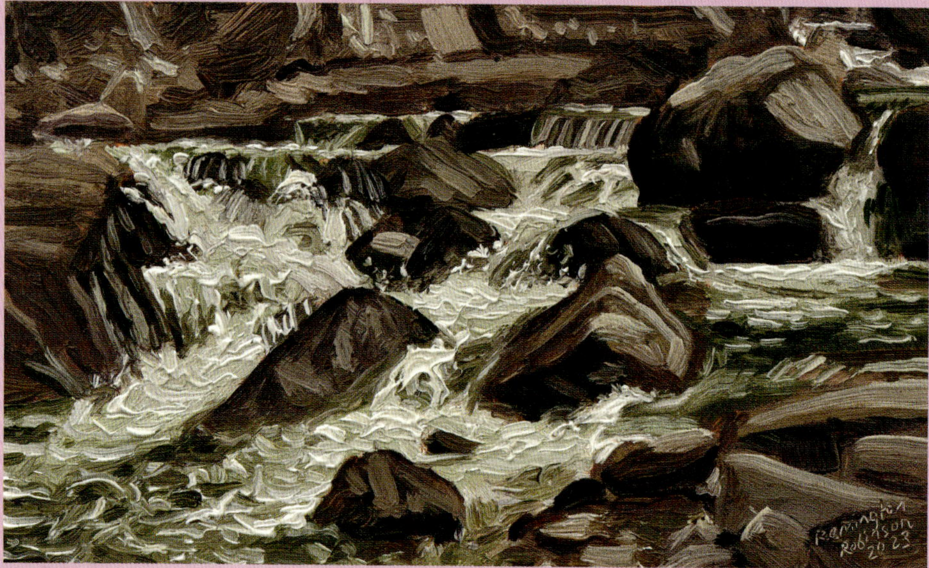

This painting of the rapids in Boulder Creek was done with secondary colors only—Pyrrole Orange, Purple Lake, and Sap Green. You can see some of the orange underpainting showing through in a few areas.

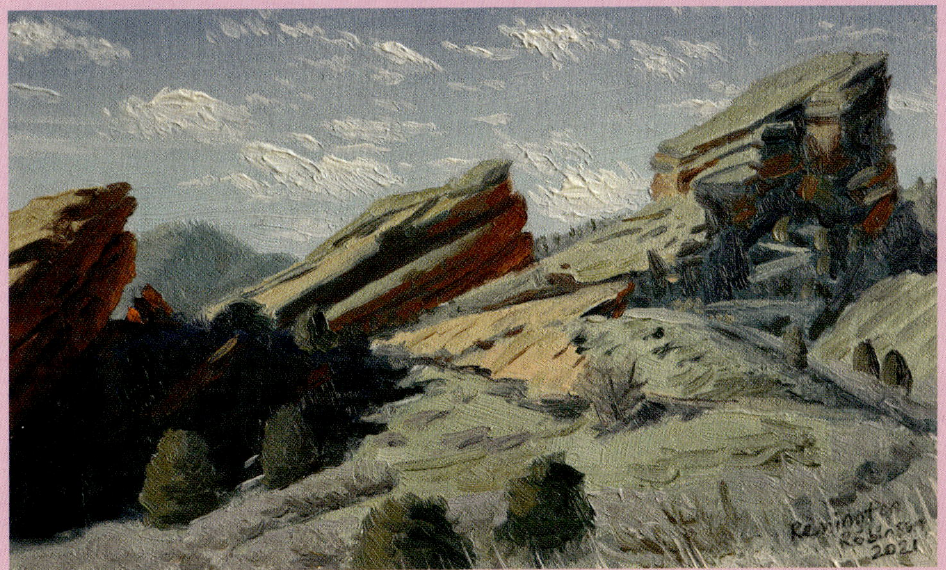

Red Rocks Park and Amphitheatre, painted in a secondary color palette of Titanium White, Pyrrole Orange, Phthalo Green, and Dioxazine Purple. The blue sky was created by mixing purple and green together, which is not supposed to be possible!

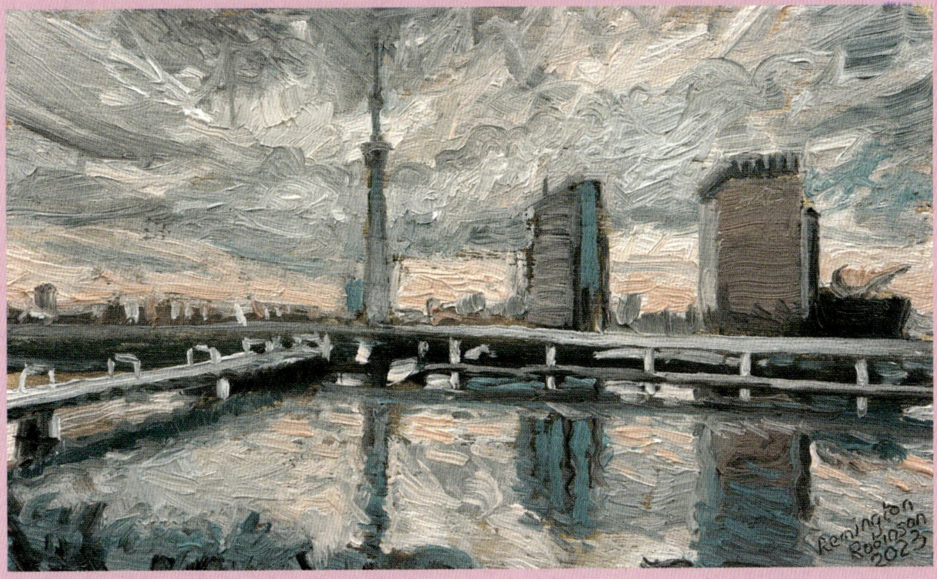

A view of the Tokyo Skytree from across the Sumida River in Tokyo, Japan. This was painted with Titanium White, Light Portrait Pink, Sepia, and Cobalt Turquoise Light.

PENCIL OVER PAINT:
HOUSE IN MY NEIGHBORHOOD

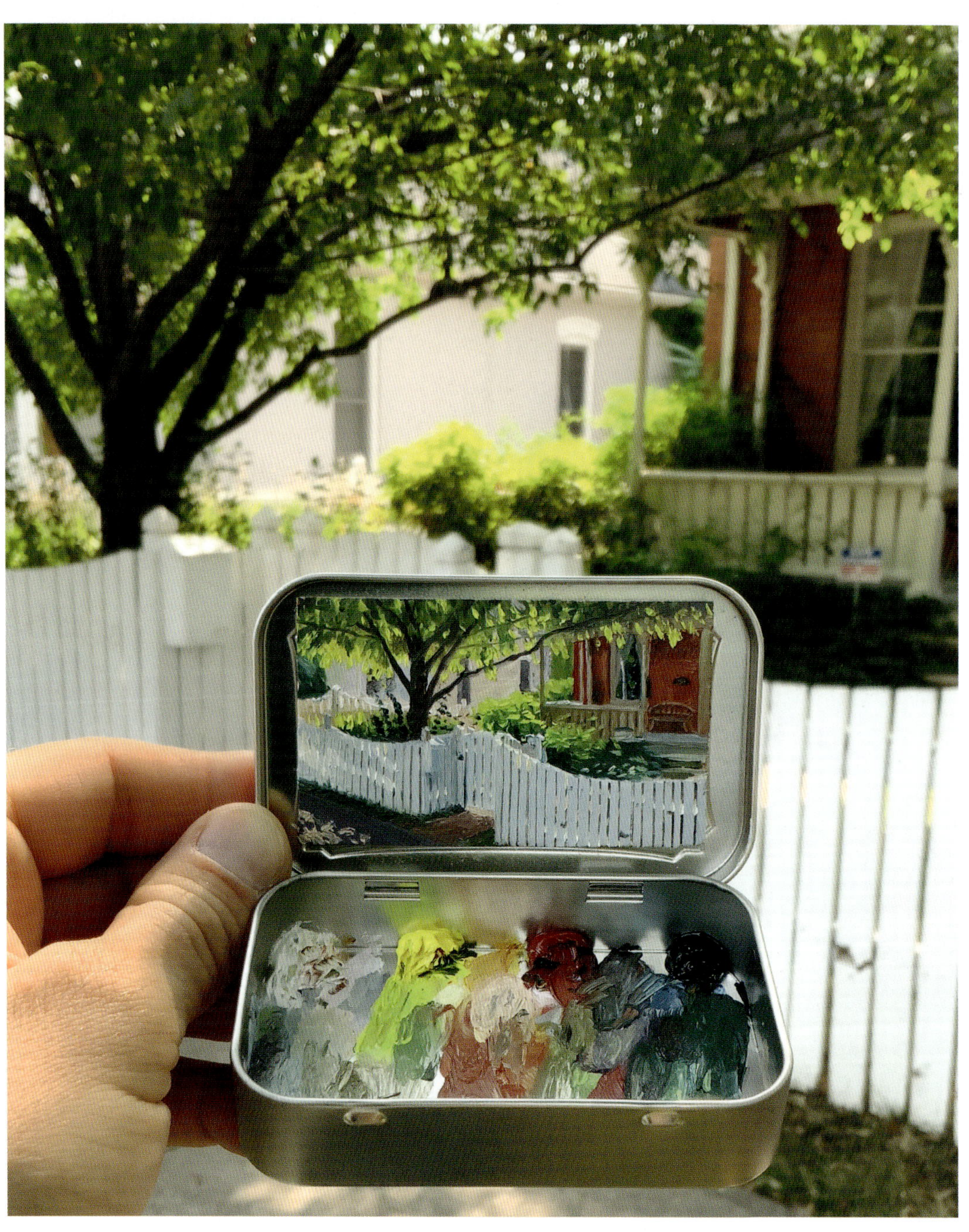

I was out on a walk one morning with my painting kit in late summer. There was a step ladder in someone's front yard with a "free" sign on it. I decided to take it with me because I didn't own a step ladder. On my way home, I saw this beautiful scene in front of a house, so I decided to stop and paint it (the step ladder came in handy to hold my materials!). The morning light on the trees, the red brick of the house, and the nice shape of the white fence all looked compelling together.

Sometimes there are details in a painting that make more sense to compose with an alternate tool, such as a pencil. There is a technique called sgraffito, *which means scratching marks into the top layer to reveal the color of the layer underneath as a way of achieving fine detail. In painting, this is usually done with white canvas, where the scratching away reveals the white of the canvas, thus producing white details.*

The technique I'm showing here is different from sgraffito because it's just drawing on the underlying substrate, plowing through the paint as you go. I find that the results are typically better if the paint you are going over is a fairly thin layer.

What's nice about this technique is that if a mistake is made, a little paint can cover it up easily. Usually if there is a thin line here or there, I will just paint it with a thin liner brush. But when there *are many lines together—in this case, the separations between the slats of the fence—using a pencil after putting paint down is a perfectly acceptable way to go. Check out the gallery on page 126 to see some more examples of paintings with pencil over paint.*

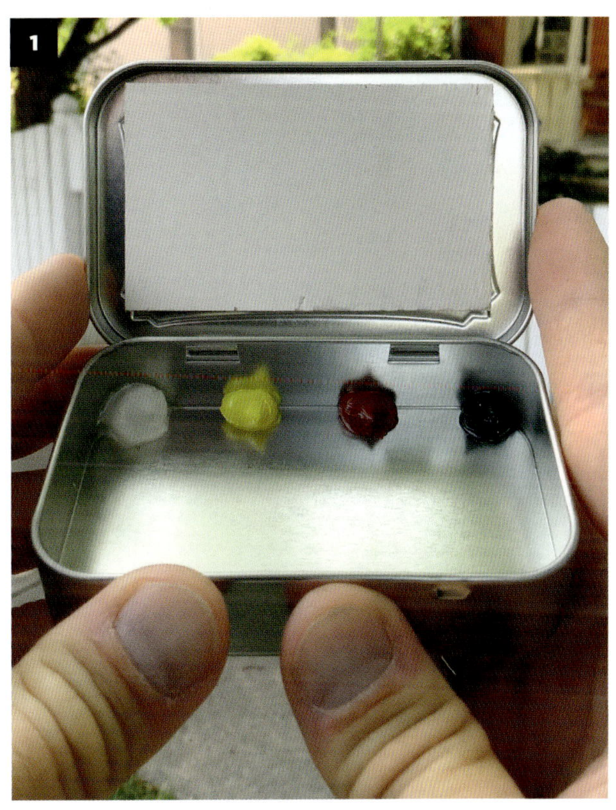

1. My color palette is a variation on the primary colors. I'm using Titanium White, Bismuth Yellow, a rusty, earthy red called Light Red, and Prussian Blue.

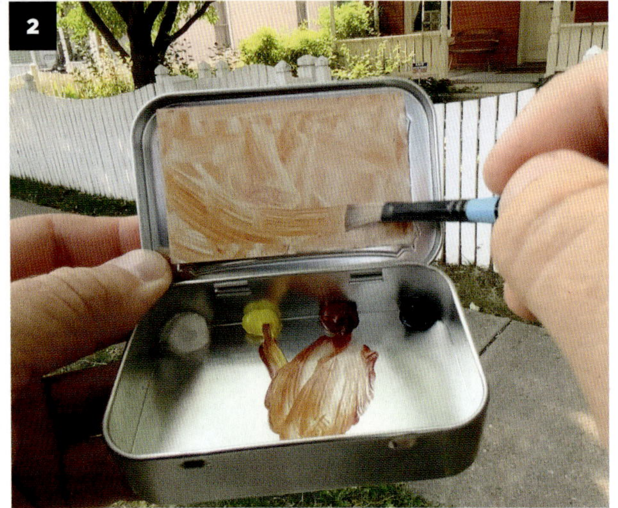

2. I first cover my whole surface with a warm, thin wash of pigment, which is able to move easily because it's diluted with odorless mineral spirits. The wetness of the surface will help the paint glide around easier as well.

3. Next, I lift away pigment for the lighter areas (page 26) and add a little pigment for the darker areas. I don't go crazy with detail at this stage because what I've done now is indication enough for me to visualize where this painting is going.

4. I mix a dark green using Prussian Blue and Bismuth Yellow, which provides contrast so I know easily where I want to go next. The contrast also shows me what I want to change, if anything, about my composition. And if I do want to change something, this is an easy stage to do it.

Here, you can see the ladder I found, which is acting as my painting station. Also, if anybody happens to walk out of the house and is wondering what I'm doing, I am fully prepared to show them that I'm just painting a beautiful scene that I noticed. The grass I'm standing on is city property, but if they have a problem with me being there, I am also prepared to pack up and leave in less than a minute. But I have found that in every case I have been involved in, people are glad to see someone out in the world painting, and are flattered that I chose their house to paint.

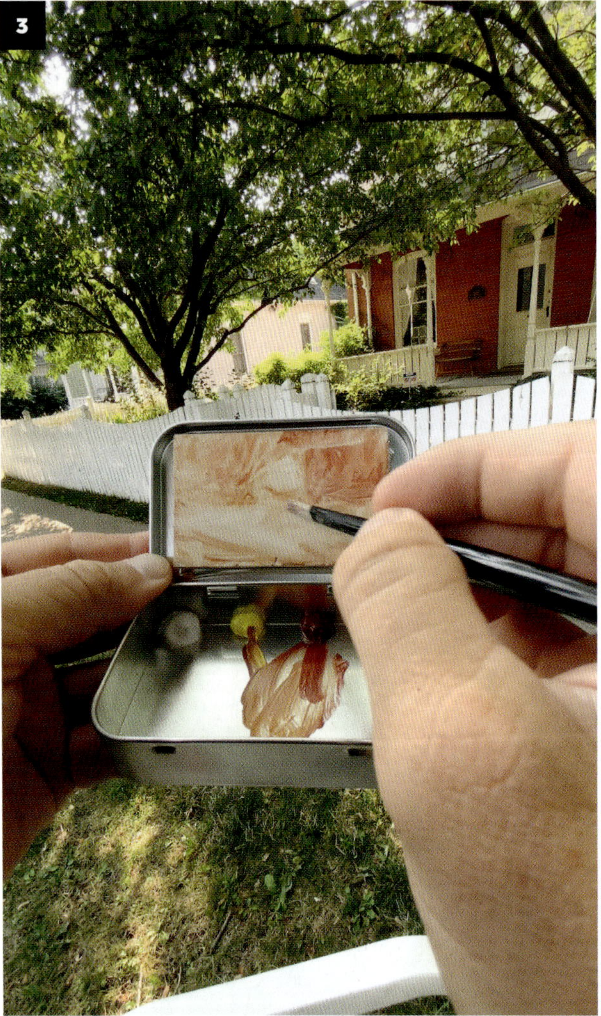

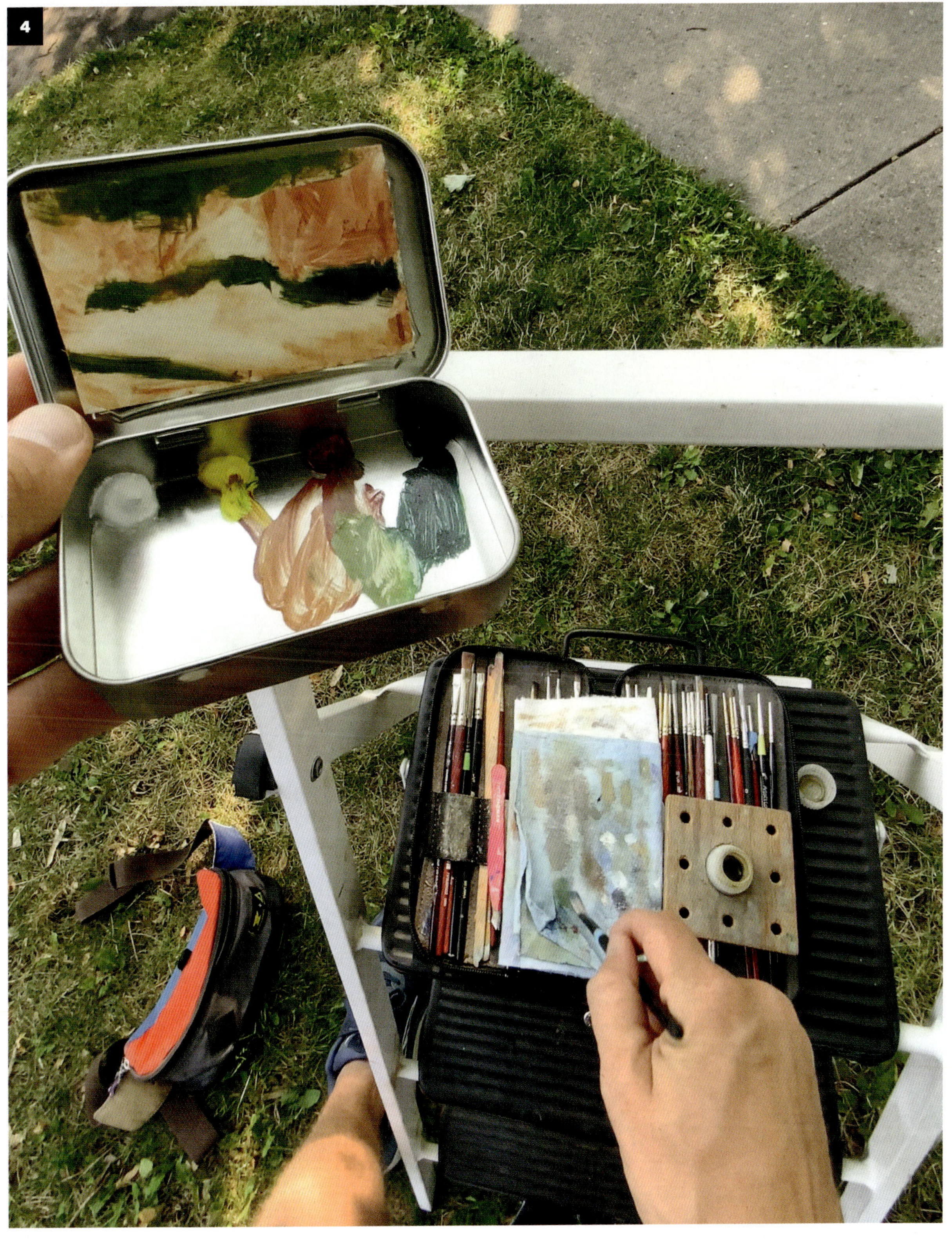

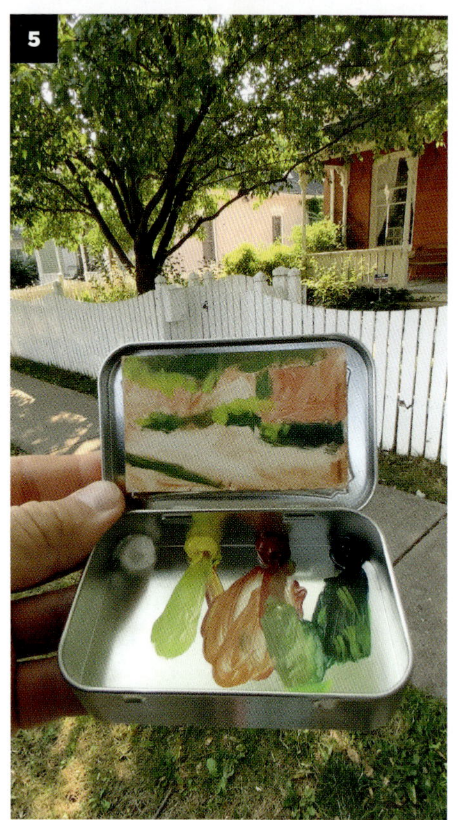

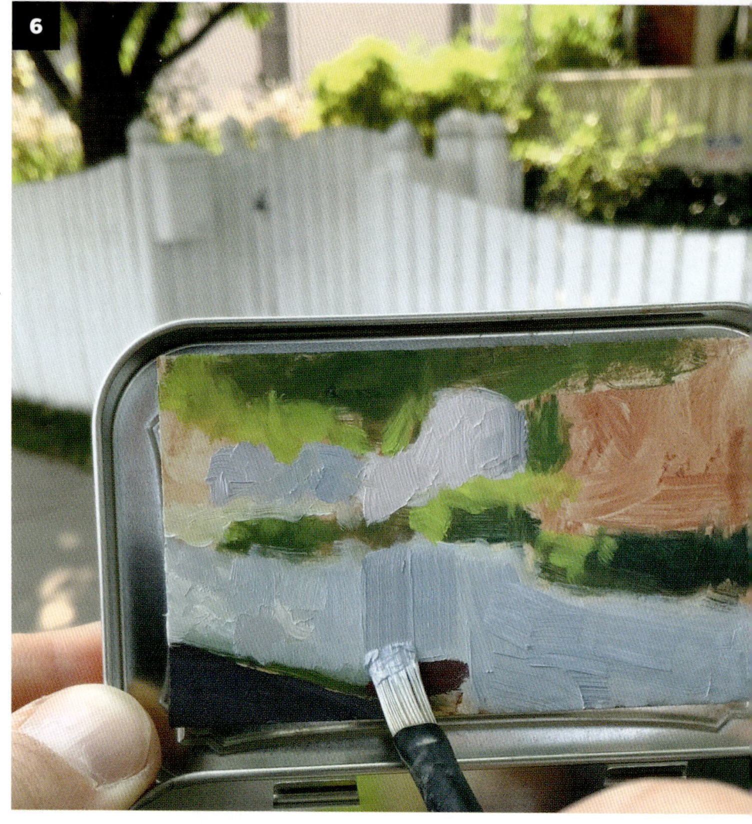

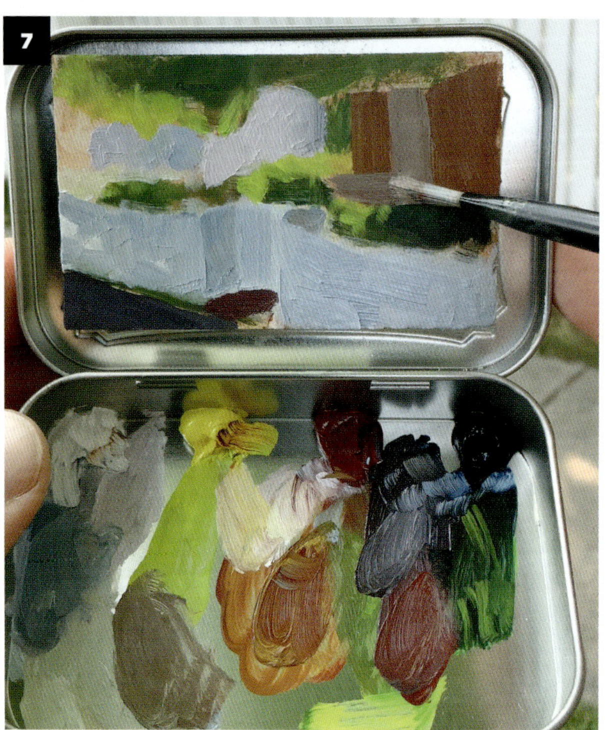

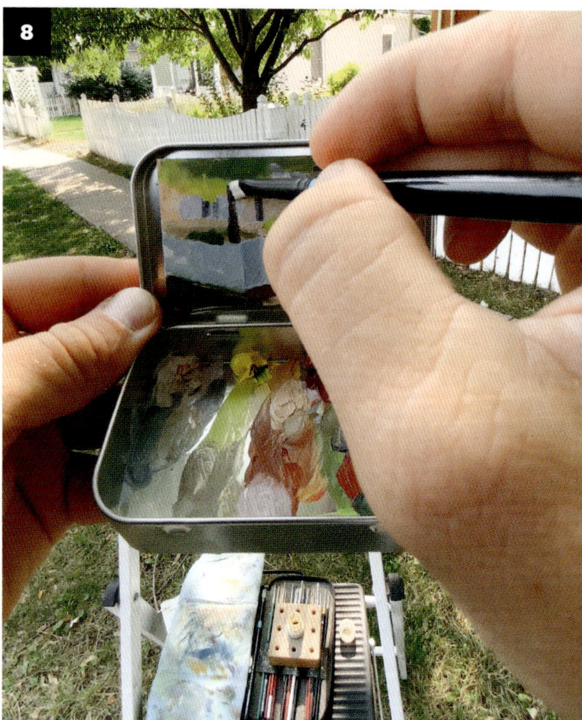

5. I've now mixed an extremely light green for the leaves by first cleaning my brush, then just barely touching that dark green before grabbing a nice amount of yellow and spreading it across my palette. I mix that together, and just that tiny touch of dark green is all that was needed to tint the yellow into a vibrant light green, which is the color that leaves like this produce when they are backlit.

6. Now for the fence. Even though it's a white fence, it's in the shade, which means I have to make a slightly muted blue. I could've mixed gray, but I think it'll look just as convincing and a little bit better if it's bluish. I mix some white with a tiny touch of blue and just a smidge of red to mute it down a bit. This is a bit of a larger mixture because that fence takes up a lot of space in my composition.

7. I notice that different faces of the fence are darker than others. I repeat the process of making the muted blue, but with more of each pigment to make it darker. I also use this color to adjust other areas of the fence and add texture within the color.

I continue blocking in the rest of my composition without getting too caught up in detail.

I also do some of the smaller blocking-in of the dark windows.

8. I'm painting the trunk of the tree with a mixture of Prussian Blue and Light Red, with an emphasis on the red to make it look more dark brown.

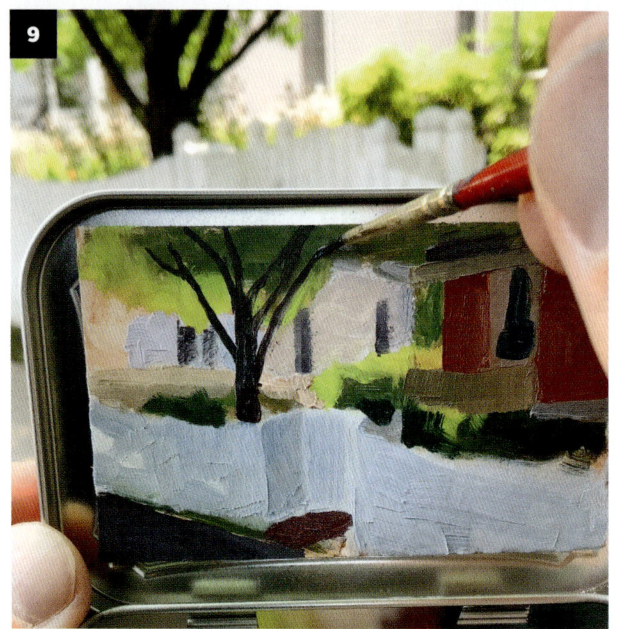

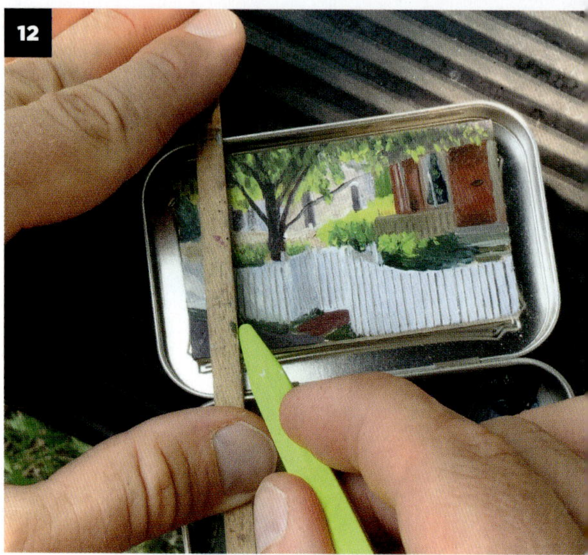

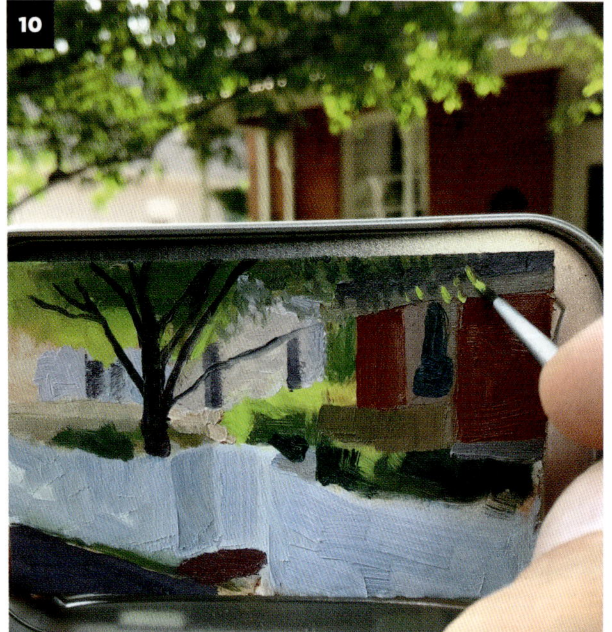

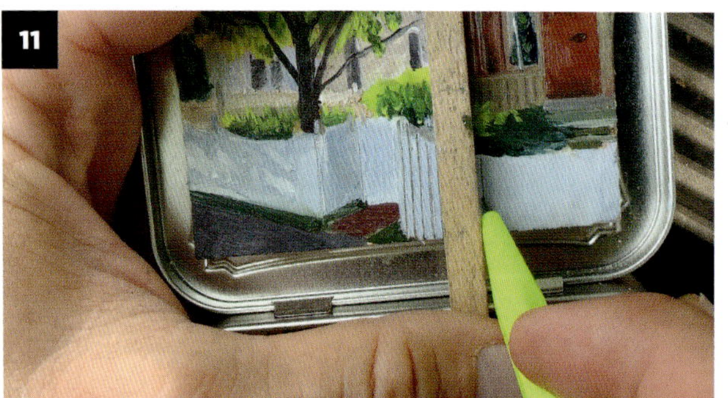

9. Here I am working with a thin round brush to paint the branches of the tree.

10. This is one of the most fun parts— painting the little individual backlit leaves with that saturated light green mixture that is relying on yellow for its light value, but no white. These backlit leaves over the dark background were one of the main reasons I chose to paint this scene in the first place.

11. I'm using a coffee stirrer stick as a straight edge to draw the slats in the fence with my pencil. The nice thing about working in a mint tin is that the edge of the tin is higher than my wood panel, so it holds a straight edge just above the surface of the painting without actually touching it. The ladder is really coming in handy here to hold my phone on the top step for recording purposes, while I use the second step as a stable working surface to make these precise pencil lines.

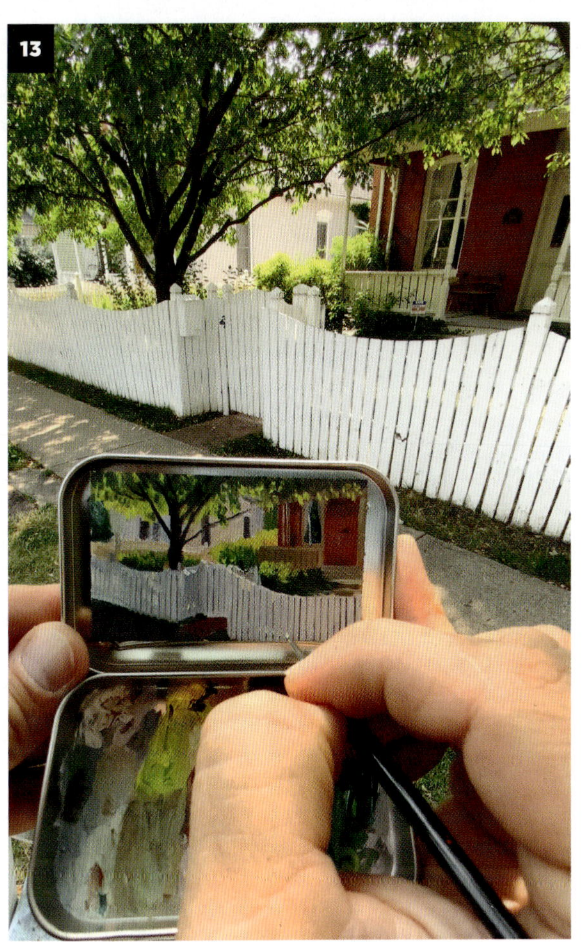 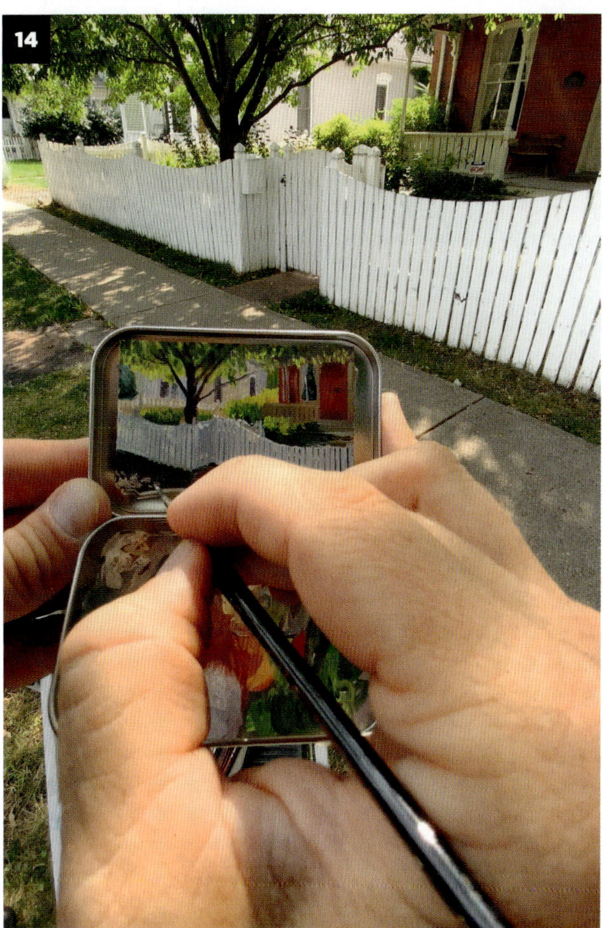

12. I'm completing the slats on the other side. Because I'm using a wood panel as my substrate, I'm not worried about poking the pencil through canvas.

13. After finishing the pencil lines, I go back in with my smallest round brush to paint some highlight details over the pencil marks to really make it look convincing. There is light bouncing all around in between all things, including the different sides of the fence slats. With realism painting in general, I find that small details like this are particularly important to achieving a realistic look.

14. One of the last things I've noticed is a little bit of dappled sunlight on the sidewalk, which I quickly paint in using a warm, light-brown color.

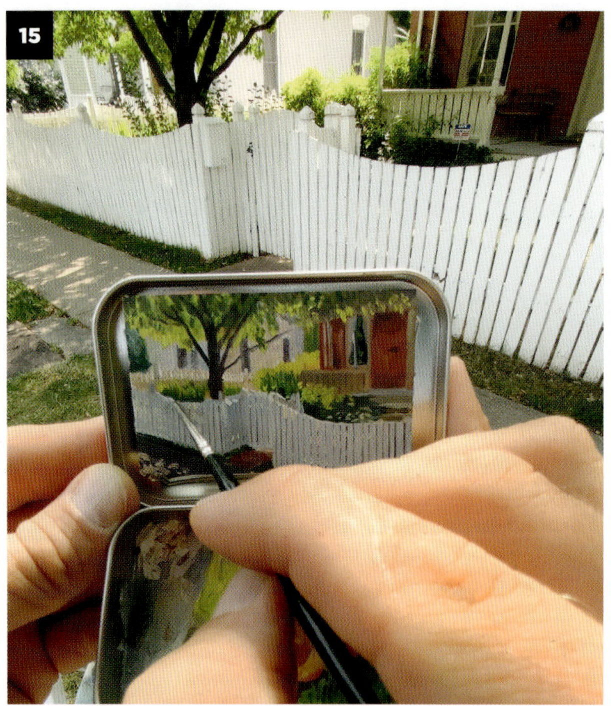

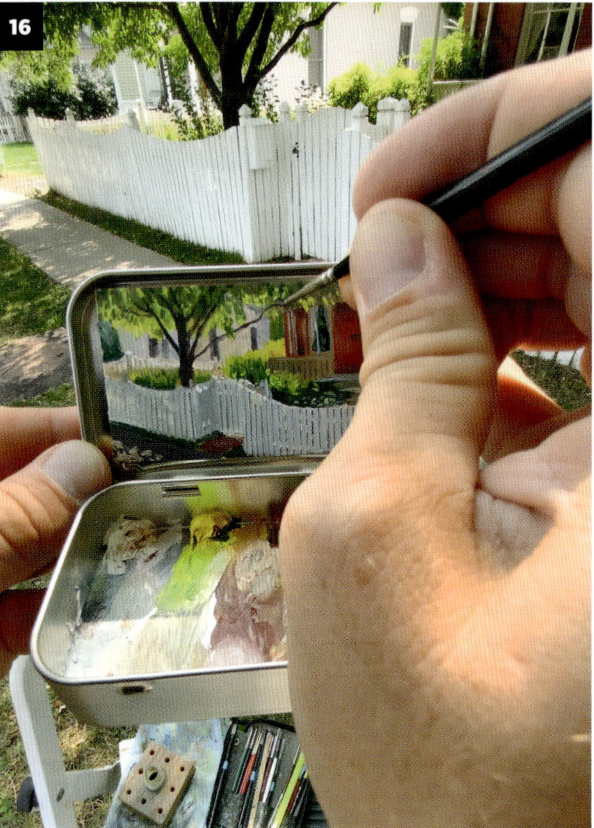

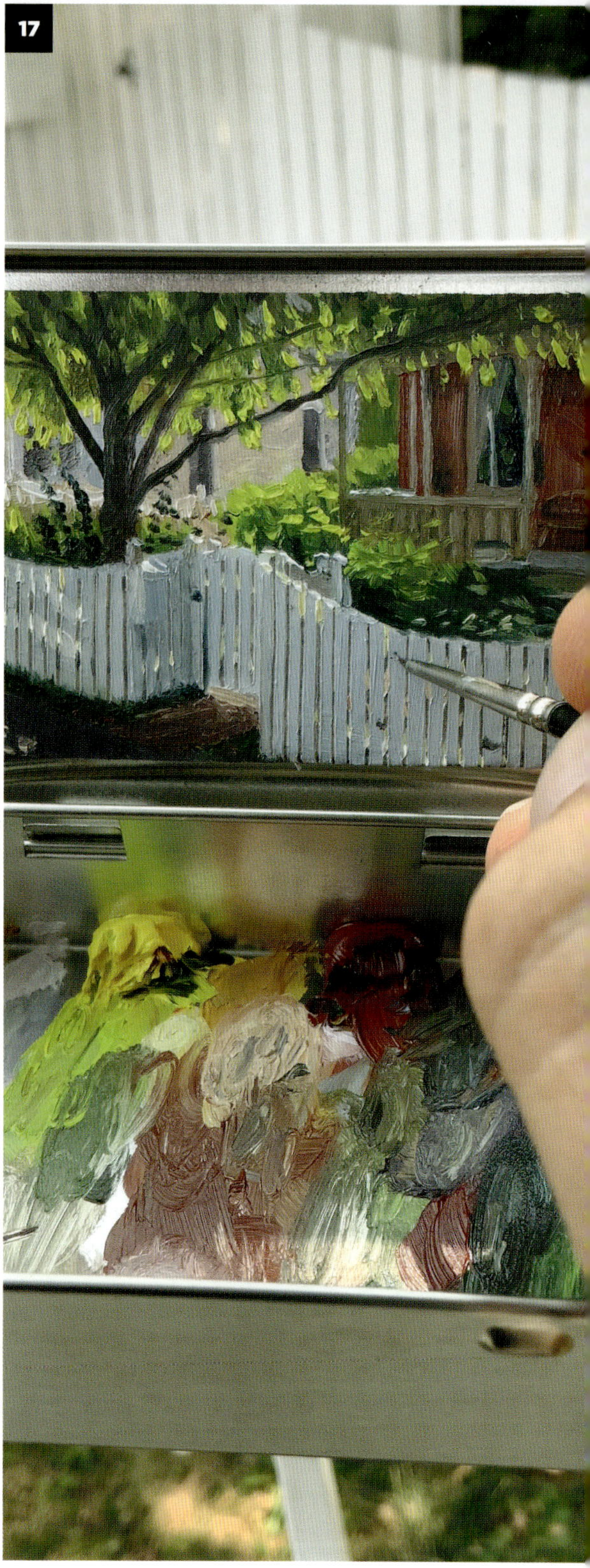

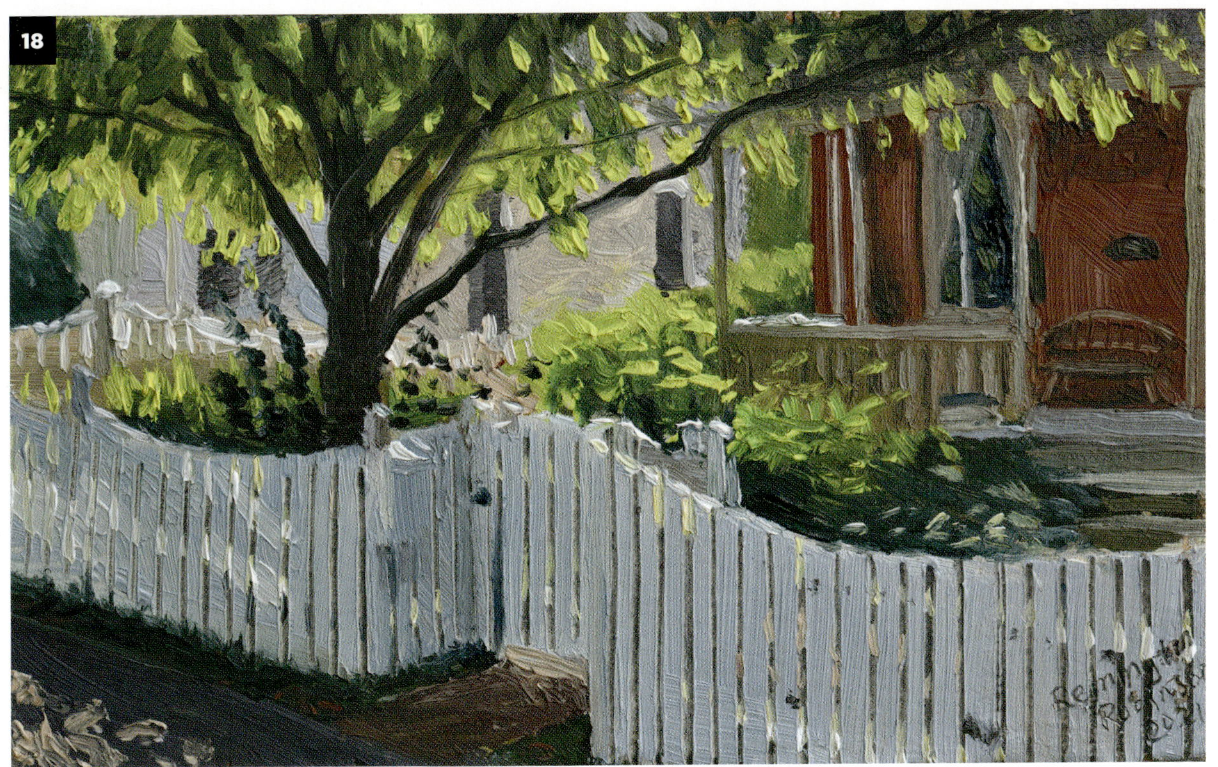

15. Skipping back over to the fence—I can't help but add more detail to it because it's just so fun!

16. I almost forgot to finish the tree branches. After that, I do a quick scan to see if there's anything else to do before calling this finished.

17. I'm noticing just a few more small details in the part of the fence that's closest to me, so I grab my smallest brush and just hit those really quickly.

18. Here's the final painting. I wouldn't recommend trying this technique with thick paint, because to me, it looks better if done over a thinly painted surface.

GALLERY: PENCIL OVER PAINT

The following is a small selection of paintings which utilize the technique of creating fine detail with a pencil over the wet paint.

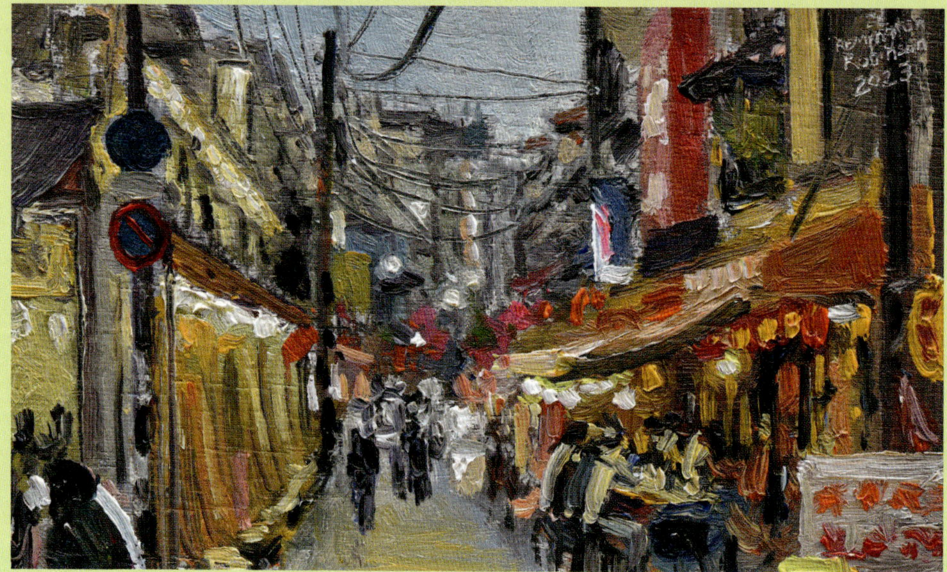

In the busy Asakusa neighborhood of Tokyo, Japan, several people are eating dinner under the awning of a restaurant. Overhead, there are many wires running through the telephone poles, which were drawn in with pencil after the background was painted in.

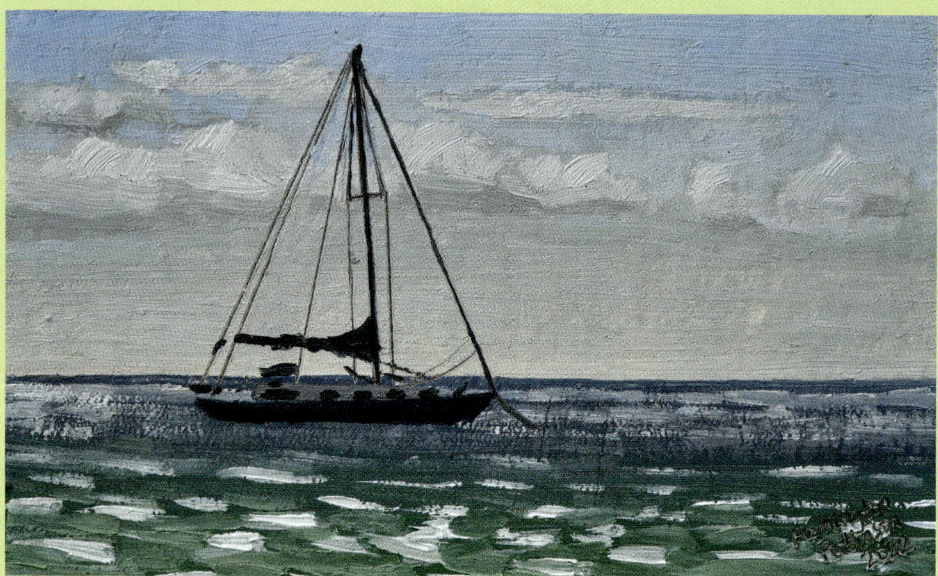

Pencil lines and a straight edge were used to create the few delicate mast lines on this sailboat anchored off the shore of Maui, Hawaii.

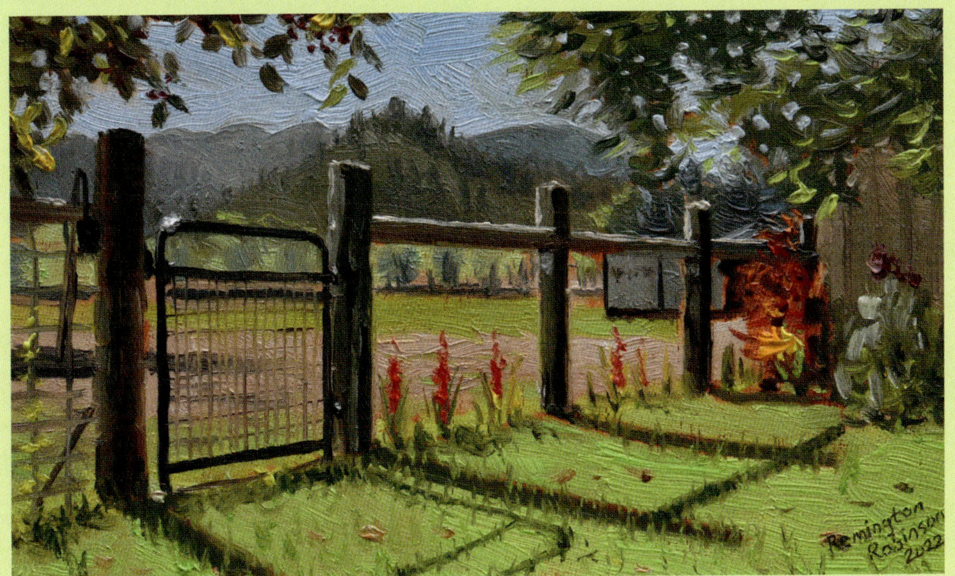

A few quick pencil lines are applied over the paint in the gate of this fence in Missoula, Montana.

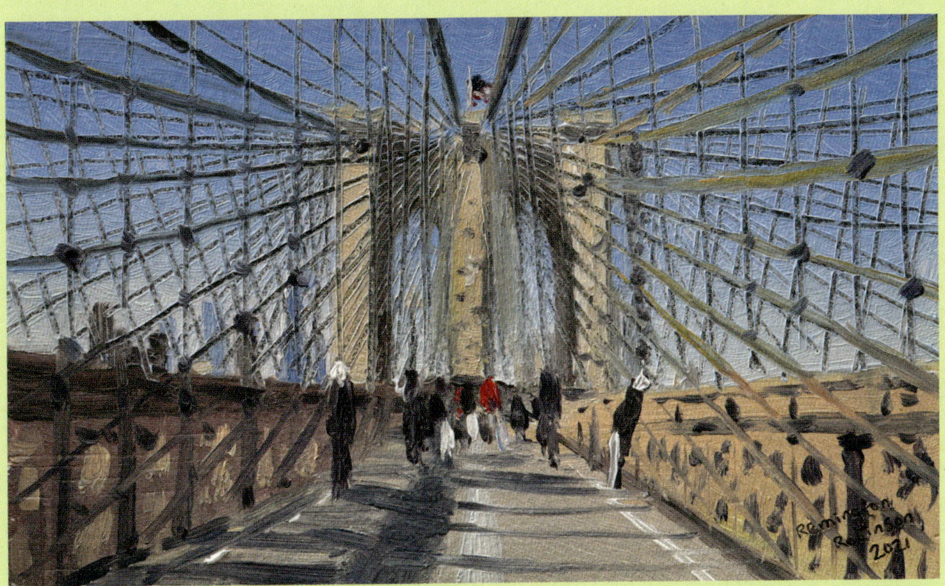

This is the Brooklyn Bridge in New York, using the technique of making pencil lines over the wet painting to achieve lots of small, thin lines.

MOVING SUBJECT: ARGENTINE TANGO

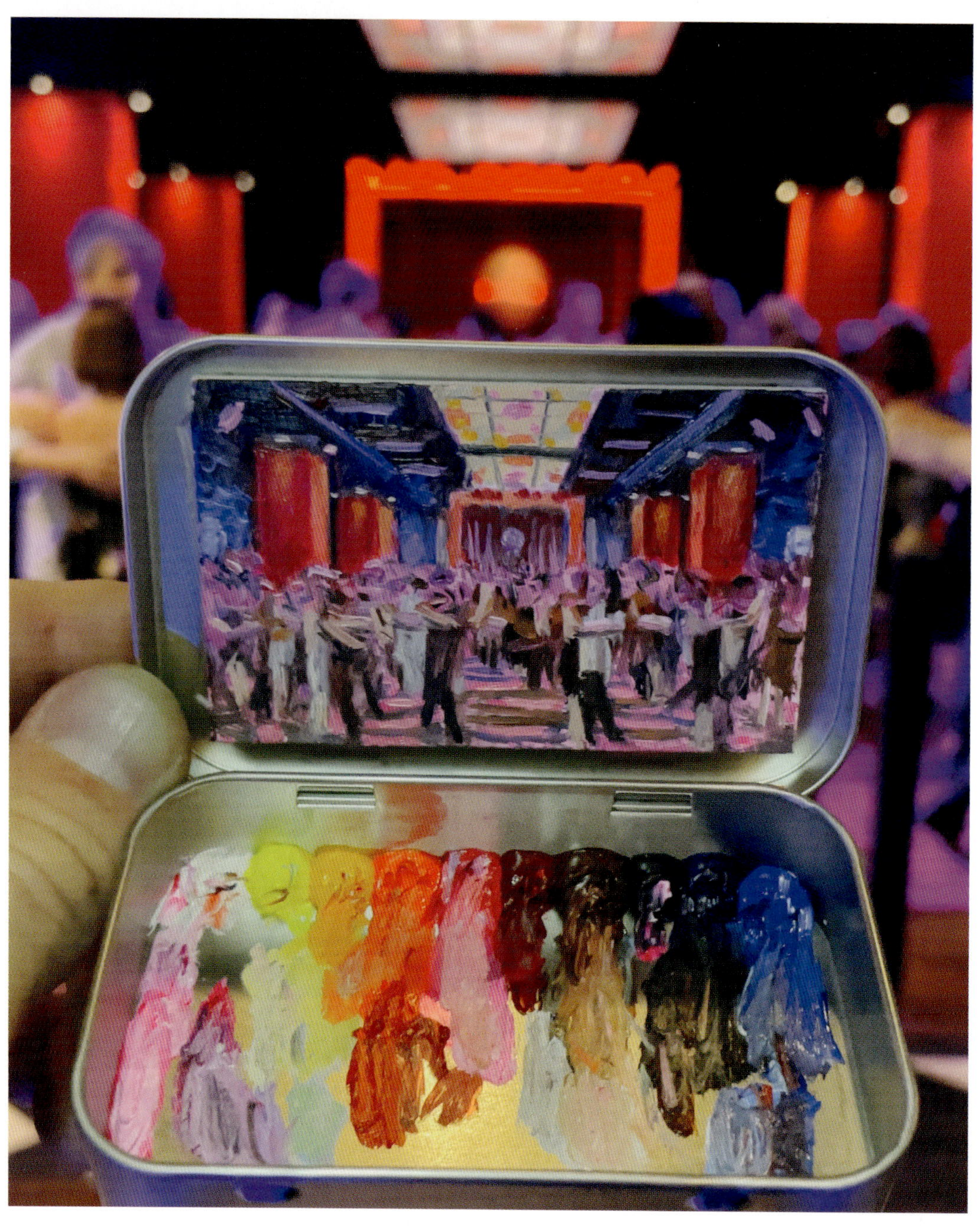

Painting any kind of moving subject matter adds an extra level of difficulty to painting from life. It's so easy to become swayed into using a photo reference as an aid. In some situations, it's almost unavoidable to use a photo reference—I also do it here and there. Attempting to paint a moving subject solely from life can be tedious and frustrating, but it can also be exhilarating and satisfying. Painting moving subjects on a small scale can also be easier to manage because of the size. Check out the gallery on page 135 to see some more examples of paintings with moving subjects.

Because my partner is a tango dancer, I have painted at many dances in the last decade. I have noticed over time that painting a large group of dancers is similar to painting a river or a waterfall. From far away, it always kind of looks the same, because even though everyone is constantly moving and shifting around, they are always located in the same area in relation to the landscape. That's a good place to start. I'll show you how I approach painting a group of people dancing at a tango dance (milonga) in Buenos Aires, Argentina.

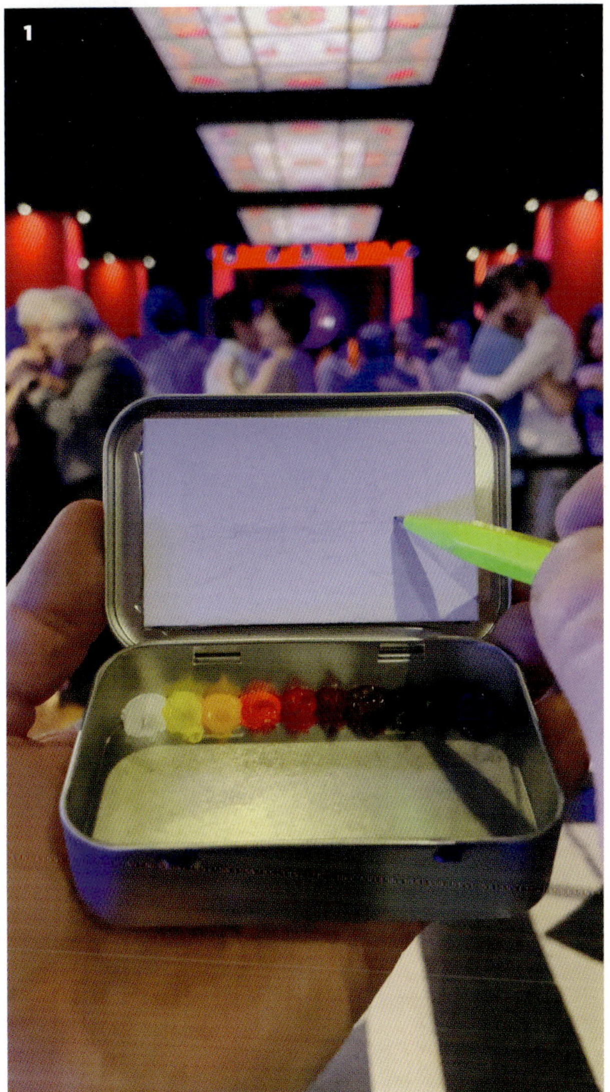

1. I'm starting this piece by sketching the structure of the room in pencil. I positioned myself at one side of the room where I can paint the room symmetrically with one-point perspective, with the vanishing point directly in the middle of my composition. This sets the stage for the dancers.

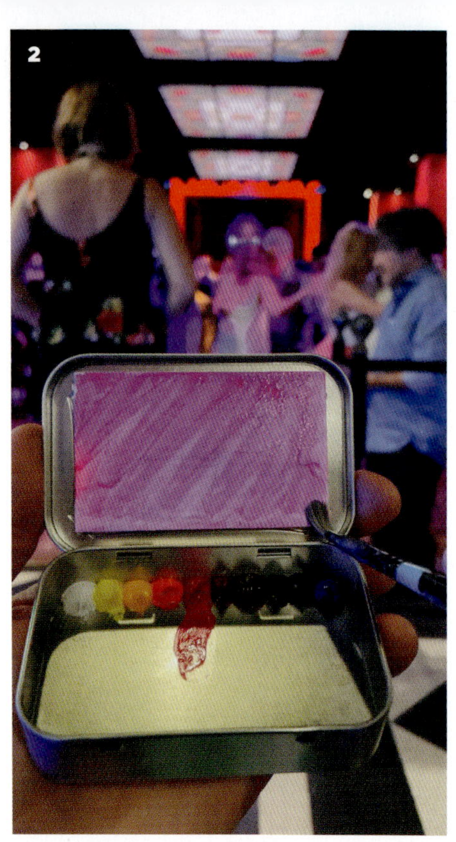

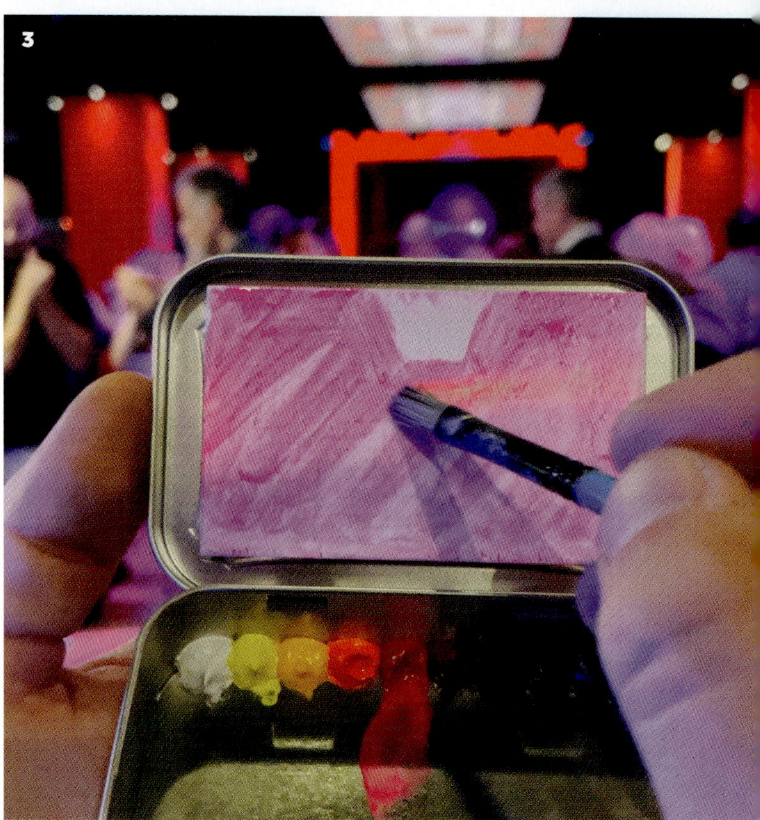

   MINI PLEIN AIR PAINTING

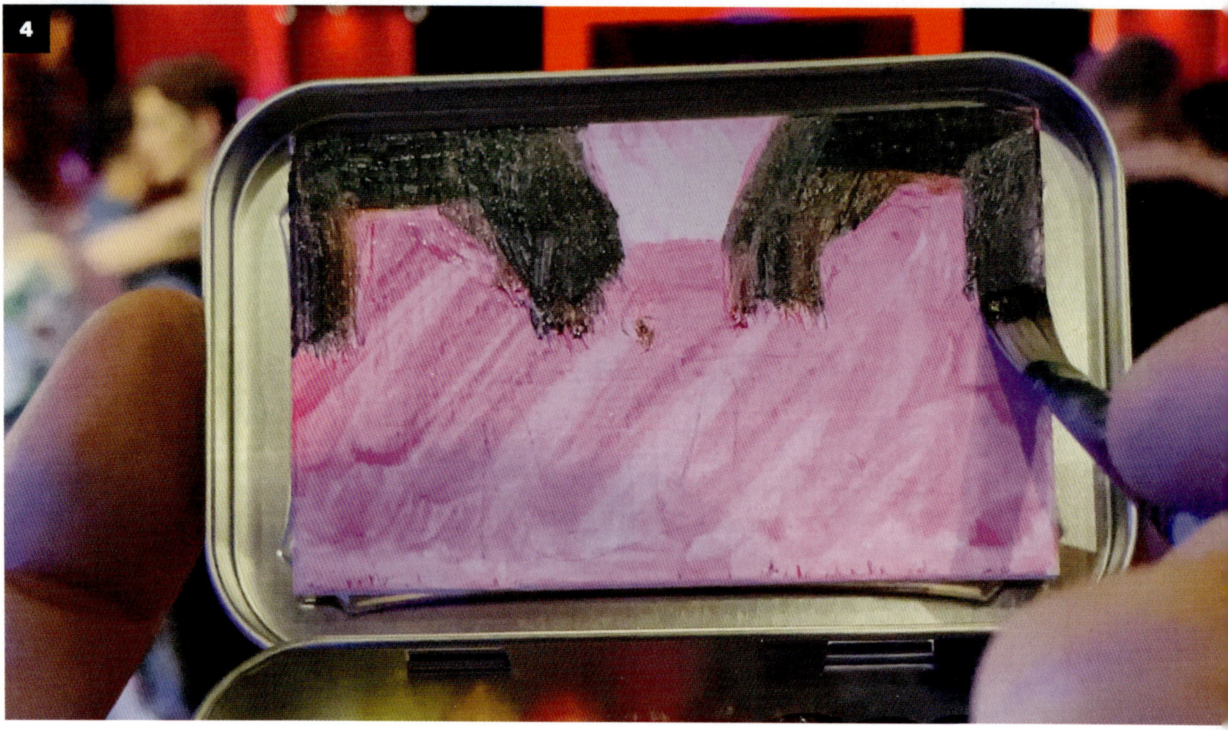

2. I continue with a light wash of Quinacridone Opera over the whole surface so that I can still see my pencil sketch underneath.

3. The brightest part of this scene is the overhead light, which I lift color away from with my brush (page 26).

4. I'm beginning the color-blocking phase by establishing the large area of black ceiling, making sure that I am maintaining the symmetry I want for my composition. The static, unchanging scene of the room can be painted like normal.

5. While I've got this dark pigment on my brush, I might as well throw in a few marks to indicate some people dancing. Right now I'm beginning to study their movement as I start to think about how I want to paint them.

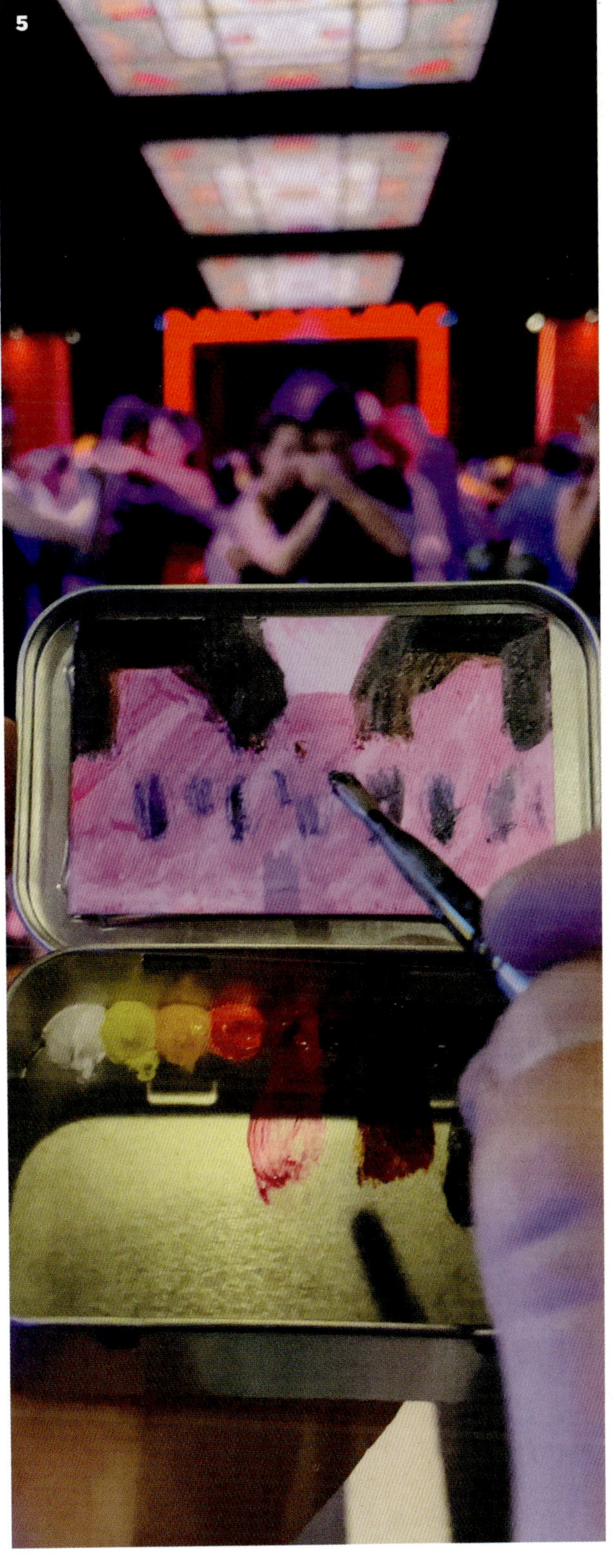

6. Continuing the blocking-in phase, I fill in a very light yellow-orange color for the overhead light, some red for the pillars on each side, and some dark blue for the dark shape in the back middle.

7. Now I am returning to continue defining the forms of the dancers. At this point, I'm using loose, gestural painting to show their movement—at least as far as I can do it at this small scale. I'm keeping in mind the proportions of the figures and their scale with respect to the size of the room. This involves quick glances back and forth to get rough shapes of heads, torsos, and legs.

8. Something that really stands out are the shadows across the floor between all the dancers. With a thin brush, I approximate the shadows and their spacing with some dark blue lines running along the ground horizontally. The shadows become thinner as they recede back into space, which I will keep in mind as I progress further into the painting and the figures become more established.

9. Now I'm starting to paint different colors of clothing in the group. In a large group of people dancing, there are typically not a lot of colors in their clothing. Black and white dominate the crowd, with blue, red, and khaki here and there. And of course, every once in a while, there will be a wild-card color. I'm also paying attention to any lighter colors that might be influenced by the color of the ambient light in the room.

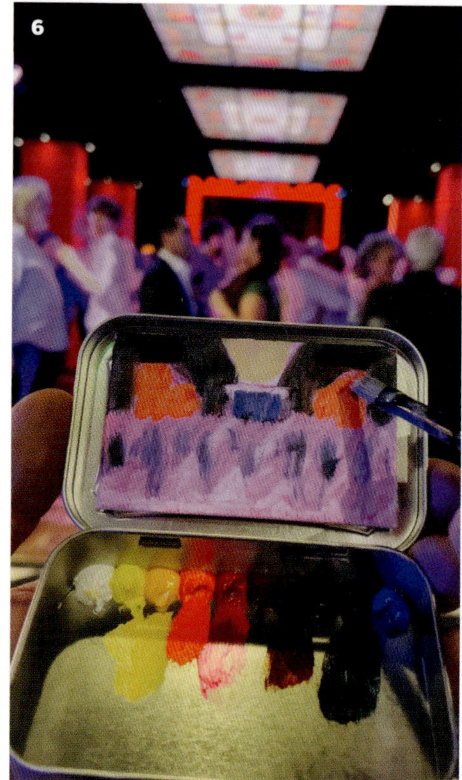

Now I'm focusing more on the heads and arms of people. A lot of these people have brown or black hair, so I indicate hair throughout that level of the painting with a dark value. As for the arms, I'm noticing that a lot of these people have their arms positioned horizontally in their embrace. The skin on their arms and faces is influenced somewhat by the pink lights.

10. Now that the positions of my figures are, for the most part, solidified, I am working more on the floor again. I have reinforced the pink with thicker paint, and I am now establishing more shadows in the few spaces in between figures where I can see more distant parts of the dance floor.

 MINI PLEIN AIR PAINTING

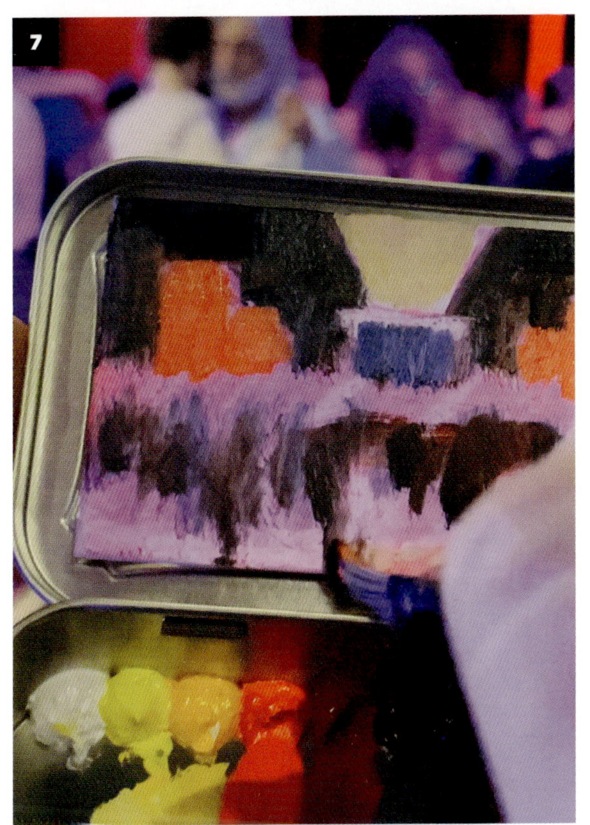

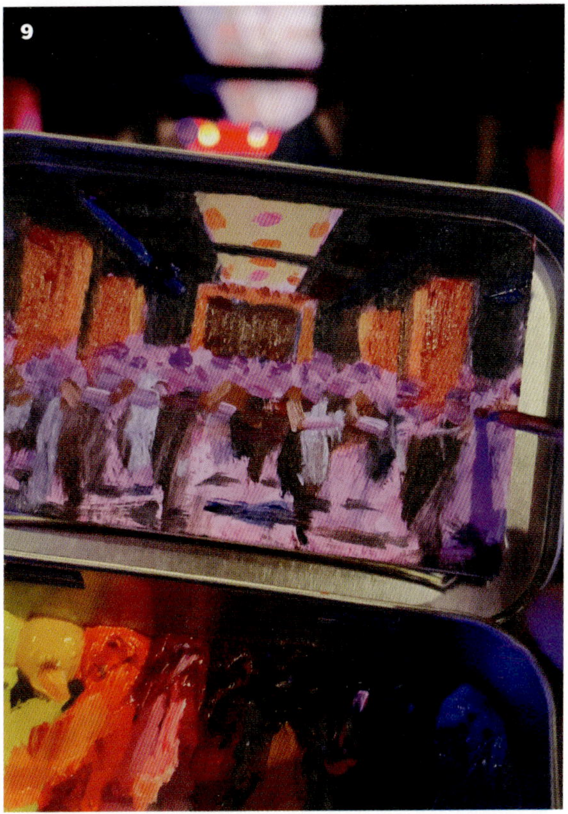

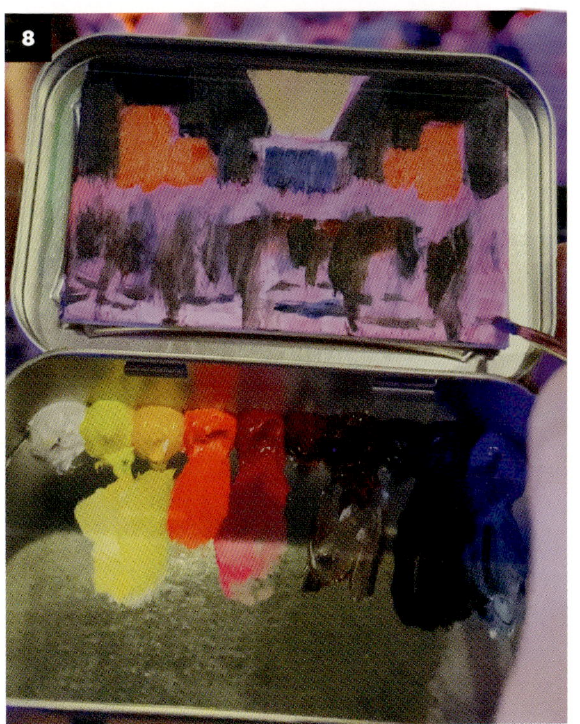

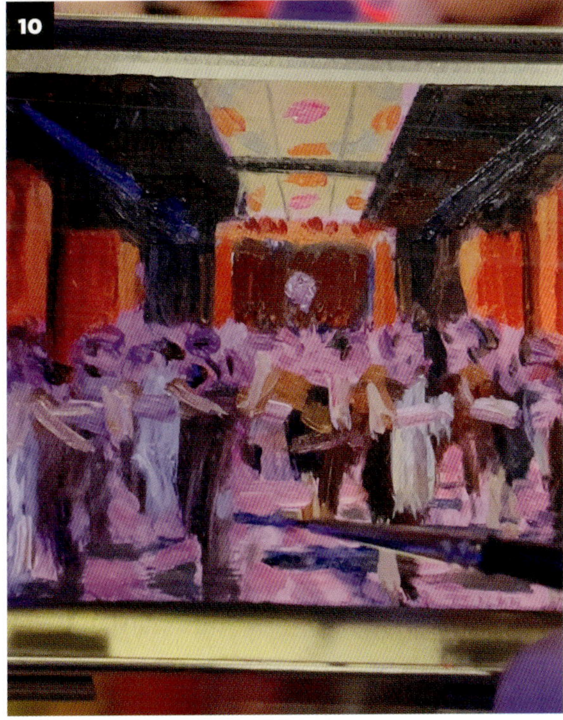

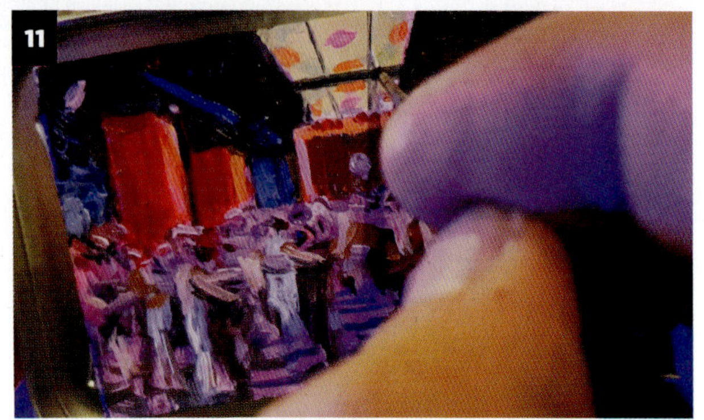 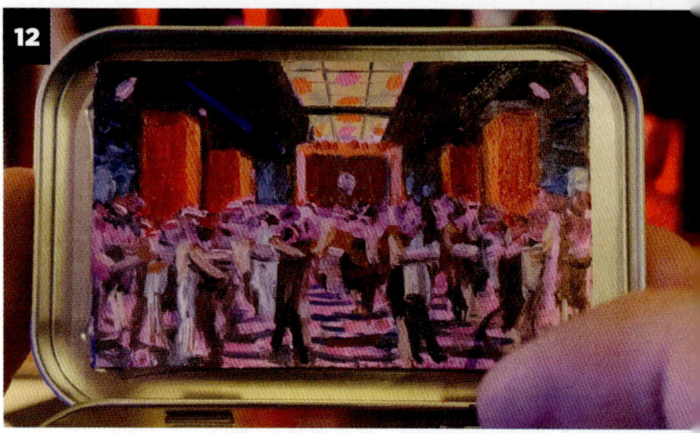

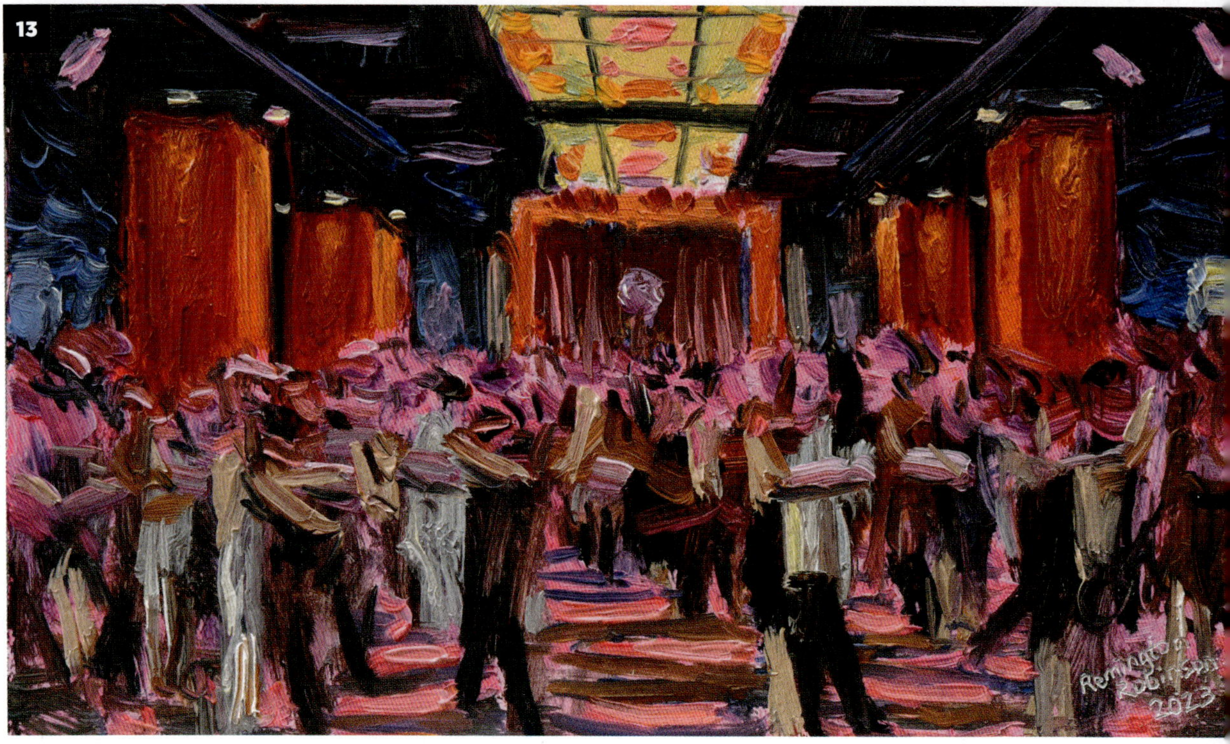

11. I am working again on the ornamental light fixture above—which looks similar to stained glass—hitting some of those details with my smallest brush.

12. I'm adding a few final details here and there on the people to make them look more like dancers, such as maybe an extended leg off to the side, or an outstretched arm.

13. This is the final painting from a tango milonga in Buenos Aires, Argentina.

The following is a small selection of paintings that capture a moving subject of some kind.

This painting of a brook trout in Gore Creek in Vail, Colorado, required more patience than usual. The fish would rise every few minutes to eat bugs floating past, and every so often would become spooked away by people tubing down the river or dogs splashing. But it would always return to the same place.

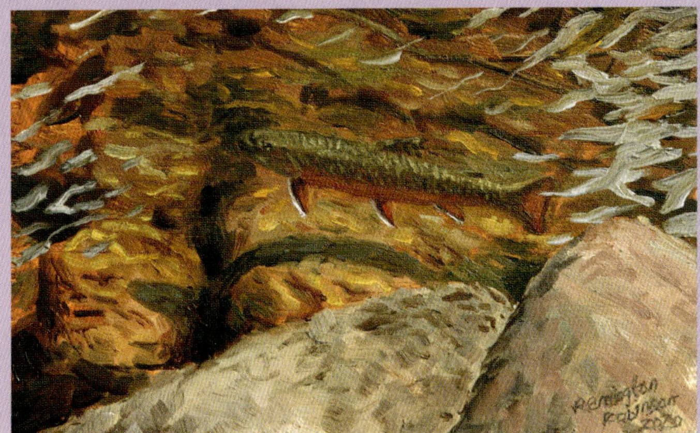

A bluegrass band and people dancing at the Gold Hill Inn in Colorado. The musicians were not moving around as much as the dancers, but the basic positioning of the different groups of people were the same the entire time.

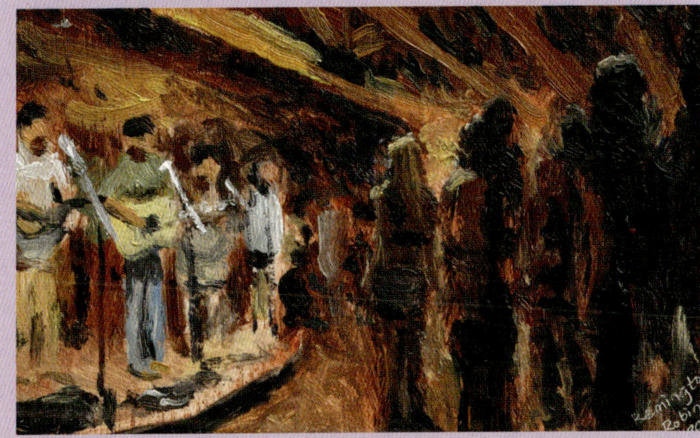

The cable cars in San Francisco, California, are continuously moving up and down Powell Street. While the rest of the cars and people on the street were painted quickly from life and from imagination, the main cable car in the foreground was painted little by little every time it came by, with a little help from a photograph.

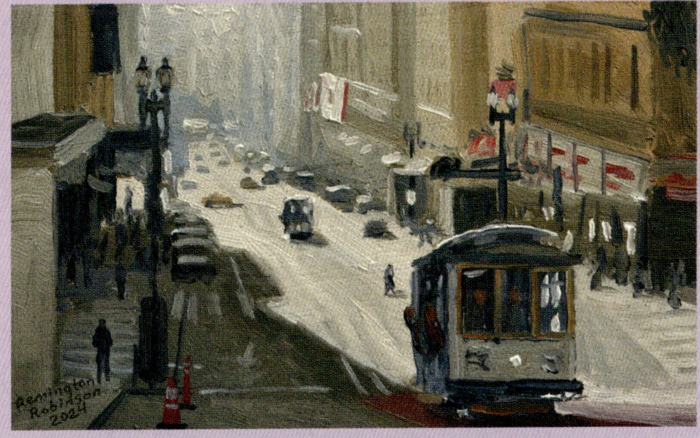

FAMILY VACATION: OLD ADIRONDACK CAMP

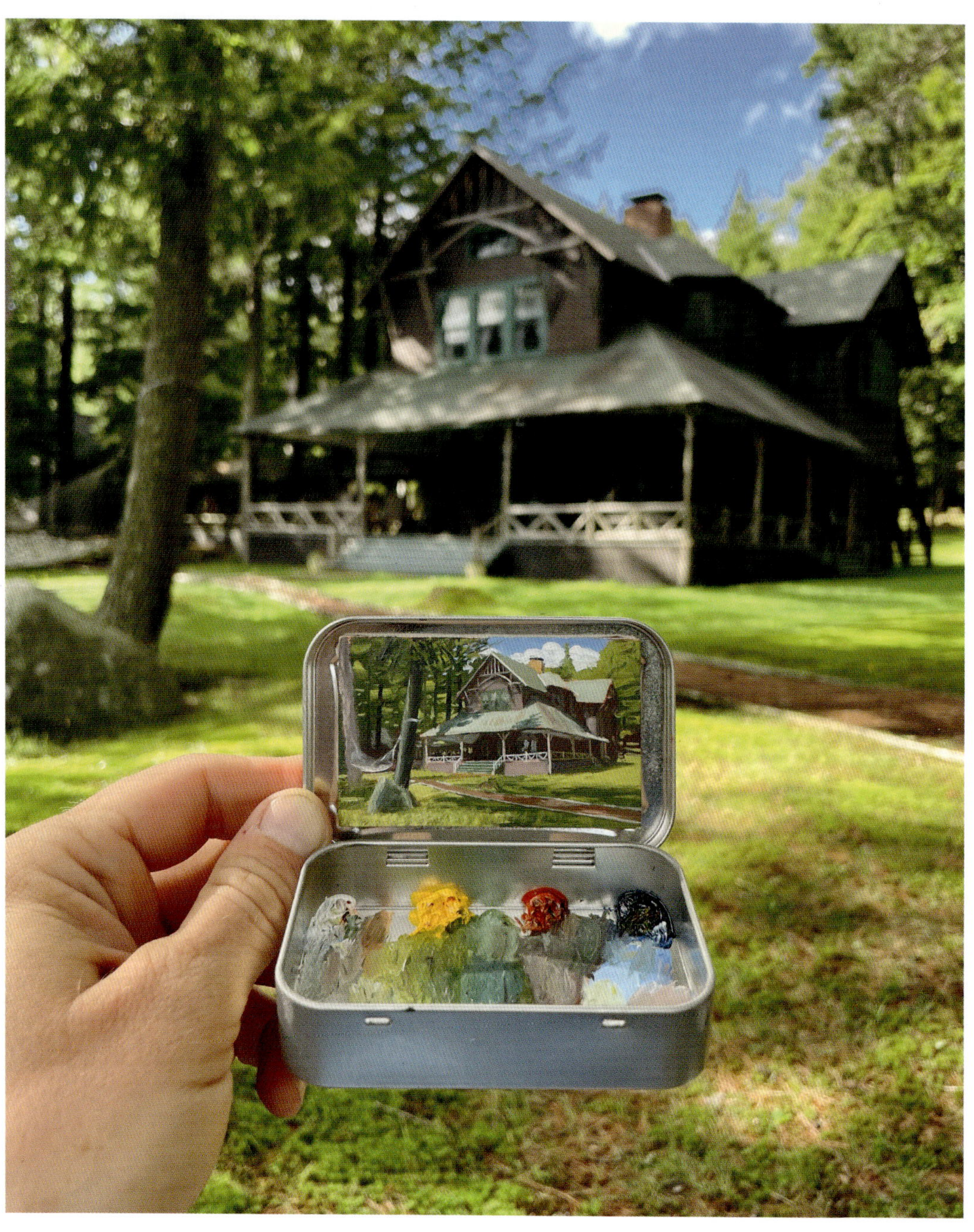

It's often the case that when I am on vacation with my family, I also want to paint the interesting places where we visit. This can sometimes be a problem, because besides wanting to paint, I also want to spend time with my family, and they with me. A good thing about miniature painting is the low time commitment, which allows for a little bit of painting to happen here and there several times during vacation. Check out the gallery on page 143 to see some more examples of paintings I did during family vacations.

A long time favorite family vacation spot of mine is an old Adirondack camp in upstate New York. The camp is historical, with distinguishing features that are typical to this style architecture, including ornamental woodwork with the bark still intact on all of the posts and railings. The serenity of nature is overwhelming in this quiet nook of the world away from most of civilization. In this final exercise, I will be painting a portrait of the main house at the camp, which was originally constructed in the late 1800s.

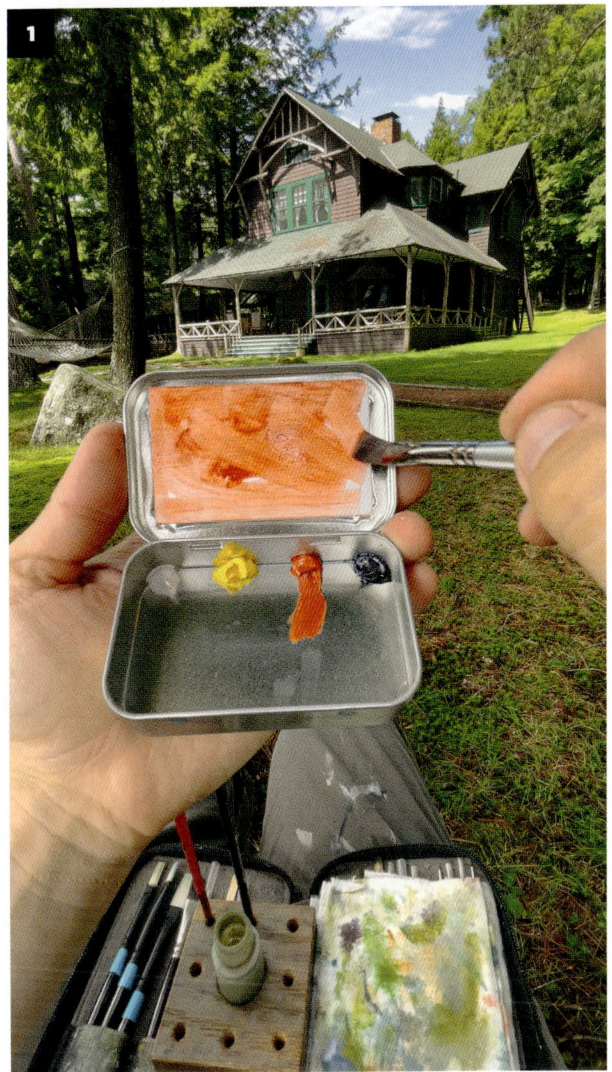

1. My color palette for this exercise consists of Titanium White, Chrome Yellow Deep, Mars Red, and Prussian Blue. I'm starting off by toning my whole surface with a thin wash of Mars Red. This is the same version of the primary color palette you might remember from the project titled "Foliage: Tree Next to the Road" on page 48.

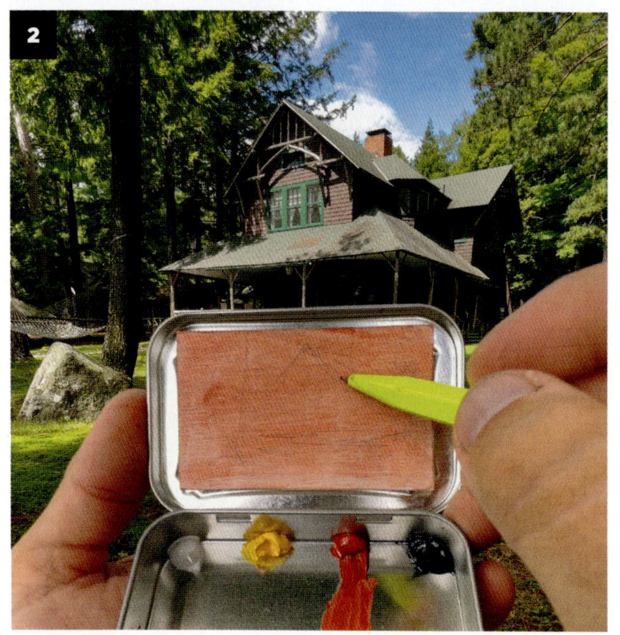

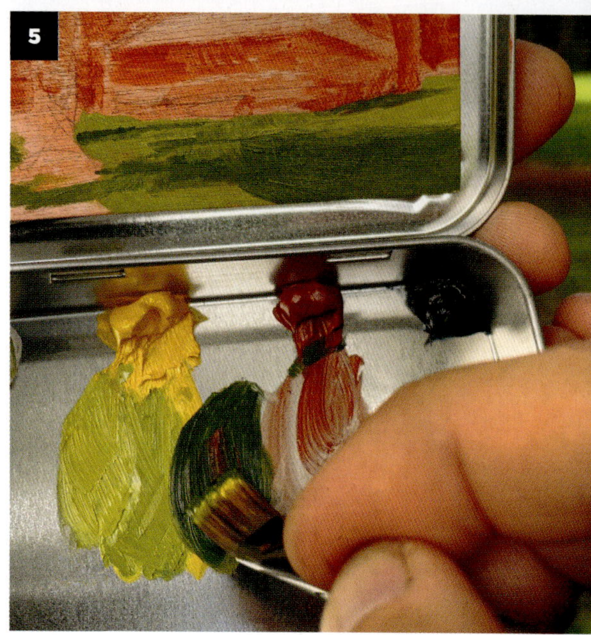

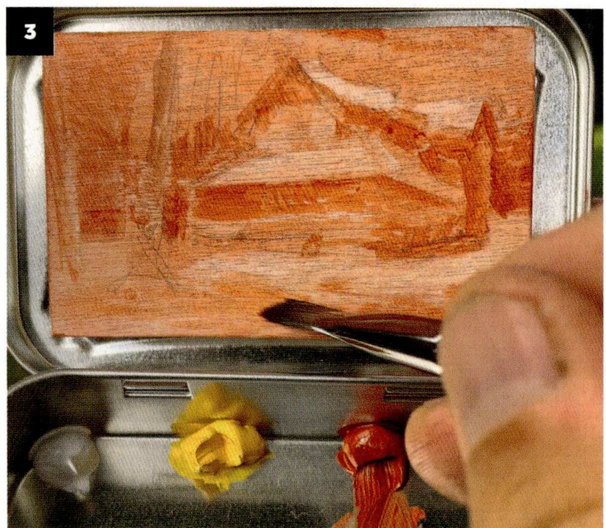

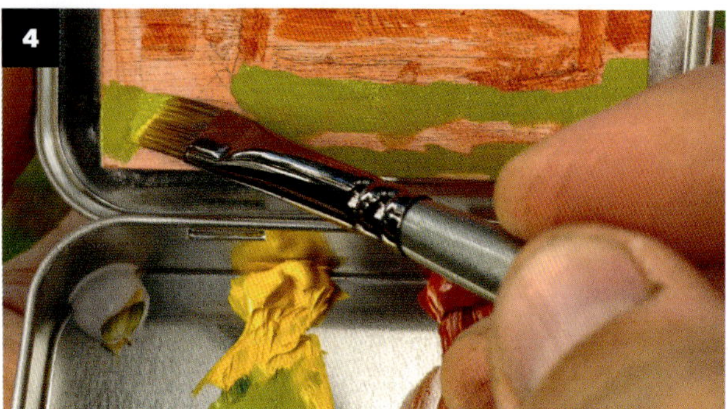

2. To make sure that my structure is accurate for the house, I take out my pencil and begin sketching my composition over the toned surface. I won't be able to erase any of these pencil marks, but I will be able to adjust once I start painting if I need to. This could be considered a two-point perspective drawing, but both of those vanishing points are off my picture plane, so I just need to eyeball it. In my composition, I want to see the whole house, but I also want to see the hammock on the left and the pine-needle path, as well as the blue sky.

3. With a large brush, I am lifting away pigment for the lighter areas (page 26) and adding more Mars Red to the darker areas.

4. Now for the color blocking. I'm starting with the color of the sunlit part of the green grass, which is Chrome Yellow Deep

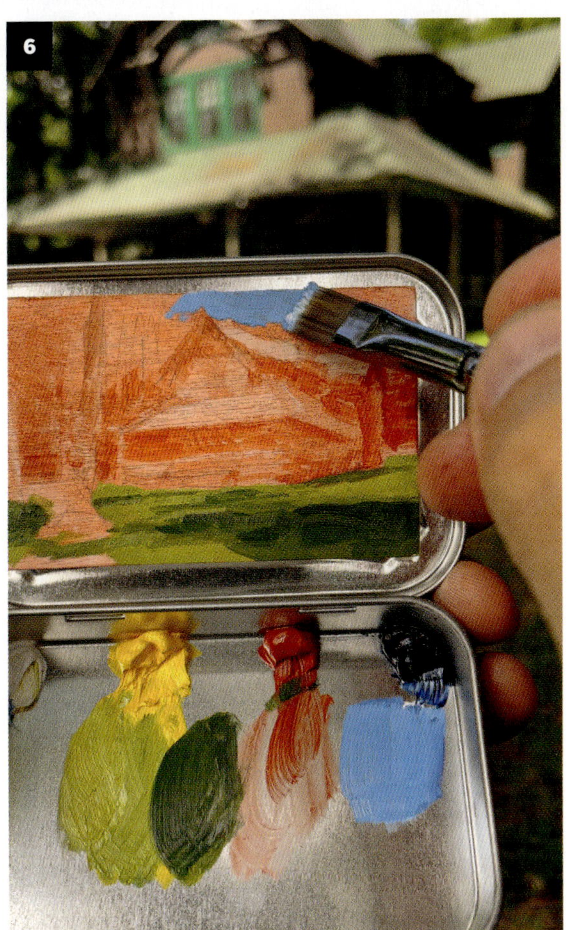 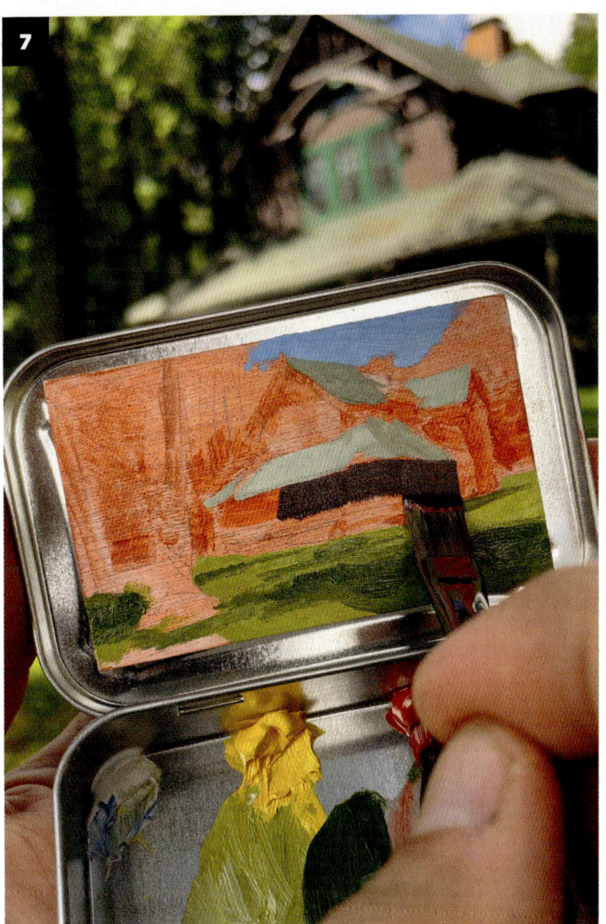

mixed with just a tiny touch of Prussian Blue to shift it into green. I've also added a bit of white to brighten it up a little.

5. Next, I am mixing the green for the shadows in the grass. This mixture involves a more liberal amount of Prussian Blue mixed into the edge of the pool of Chrome Yellow Deep in my palette. To darken it even more, I add a little bit of Mars Red.

6. The deep blue of the sky is just Titanium White and Prussian Blue mixed together.

7. To continue the blocking-in process, I have mixed some colors for the different planes of the roof, which is a light green that has more blue in it than the light green of the grass, and a lot more white. I am also beginning to block in the dark shadow underneath the wraparound porch.

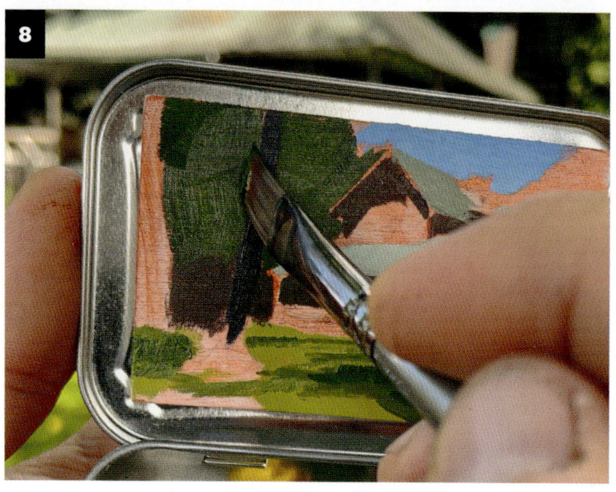

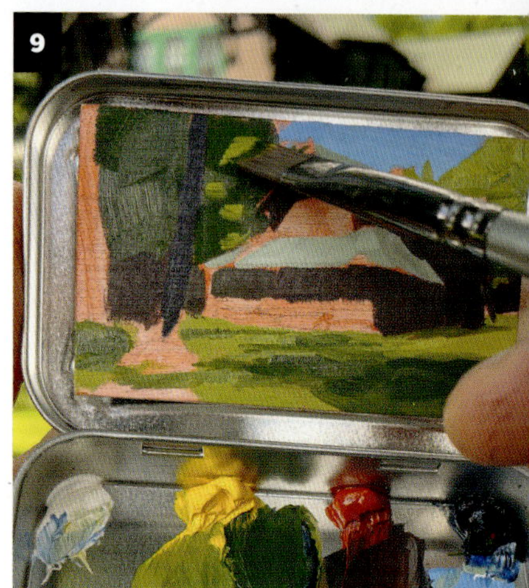

8. Now I am filling in that large area of deep green for the tall evergreen trees near the house. The dark brown color I mixed in the previous step was used for the shadows all over the building as well as shadows in the woods at ground level.

9. With a slightly darker tinted version of the light green grass color, I am now adding the large highlight areas in the trees.

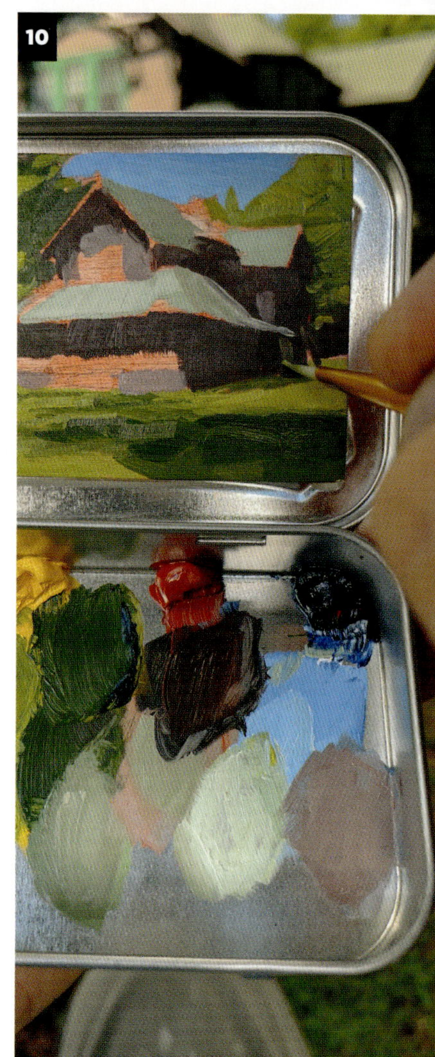

10. The parts of the brown siding of the house that are illuminated by sunlight do not look brown, but somehow a warm, purple color. I start with Mars Red and add a little bit of Prussian Blue to tint it purple, and add a tiny bit of yellow to warm it up. Then I add some white to lighten it up to the appropriate value and block in those areas on the house.

11. As I continue with the details, I notice the ceiling in the wraparound porch, which is painted white, but is a muted bluish green from the reflected light coming off of the green porch illuminated by the sun. Some other details I've painted in: shading on the left side of that tree behind the rock, which shows you where the sunlight is coming from, as well as some tree shadows landing on the roof of the front porch of the house. I've begun to build up a billowing

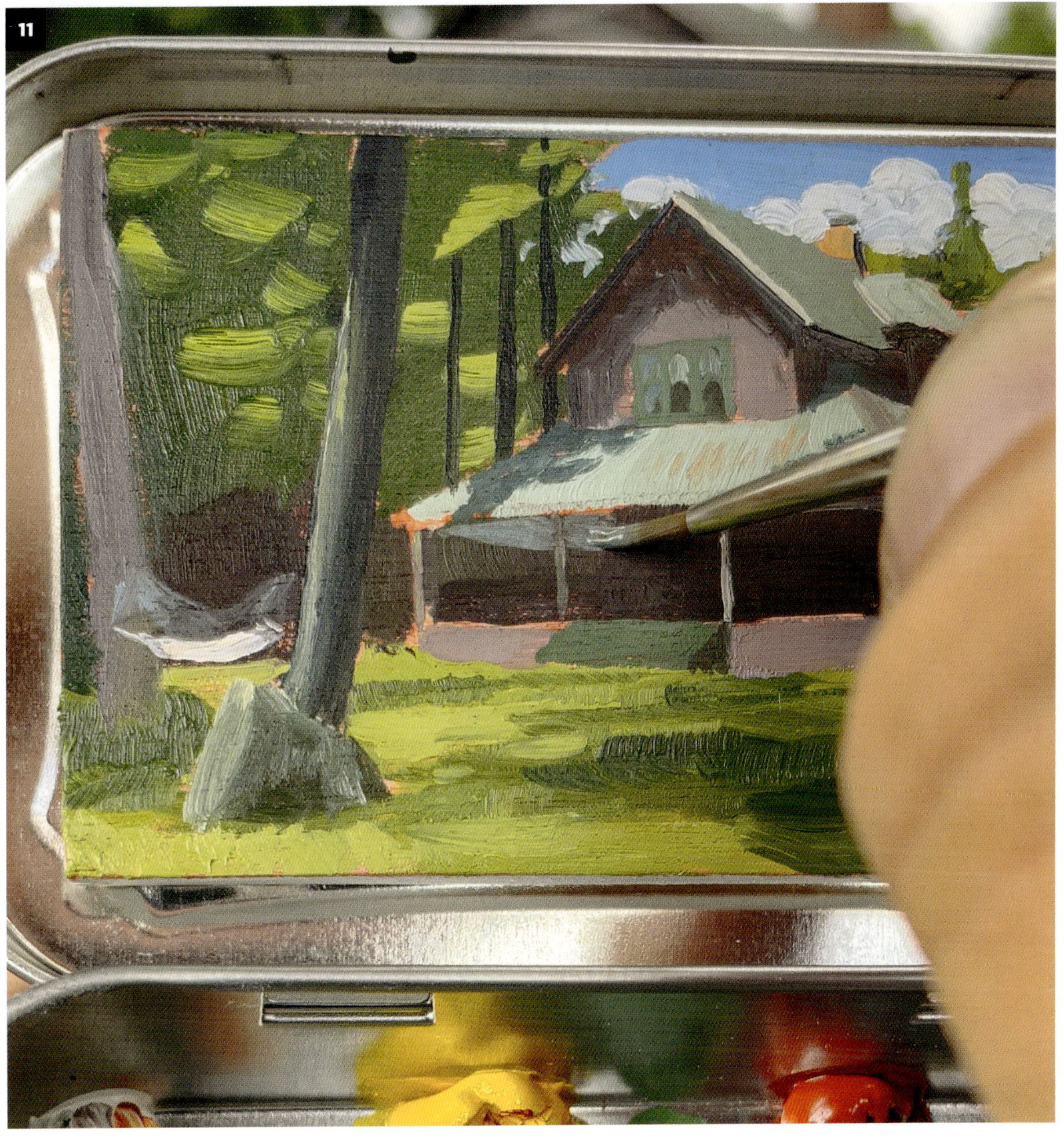

white cloud in the sky. The tree trunks are coming together, and I've added some brown-ish-orange streaks on the roof, which are a combination of pine needles that have landed and collected there, as well as some natural aging of the roof in those areas where water runs down it.

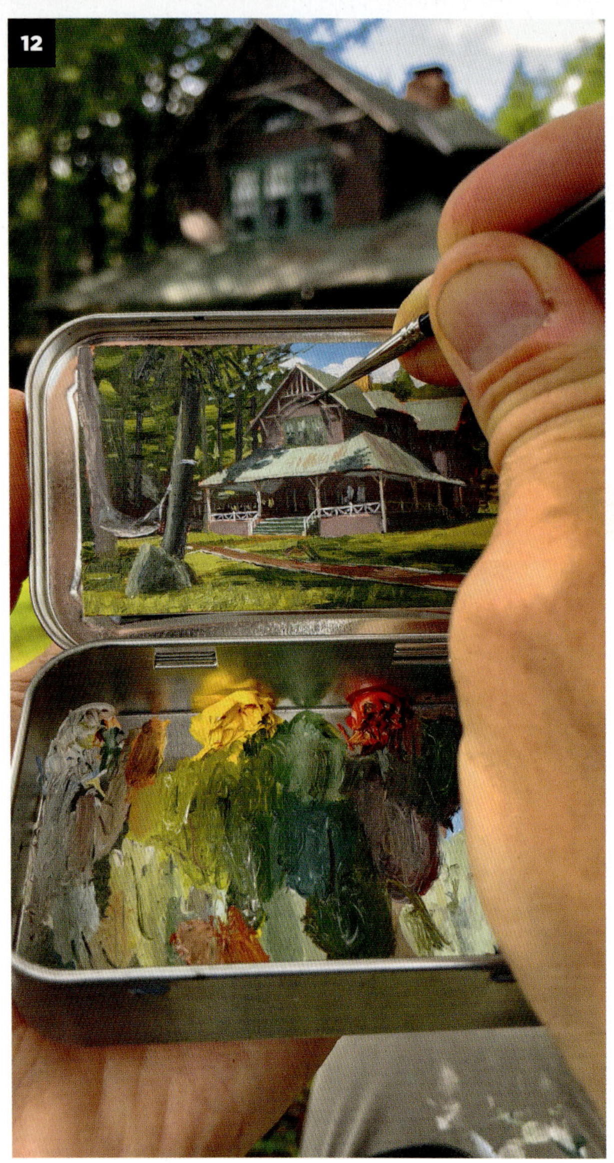 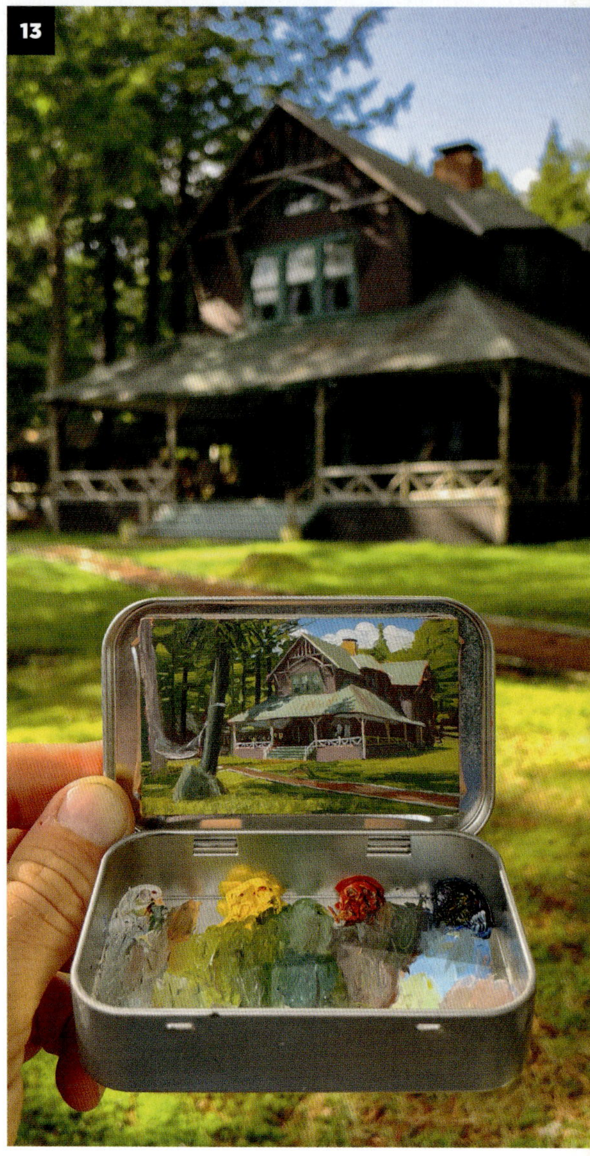

12. On the porch of this house, as well as on the overhang of the roof, there are decorative embellishments of natural timber—in some places, it even still has its bark. I am painstakingly trying to recreate all of that with my brand-new, super-thin liner brush.

13. To finish this painting off, I've finalized the details of all of the timber ornamentation and its shadows, the pine needle path, texture in the trees, and any other small details that I hadn't painted yet, while leaving out some details that are just too small to make a difference.

GALLERY: FAMILY VACATION

The following is a small selection of paintings I made while on vacation with my family in the Adirondacks in upstate New York.

The final painting of the old main house on the old Adirondack camp.

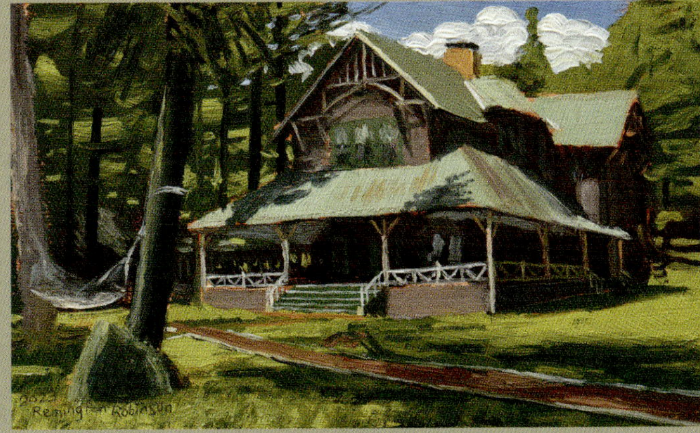

The full-size billiard table in the upstairs part of the boathouse if a frequent hangout at night after the early-risers retire for the evening. The fireplace and the canoes overhead make it feel rustic and cozy.

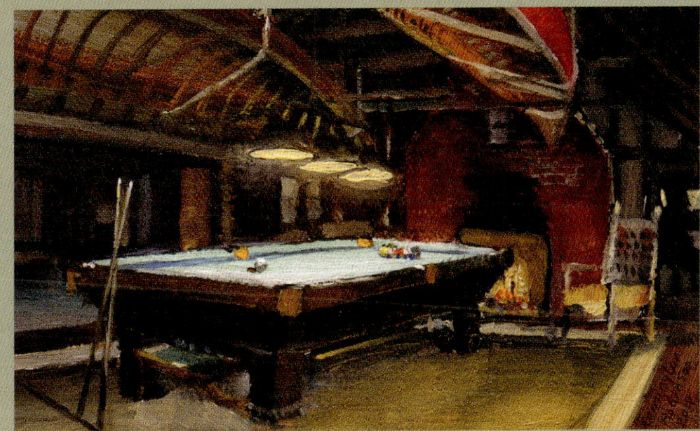

A view of a hammock amongst the towering white pines and an island out on the lake.

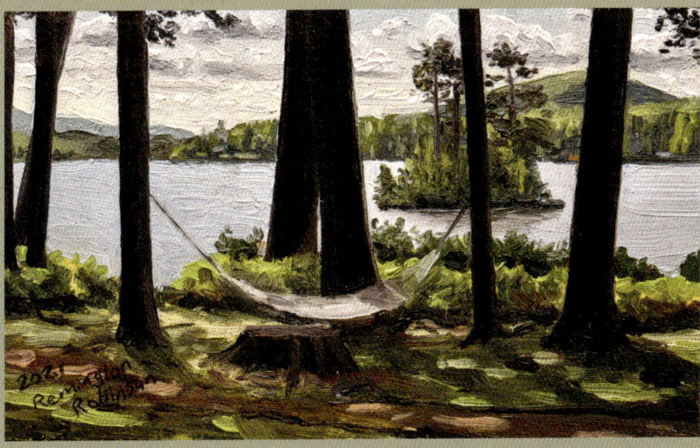

ABOUT THE AUTHOR

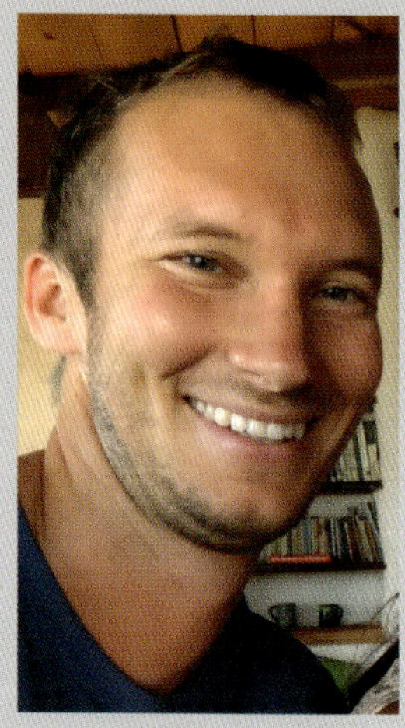

REMINGTON ROBINSON (b. 1986) grew up in Chagrin Falls, Ohio. In 2004, he moved to Boulder, Colorado, for college, graduating in 2010 from Rocky Mountain College of Art + Design in Lakewood, Colorado, with a BFA in painting and drawing. In 2016 he started *plein air* painting for fun, and in 2017, he first painted miniatures in mint tins, having painted over 1000 mini paintings as of the publishing of this book (2024).

ACKNOWLEDGMENTS

I would like to thank my partner, Tara Fortier, for her thoughtful insights, for being a loving and supportive partner for the past 11 years, and for inviting me along to her many work conferences abroad which have provided the largest opportunity for me to paint all over the world. I also thank her daughter, Lucia, for being a growing light in my life ever since she was just 3 years old, and whom at this point I now truly consider to be a daughter of my own. Many thanks to my parents, Frank Robinson (1956–2017) and Kathy Spresser, as well as my stepdad Mark Spresser; my siblings Kate, Luke, and Mag for being the best of sibling friends one could hope for. Thanks also to all other friends and relatives for being such positive and supportive companions throughout my life. In particular, I want to thank my high school art teacher, David King, for teaching me the fundamentals of painting, Caroline Polachek for her creative influence when we were in college together, as well as Colin Frager for all of the help during the early stages of my art career. Thank you to Instagram for connecting me and my work to the world, and thank you to Quarto and Walter Foster for publishing this book. I especially want to thank 'Billy' Eduard Albert Meier and all my FIGU friends for the continuous inspiration to think for myself and to be forever searching and curious about the nature of reality and the laws that govern our universe, as well as the inner workings of the psyche and the consciousness.

Last but not least—and this may sound strange—I want to take this opportunity to thank my own highest self, my own innermost creative-energetic self. Sometimes my ego gets in the way and drowns out the positive impulses from my innermost self. However, because of my innermost self, I am always striving to think for myself, to be conscious and attentive of my own thoughts and feelings, my knowledge, my wisdom, and my ability, in order to lead everything to harmonize with the success that I know is possible, to the best of my capabilities. The best form of self-love is to be your own best friend and to not only act on good advice from others, but to act on the best knowledge we each have within ourselves, in order to be the most successful we can be. If we don't each act on our own impulses to help ourselves to achieve our own successes, then all help in the form of outside opportunities, encouragement, and inspiration mean nothing. There is a saying, "you can lead a horse to water, but you can't make it drink." There are key situations in life where opportunities come and go, and it's up to each individual to choose to be one's own best friend, and take those opportunities and run with them, or to self-sabotage.